UNPLUGGED

MY JOURNEY INTO THE DARK WORLD OF VIDEO GAME ADDICTION

RYAN G. VAN CLEAVE, PH.D.

Health Communications, Inc.
Deerfield Beach, Florida

www.hcibooks.com

Library of Congress Cataloging-in-Publication Data

Van Cleave, Ryan G., 1972-
Unplugged : my journey into the dark world of video game addiction /
Ryan G. Van Cleave.
p. cm.
Includes index.
ISBN-13: 978-0-7573-1362-2
ISBN-10: 0-7573-1362-0
1. Video game addiction. 2. Video games—Psychological aspects. I. Title.
RC569.5.V53V36 2010
616.85'84—dc22

2010011264

Publisher: Health Communications, Inc.
3201 S.W. 15th Street
Deerfield Beach, FL 33442–8190

Cover design by Larissa Hise Henoch
Interior design by Lawna Patterson Oldfield
Interior formatting by Dawn Von Strolley Grove

Contents

"Space Invaders proved so addictive that it not only inaugurated an entire video game paradigm, it caused a nationwide coin shortage in Japan."

—Chris Green

"You know you're a serious World of Warcraft player when the game starts interfering with your life. You know you're an addict when your life starts interfering with the game."

—Anonymous

Foreword

> "Certain individuals use certain substances in certain ways, thought at certain times to be unacceptable by certain other individuals for reasons both certain and uncertain."
>
> —MILTON BURGLASS AND HOWARD SHAFFER, 1984

The definition of what constitutes addiction has been a matter of great debate for decades. And it's why I will have a job for life. Addiction means different things to different people, but for many, the concept of addiction involves taking drugs. Therefore, most official definitions concentrate on the ingestion of a substance. This book challenges that traditional view.

Ryan Van Cleave's confessional and sometimes self-deprecating story of his own addiction to the online game *World of Warcraft* will take you on an emotional roller-coaster ride. This open and honest account of Ryan's descent into the "darkest side of the digital world" may make you laugh, cry, and disbelieve—but whatever your reaction, you won't forget. The book conjures up wonderful imagery that many of us will empathize with. (Like Ryan, I am a published poet who, in the 1980s, viewed university as a place to "play video games, chase girls, and play guitar." However, unlike

Ryan, I was able to focus on what was most important!)

Research into online gaming addiction is a relatively new area of psychological study. I have studied behavioral addictions for twenty-three years, and I published my first academic paper on video-game addiction back in 1991. More recently, I have spent a great deal of time researching the excessive playing of online games like *Everquest* (known colloquially by many of its users as *Evercrack*). Similarly, Ryan refers to *World of Warcraft* as *World of Warcrack*. He also describes WoW as "digital heroin." This is not only emotive but also puts into two words what his experience with *World of Warcraft* was all about.

How could something so innocuous as an online game compromise everything in his life? What's more, how could it take a man to the brink of suicide? Despite the traditional idea that addictions are usually about drugs, there is now a growing scientific movement that views a number of behaviors as potentially addictive. These so-called "behavioral addictions" include gambling, overeating, sex, exercise, video-game playing, love, work, and Internet use. Such diversity has led to new, all-encompassing definitions of what constitutes an addictive behavior. One definition published in the *Annual Review of Psychology* defines addictive behavior as:

> A repetitive habit pattern that increases the risk of disease and/or associated personal and social problems. Addictive behaviors are often experienced subjectively as 'loss of control'—the behavior contrives to occur despite volitional attempts to abstain or moderate use. These habit patterns are typically characterized by immediate gratification (short term reward), often coupled with delayed deleterious effects (long term costs). Attempts to change an addictive behavior (via treatment or self initiation) are typically marked with high relapse rates.

In my research, I view addictive behavior as any action that features what I believe are the six core components of addiction (salience, mood modification, tolerance, withdrawal symptoms, conflict, and relapse). I have consistently argued that any behavior that fulfills these six criteria can be operationally defined as an addiction. In the case of online gaming addiction, these would be:

Salience. This occurs when online gaming becomes the most important activity in the person's life and dominates thinking (pre-occupations and cognitive distortions), feelings (cravings), and behavior (deterioration of socialized behavior). For instance, even if the person is not actually gaming online, he/she will be thinking about and planning for the next session.

Mood modification. These are the subjective experiences that people report as a consequence of engaging in online gaming and can be seen as a coping strategy (i.e., they experience an arousing "buzz" or a "high" or paradoxically tranquilizing feel of "escape" or "numbing").

Tolerance. Increasing amounts of online gaming are required to achieve the former mood-modifying effects. For someone engaged in online gaming, this means a gradual build up of the amount of the time spent online, engaged in the behavior.

Withdrawal symptoms. Unpleasant feeling states and/or physical effects that occur when online gaming is discontinued or suddenly reduced (e.g., the shakes, moodiness, irritability, etc.).

Conflict. Conflicts between the online gamer and those around him (interpersonal conflict), conflicts with other activities (job, schoolwork, social life, hobbies, and interests) or from within the individual him- or herself (intrapsychic conflict and/or subjective feelings of loss of control), which are concerned with spending too much time engaged in online gaming.

Relapse. Repeated reversions to earlier patterns of online gaming. Patterns typical of the height of excessive online gaming are quickly restored after periods of abstinence or control.

Once you've read this book, you'll realize that Ryan's obsession met these criteria and that he was addicted to *World of Warcraft* in the same way that other people are addicted to alcohol and other drugs. His unadulterated first-person account gets to the heart of what it is to be addicted. He compromised everything in his life to play a game, putting "things off until tomorrow so [he] could enjoy the enjoyment of now."

One of the reasons I got into this line of research was my own experience with gaming, which echoes some of Ryan's early experiences. Ryan talks of his introduction to playing video games on a Commodore 64 and his obsession with *Tetris*. When I was fourteen years old, I would spend all day every day during the school holidays playing *Donkey Kong* on my dad's Commodore 64. Ten years later, I'd spend several hours every evening playing *Tetris* into the small hours as a way of relieving the stress of my first lecturing post. When Ryan talks of the "ridiculous burst of satisfaction" from playing *Tetris,* I know exactly what he means. Online games provide a fantastic means of escape—especially when things aren't going right in your life. As well as providing euphoria, excitement, arousal, a buzz, and a "high," the playing of online games can (somewhat paradoxically) help the player numb, destress, relax, and "zone out." They make people feel better through the adoption of another persona—at least in the short term. As Ryan describes, games left him "open to pretending to be anyone [he] wanted to be."

It may be easier to understand online gaming addiction by considering what we psychologists call the partial reinforcement effect (PRE). This is a critical psychological ingredient of gaming addiction whereby the reinforcement is intermittent (i.e., people keep responding in the absence of reinforcement hoping that another reward is just around the corner). Knowledge about the PRE gives the game designer an edge in designing appealing games. Instant reinforcement is satisfying. The magnitude of the reinforcement (e.g., high points score for doing something in-game) is also important. Large rewards lead to fast responding and greater resistance to extinction, thereby leading to increased "addiction."

Online gaming involves multiple reinforcements in what I call "the kitchen sink approach." Generally speaking, in video games, different features provide a different reward to different people. The rewards might be intrinsic (such as improving your highest score, beating your friend's high score, getting your name on the "hall of fame," or mastering the game) or extrinsic (such as peer admiration). As Ryan points out, in online gaming there is no end to the game and there is the potential for gamers to play endlessly against (and with) other real people. This can be immensely rewarding and psychologically engrossing. While I ought to stress that just playing excessively doesn't necessarily make someone an addict, for some, the partial reinforcement effect may lead to addiction where online gaming becomes the single most important thing in those people's lives, so important that they compromise and neglect everything else. While there is little empirical evidence from research indicating how the addiction establishes itself and what people are actually addicted to, Ryan provides in detail the roots of his addiction in his childhood. Worldwide, there are currently very few practitioners who specialize in the treatment of online gaming addiction. This may be because there are relatively few players who are genuinely addicted to playing who have actually sought professional help. Perhaps Ryan's story will help raise awareness and kick start some empirical treatment trials to be carried out.

Thankfully, Ryan has overcome his addiction. Ryan was lucky. He faced his demons and overcame the urge to kill himself. Although Ryan's story was extreme and perhaps does not necessarily represent the experiences of other heavy gamers, his addiction was as real and as ever present as other more traditional addictions such as those to alcohol and drugs.

—**Mark Griffiths, Ph.D.**, Director
International Gaming Research Unit
Nottingham Trent University, United Kingdom

Acknowledgments

In addition to my own experiences as an addiction and recovery consultant and a video game addict, I often drew on the expertise of more digital culture and video game addiction experts than can be easily named. Thanks to all of them for their encouragement, advice, and support. Special appreciation goes to Professor Eric Gingrich for his assistance at crucial times in this book's development. Much gratitude and appreciation also goes to Dr. Mark Griffiths for encouraging me with this book and offering to write the foreword.

A very special thank you goes to my literary agent superstar, Claire Gerus, whose tireless efforts and shrewd advice have proven of immeasurable value to me throughout the years. This book would not be possible without her. Special thanks, too, is due to Carol Rosenberg of HCI. Her unwavering confidence in this project was a godsend. Thanks also go to Kim Weiss, Christian Blonshine, and Nicole Haye at HCI for their efforts to help get this book into the hands of those who need it. Freelance publicist Maryglenn McCombs, too, played an important role in getting *Unplugged* out into the world. Her work is greatly appreciated.

Also, I owe a very special "Thank you!" to everyone who contributed to the interviews in the appendices. I wish that video game addiction didn't carry the type of shame and stigma that makes people choose to remain anonymous when sharing their stories—

perhaps the publication of *Unplugged* will work to change that perception. In any case, thank you for having the courage to speak up and share those important stories in this book.

Thanks also to Rob, who is my best friend whether I'm playing World of Warcraft or not. Everyone should be so lucky as to have someone like him in their lives.

Finally, thanks to my family, for their unfailing love and support. It means the world to me.

Introduction

My wife said she'd kill me if I told my whole story, but here's the problem—if I don't take responsibility for my own damn life, I might as well have Geronimoed into the Potomac. Every single day for the past twenty-five years, I'd been doing myself in with lies, half-truths, "spin," and ego-enforced self-blindness. The stories I told myself were so immaculate compared to the gritty yuck of my day-to-day existence. Why wouldn't I believe those instead?

I don't intend to "James Frey" my way into that wishy-washy world of gray, where most of us truly eat, drink, screw, and lie to ourselves about the sketchy, better-than-reality narrative of our lives. Honestly, though, I was so plugged into virtual worlds that I'm not sure I recall what truly happened in real life. I missed out on a ton of it. Worse, I've gotten so clever at covering up the truth—call it a reflex now, nearly as automatic as breathing—that I'm not even sure I have the ability to be one hundred percent straight with myself anymore. You can be assured, though, that I am relating the events *exactly* as I remember them.

When you can walk into the local Media Play and grab a World of Warcraft 60-day prepaid game card off the New Arrivals rack and buy it when your wife's in the bathroom only to have her ask you in the car if you bought anything and you eye her dead-on and say "Nope" as you run your fingers down the slick spine of that plastic box that you now hug to your chest beneath your shirt, and somehow you *mean* "nope" and believe "nope" too, well . . .

It's like putting your mouth around the mouth of a gun.

❖

If you haven't figured it out yet, you're not going to like me. And I don't blame you a bit, but I'm going to tell you what I did anyway. With 11.5 million World of Warcraft subscribers and tens of millions more playing other video games like their lives depend on it, there's a lot at stake. And that's not even considering console-system games, like the Nintendo Wii (1.26 million units sold in November 2009 alone) and the Xbox 360 (820,000 sold during that same month), which are overtaking baseball to become America's greatest pastime.

So I have to confess my descent into the darkest side of the digital world via my addiction to Warcraft because 65 percent of American households play computer or video games, and . . .

- Because the average age of the most frequent game purchaser is forty.
- Because in 2008, 26% of Americans over the age of fifty played video games, an increase from 9% in 1999.
- Because 63% of parents believe video games are a positive part of their children's lives.
- Because a 2007 study by the AMA reports that close to 90% of American youngsters play video games and as many as 15% of them—more than 5 million kids—may be addicted.
- According to a May 2009 study in *Psychological Science*, a top peer-reviewed publication, about 8.5% of American youth between 8 and 18 show symptoms of video game addiction.

The average game player is thirty-five years old and has been playing games for thirteen years, statistics show. That's me those statistics are talking about. And those numbers barely hint at the hard facts that underpin the dark, squiriming truth of what it means to be addicted to video games.

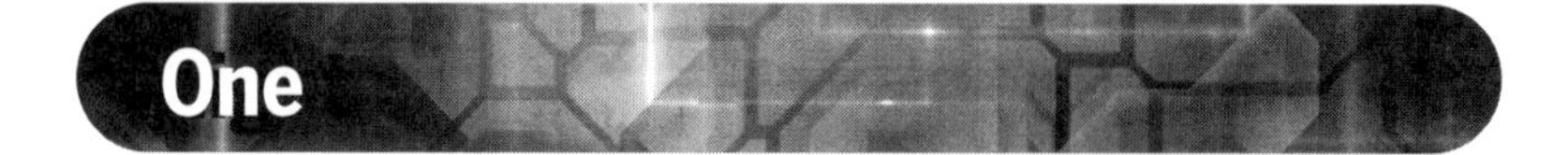

One

ADMITTING I'M A VIDEO GAME JUNKIE

The truth is rarely pure and never simple.

—OSCAR WILDE

December 31, 2007. I'm standing on the Arlington Memorial Bridge, maybe an eighth of a mile from the Lincoln Memorial loop-de-loop, and the mid-teens windchill has my breath coming in gasps. My asthma gives me a rough enough time, thanks to the 235 pounds my five-foot-nine frame heaves about daily. Tonight I've forced myself to march out into the 9:00 PM darkness to where few cars dare to go, thanks to the intermittent freezing rain. Even my thick-soled Colorado hiking boots are having a difficult time gripping the slickness.

I told my wife I was heading to CVS for cough drops. Instead of stopping at the drugstore at 23rd and C Street, however, I just kept plodding along, head hunched against the cold and the wet. Yeah, I was unsure of my destination. But damned if I was going to head back home to another bout of the "What the hell's wrong with you?"

one-upmanship that always leaves me on the losing end.

I'm focusing on the plink-plink of rain against icy ground and the crunch of my boots as I head farther away from home. For as long as I can recall, I've been my own best company. I enjoy long walks to nowhere, although lately that's proved to be less calming than ever, thanks to my perpetually unquiet mind.

For three years, every thought has been dominated by a single focus: the World of Warcraft, a massively multiplayer online computer game (MMOG), also called a massively multiplayer online role-playing game (MMORPG), in which players control characters who explore a huge virtual world, battle monsters and other players, socialize in enormous cities, and complete quests for money, fame, experience, and loot.

While others are living normal lives, I'm actively occupying my alternate world. I inventory my characters. I prioritize quests. I mull over high-powered weapon trades. I reimagine my gaming group's website. I fret about the battleground honor I need to earn. I consider how many real-world dollars I can afford to spend to buy in-game equipment on eBay or from gold farmers (people who make a career out of playing video games simply to sell acquired virtual loot for real-world cash).

Consumed by this never-ending, breathtaking virtual universe that I discovered by accident three years earlier, I might as well have been clicking away with my mouse in front of my twenty-one-inch screen even here, dozens of blocks from my home machine, as if an unseen digital umbilical cord is keeping me eternally wired to the game that demands my every waking moment.

Halfway across the bridge, I stop. My brain is telling me to climb up on the barrier. In fact, it's insisting on it, ridiculous as it seems for a thirty-five-year-old professor to huff his way up a frozen concrete barrier on this D.C. bridge. I haven't climbed a tree or a fence or anything for fifteen years, but muscle memory serves me well. As a child, I squirreled up the fifty-foot pines behind our Menomonee Falls, Wisconsin, house and the crab apple tree out front. The neighbor's slag-rock chimney was fair game, too.

Now, standing atop the barrier between safety and the plummet to certain icy death, my brain is holding me hostage, despite my crippling fear of heights. My kids hate me. My wife is threatening (again) to leave me. My friends no longer bother to call. My parents are so mad at me, they don't bother to visit their only grandchildren anymore, even here in D.C., a tourist paradise they've longed to visit for years. I haven't written anything in countless months. I have no job prospects for the next academic year. And I am perpetually exhausted from skipping sleep so I can play more Warcraft, the latest video game to have a choke hold on me.

"You're not good enough. You'll never be good enough," my brain insists, flogging me with feelings of worthlessness, well-earned shame, regret, despair, and panic that I'll forever remain unloved, alone, and scrambling for a glimmer of meaning in my life.

My head turns swimmy, and for a moment I can't see straight.

This is absurd—leaping to one's death at the apex of winter on a bodiless bridge. James Stewart even contemplated the same swan-dive scenario in *It's a Wonderful Life* (admittedly on a much less historically significant bridge). Only he had a guardian angel flitting around, ready to pull a Walt Disney abracadabra and make everything terrific. I can't shake the idea that if I had my own guardian angel, I'd snatch her out of the air by her gossamer wings, smash her in the chest with a balled-up fist, and steal her lunch money to cover another month's subscription to Warcraft.

The wind blows a strand of hair across my eyes, and I push it back, noticing how greasy and matted my hair has become. It might've been two, maybe three, days since I'd showered. That's what a recent eighteen-hour stretch of gaming, followed closely by another five-hour stretch, does—you skimp on nonessentials, cutting every corner you dare to squirrel away a little more game time.

God, it's cold.

A semi roars at me from the Arlington side, and for a moment I'm sure he'll phone 911 about the nut-job pirouetting on the bridge railing. But whether the guy was fiddling too intently with the XM radio tuner or was simply too amped on NoDoz and cheap cigarettes, speeding along to a New Year's Eve party, he keeps driving. Within twenty seconds, the crimson glow of his taillights vanish around the bend.

Want to know why I haven't already jumped into the Potomac? It's because the distant memory of the old, responsible me whispers that I've been too lazy to have increased my insurance from my prefatherhood years. The current cash payout wouldn't be enough to really make a difference for my wife and my two daughters.

My messed-up brain screams at me to do it anyway and let them reap what they have sown for not supporting me. For not loving me unconditionally. For not understanding. For screaming at me endlessly to "stop playing that fucking game," the one thing in life that gives me any sense of satisfaction, joy, accomplishment, and purpose.

Screw them all, my brain tells me again, persuasively.

But there's a difference between wanting to die and wanting the tumult in your life to die. Sometimes the only way to imagine that all that crap will cease is to imagine yourself dead, at peace, one with God and the universe and all that. Enter the suicidal gesture and my current dilemma: to go for it or to step down and face the hell that my life has become.

Shit.

A moment of clarity arises, like the tip of an iceberg in a swirling sea of confusion. I don't want to die. And getting to this point is, I now realize, what this late-night walk was all about.

And then comes God's little "haha."

I slip.

Right as I'm trying to clamber back onto the safe side of the walkway area, my left heel catches a patch of invisible ice, and my leg shoots out in cartoon fashion. For a moment, I am Wile E. Coyote minus a little sign that reads YIKES! as I hang in the air, defying gravity. Then reality returns, and I collapse onto my back, WWF-style, the wind expelled forcibly from my chest in a rush.

I begin to slide the wrong way off the ice-shellacked railing, the Potomac suddenly a big dark magnet and me a huge lump of iron slag. One of my boots tears loose and heel-over-toes all the way down until it's lost in the swirl of wind-stirred water, which is frigid enough to kill a man faster than being shot in the gut.

It's not hypothermia that kills you, I've learned from one of those Discovery Channel shows, but cold shock. You inhale the water, which leads to heart attack, stroke, panic, gasping, and hyperventilation. Next on the agenda: rapid drowning.

Hypothermia operates on a scale of hours; cold shock takes mere minutes.

Oh, my God, this is it.

I manage to hook one elbow through the concrete pillar and try to hoist myself up, but my body feels leaden, even without the rain weighing me down more than I ever imagined.

I begin to holler for help, my voice faltering as my asthma flares, making each gasp for breath a blinding chore.

Of course, I didn't carry an inhaler with me because I didn't have one, so poorly insured are we here in D.C. With our Clemson, South Carolina, house sitting vacant and unsold since July 2009, I couldn't afford the Proventil or Advair anymore, but now I wish I'd splurged on it and committed to eating Ramen noodles for a month for a single deep puff of that miraculous, oxygen-giving medicine.

Two cars now worm their way carefully onto the bridge, one in each direction. I can't make out the Arlington-bound one, but the other is a fancy Lexus, dazzling red like the color of arterial blood. Eyes wet from wind-whipped tears, I try again to scream for help, but nothing short of a gunshot or nuclear boom will attract anyone's notice tonight as people hustle from party to party.

The idea that I might not again enjoy spoon-feeding my one-year-old her beloved sour cream, read *The Lord of the Rings* trilogy again over a lazy weekend, or watch the final season of *Seinfeld* that I'd managed to miss on TV began nagging at me.

I peered down at the waters below.

No, I wasn't ready to die. Not tonight.

With one leg over the top, I shifted my weight until I precariously got my body to move in the correct direction. Farther. Farther. Then gravity took charge, and I spilled over in a heap toward the pavement, where I lay inert and exhausted, wondering if I'd ever walk again. The tendrils of pain shooting up my legs and back suggested permanent disability. Perhaps I'd be wheelchair-bound.

I fumbled for my cell phone but realized that in my haste to leave that evening, I'd left it atop the mantel in my office at home.

I sat up gingerly, shaking—not because of the cold working through my coat and clothes, but because the decision not to jump had nothing to do with family, financials, or revenge.

It was Warcraft. I was scheduled for a ten-man raid on Karazhan (a top-level dungeon with some of the best loot in the game) at 11:00 PM with my guildmates, and I couldn't bear the thought of missing it—even if that meant gluing my eyes to my laptop while my kids and my wife watched Dick Clark mumble in the new year on TV, or postponing the ER visit to handle my aching frosty feet until the next morning.

That's when I realized I was already dead.

RANGE WARS, OR HOW I GOT HOOKED

Of course it's the same old story.
Truth is usually the same old story.

—MARGARET THATCHER

I was a big reader in elementary school and devoured stacks of books by the week. We also had an Atari, and I regularly thumped my brother in 01 Combat and Yar's Revenge. But nothing snared my attention like the miraculous, better-than-real-life worlds I discovered through J.R.R. Tolkien, C. S. Lewis, Marion Zimmer Bradley, Stephen King, Robert Cormier, Ray Bradbury, and Harper Lee. I whipped through Jerry Spinelli, Richard Peck, Virginia Hamilton, Piers Anthony, Isaac Asimov, and Gary Paulsen, and I was constantly searching for new literary thrills.

When my folks confessed that my dad had a job offer—by "offer," I mean a move to Chicago to "keep your sales job at Amoco or be out of work" demand at age fifty-one—we were gone within three weeks. Just after breaking the big news, my mom took me to the Northridge Mall's Waldenbooks. She knew that I didn't make friends easily and that moving would most likely be the death of my already tentative social life. Everyone knew that.

It was no surprise, then, that she bought me a book by way of apology. When I flipped through Terry Brooks's *The Elfstones of Shannara* but still refused to get excited about the Chicago move, she gave in and bought me Zaxxon, an Atari game, from the electronics store next to JC Penney's. Anything to shut up my whining.

My brother, Aron, on the other hand, was a people magnet. Tall and lean, he had the same type of charisma that made Barack Obama a viable candidate to replace George W. Bush. People listened to my brother. People responded to him. People simply liked to be around him. Even when he wasn't playing bass in popular local rock bands, he had groupies.

Me? I usually remained ignored in a corner, unable to manifest even the dimmest glow to compete with his brilliant shine.

And so the four of us moved that March from a brick ranch-style home in Menomonee Falls, Wisconsin, to a brick ranch-style home in Palatine, Illinois, an affluent northwestern suburb of Chicago full of stressed-out, mid-level white-collar folks who occasionally went crazy. What made Palatine famous wasn't its connection to rocker Ted Nugent, science fiction writer Frederick Pohl, or *That '70s Show* alum Christina Moore, but the Brown's Chicken massacre, in which two assailants robbed the restaurant and murdered all seven employees back in 1993. That crime went unsolved for nearly a decade before an ex-girlfriend of one of the murderers turned them in.

Honestly, Palatine wasn't the worst place to live. Still, I was shell-shocked by the experience (my father even whispered to my mom that I was walking around with a "stunned Vietnam vet" look), so my parents didn't make me go to school for a few weeks after we'd finished unpacking. I just sat alone in the basement in the dark and played Zaxxon so much that we had to replace one of the joysticks when the button wore out.

I kept telling myself it was stupid to be wasting days trying to top my own high score on a video game. But I kept playing as if I were on the cusp of some crucial understanding that I'd never receive if I reentered the regular world of my father—the world that made families move, forced people to cut back on their retirement savings and book purchases, and drained the joy from my eyes. What I'd learned about the real world was that it meant misery.

By the end of March, my folks genuinely feared truant officers busting down the doors to look for me. I finally reported to Virginia Lake Elementary School, where I attended classes for the last few months of sixth grade. In Wisconsin, I'd been in the gifted and talented program, which meant that they taught us German in third grade, we designed our own role-playing murder mysteries in fourth grade, and we regularly got yanked out of the humdrum classes to build gigantic rat mazes with 3,000 toilet paper rolls and work with BASIC on an Apple IIe computer. Our favorite pastime, though, was playing the Oregon Trail as a team. We learned a little bit about nineteenth-century pioneer life, but the best part was the hilarious ways we died: diarrhea, snakebite, exhaustion. And my favorite? "You have died of dysentery," a phrase that found its way onto T-shirts and into Internet lingo.

What "gifted and talented" translated into in Illinois education-speak was "retarded." Despite my protests and my 130-plus IQ, I was sentenced to a sixth-grade class where the average brain fizzled away at perhaps seventy-five watts. The administrators wouldn't make a change without transcripts and records and things we didn't have handy. My parents finally just told me, "It's only for two months. Just go with it."

Even worse, Virginia Lake was a K–6 school, versus my Wisconsin school, which had been grades 6–8. I mean, really, I suddenly had recess again? Twice a day, too? And there were barely any quizzes or tests, because the adults in charge didn't want any kids feeling bad if they did poorly. I was dying of intellectual dysentery.

My new teacher, Mr. Porto—it's not hard to imagine how we had fun with *that* name, especially with his thin, 1970s-style porn-star moustache—came up with an ingenious way of rewarding good behavior. Like a scientist doling out food pellets to his best maze-running rats, Mr. Porto let us accumulate photocopied play money, "Virginia Bucks" (VBs), through our academic and social successes. At the end of the year, we could spend it on "all sorts of nifty prizes"—that is, the crap he found when clearing out his garage and school desk drawers. Score a perfect 100 on a book report, get two VBs (STDs, we joked). Clean up after yourself, really spic-and-span, and get one VB. Win the weekly spelling bee, get five VBs.

During the last seven weeks of classes, I accumulated more than 200 Virginia Bucks while burning through afternoon and evening sessions of Atari by myself. The other kids, who'd all been there the entire year, barely had that many combined, because you lost bucks when you screwed up, swore, or acted in "any way that proves detrimental to the class."

During the big auction day that followed, I bought a stuffed green bear just because a girl who told me I "looked lame" wanted it. And I bought a corncob doll of an old lady sitting in a red-wire rocker for my mother. The rest of the Virginia Bucks I threw in the trash after my last day at Virginia Lake.

Mr. Porto saw, but I didn't care. Although he wanted to be like the hip and nurturing know-it-all star of *Welcome Back, Kotter* (who, curiously, had a porn-star moustache as well), Mr. Porto wasn't, and the smug superiority he exuded from thinking he was the best teacher on the planet irked me. That's why I did it.

I also did it because I was angry we'd moved, angry I was alone, angry my brother already had a cadre of friends, and angry in general. I seethed for no particular reason, or I seethed for every reason—depending on how you viewed it.

❖

One late April afternoon in Virginia Lake Elementary's library, a semicircular room with too few bookshelves and too many rubber-mat play areas, I found myself skipping the chill air of lunchtime recess and scanning the book spines for anything worth checking out. After a week of watching the other sixth graders play Butts Up, I knew this wasn't my crowd. Butts Up was a ridiculous game in which whoever was *it* would crouch against a brick wall and cower while other players zinged a tennis ball at his butt. Everyone kept throwing until someone hit a "butt bull's-eye." The *it* then got up to locate the offending ball and whipped it at the skull of anyone, who, if hit on any part of his body, then became *it*. There might've been other rules, but that's primarily what occurred.

Maybe I avoided recess because the two most popular kids in our grade were from one of the new housing developments in town (likely subsidized through government agencies, I realize now). Both were bigger and more mean-spirited than the rest of us. Ralph, the tall one with a long nose and a natural wave to his big head of hair, would chuck the ball right into the face of the nonparticipants who were bouncing a kickball or cracking jokes in a circle nearby. Often there'd be a bloody nose or even torn-up knees from someone getting knocked flat.

"*Por supuesto*!" he'd yell, laughing. And everyone else who wasn't bleeding from the nose or the mouth would laugh, too.

As I said, not my crowd.

The library was near the cafeteria, so it stank of pizza sauce, spilled milk, and graham crackers, which were routinely crushed into the industrial gray carpet by the feet of first and second graders. For me, though, the library was a refuge. The hall monitor didn't even stop me any longer when I swapped recess for the muggy, booky warmth of this small room.

In one of the reading nooks, I had rediscovered Tolkien's *The Hobbit*, a book I'd read a few years back but that hadn't made an impression on me. This time, the lovely writing caught me. I was captivated by Bilbo as he rode the barrels down the river toward Lake Town and helped the dwarves destroy Smaug the Magnificent.

"What are you reading?" came a voice from above, startling me.

I shut the book so quickly that I pinched my finger. The voice didn't come from the librarian, Ms. McGee, a potbellied, middle-aged woman from Indiana who routinely ignored me if she wasn't out sneaking a smoke. This woman was a teacher. You could just tell by the way she radiated authority and a sense of propriety. My father would've called her "a lady with demeanor," meaning that she radiated class.

"Just some Tolkien," I said, fearing I'd lost track of time and was about to be nailed for not returning to class promptly.

"I see," she said, pursing her lips as she peered down at me where I sat Indian-style on the floor. I realized that I should probably get up, only my legs had fallen asleep because I'd been in that reading nook so long. I struggled past the pins and needles to get my legs moving, nearly falling twice. It must've been a ridiculous thing to witness.

She finally said, "I haven't read him in a long, long time."

"It's good." It was. Reading a terrific book gave me a real buzz, not unlike what Dewar's, one-night stands, or late-night WoW (World of Warcraft) would later provide for me. Sometimes I wonder what would have become of me had I found those vices at this point in my life. Annihilation, most likely.

Kind of eyeing me up, she said, "You know, I've seen you in here before."

Here comes the boom, I feared. I imagined detention, suspension, or any number of scares I had little experience in but was routinely warned about. Ralph knew about detention and told us horror stories: whippings with a belt; yelling like a drill sergeant so close to your face you could feel the heat; the wet of the teacher's breath on your cheeks. Of course, I now suspect that Ralph was beaten at home instead of during detention—he had the strap marks to show it. One time during Butts Up, a windblast sent his shirt up over his head, and we all saw the vertical lines of raw, angry skin. At age eleven, I was petrified by that kind of violence.

"I'm late for class," I said. I slipped the Tolkien onto the returns counter. "I should be going."

"I'll write you a pass, if that's what you're worried about," she said.

I gave her a better once-over, taking in the smile lines of her cheeks, the hint of blue eye shadow on her eyelids, the spill of a single blond ringlet from a topknot, the length of her slender, distance-runner's body. Even her black-ribbed kimono shirt, the V surprisingly deep, suggested she wasn't like most of the teaching stiffs I'd encountered.

She smiled—though thinking about it now, I suspect it was more of a smirk.

"I'll take that pass," I said, testing her.

"Tell you what. If you head straight back to class right now, you won't need a pass. But sometime you should swing by my studio and see the game I've been working on: Range Wars. It's loosely based on Tolkien's work."

"A video game?"

She laughed. "For the Commodore 64, yes. I've been working on it for two years. I could use a fresh tester to see where it's buggy. So come by sometime and help me out, okay?"

The way she phrased it, it didn't sound like a question.

"Sure," I said, trying to imagine what Range Wars was like. I loved Tolkien. Most of my teachers didn't read anything worth reading. "What do you think of Bilbo?" I had asked Mr. Porto not even a week earlier. His response: "Billboards?"

❖

I had debated for a few days about going to her studio, yet on Saturday afternoon there I was in the suddenly warm air of early May, riding my blue Ross ten-speed along Mill Valley Road and trying to locate number 913, where Mrs. Monroe lived and had her computer studio. We'd had a few good chats at school about her old Dungeons & Dragons playing group and her stint as a freelance artist. We both laughed about the Oregon Trail, which she'd played a good deal, too. She always steered the conversation to her masterpiece computer game Range Wars, repeating that I'd be crazy not to see it, the graphics and animation "were so mint."

To a budding video game junkie who was dissatisfied by the current retail game offerings, this was a powerful persuasion.

Number 913 was a big colonial-style house with fat pillars and a long crushed gravel driveway. Ten minutes of self-discussion later, I put my bike up against one of the white pillars and rang the doorbell. I thought of how the other kids would razz me if they knew I hung out with a teacher—and on the weekend, yet, instead of riding my bike, tossing a football, or seeing the Bulls take on the Lakers on TV.

A brass pot of amaryllis sat on the porch to the left of the door, thickening the air with its heavy scent. My mother had amaryills on our back porch, although hers kept dying no matter what she tried. I rubbed my nose and tried not to sneeze.

Mrs. Monroe appeared darkly tanned, as if she'd spent the whole week beside a pool, baking herself in sunlight. And her hair color had altered—almond brown now, with natural-looking red and gold highlights.

"Hey, there. So glad you finally made it."

I followed her inside, leaving my bike out front. I considered chaining it up—a habit I'd developed after having my Huffy stolen right off the school lot in Wisconsin a year earlier—but then realized how dumb that'd look.

"Thanks," I said, as if she'd paid me a compliment.

"So. What shall we do?" she asked, her hands on her hips.

"I'd love to see that game," I told her honestly.

Mrs. Monroe laughed quietly. "Of course," she said.

She pulled me through the foyer into the front room, tugging hard on the sleeve of my Van Halen 1984 black T-shirt, which I'd inherited from my brother when he hit his latest growth spurt. I began to wonder if I should've dressed up. Were jeans shorts and a lousy T-shirt appropriate for a teacher's house?

"C'mon," she said, laughing again. "Let me show you the place first."

All through the house, mahogany paneling gleamed on the wainscoting, and ornate plaster moldings adorned the ceilings. Nearly every room had some sort of mirror on the wall, too, which I found a little weird since I was nearly vampirelike in my tendency to avoid them. A little preteen acne had made me amazingly self-conscious. I didn't understand that this was the house of someone who wanted to be surrounded by beautiful costly things. Few eleven-year-olds recognize the difference between surface and substance, gesture and reality.

The dining room walls were covered with fine white silk, and the original cherrywood sideboards, filled with bone china and polished silver, stood against them as if they had been there for a century. My mother was an Iowa farm girl. Our house was covered in rusty scythes, harness hooks, and plow blades. Here a bulbous crystal chandelier hung in the center of the room, each of the hundreds of pendants brightly polished and glistening with its own light. The round table in the middle was certainly big enough for ten to eat at comfortably, I noted.

The effect was mesmerizing. Even a dumb kid could see how beautiful her house was. I scratched at a budding zit on the back of my neck and tried to think about what I was feeling. Impressed? As if I were on some kind of expensive vacation to a resort my family couldn't afford? A little awestruck?

We drew to a stop in the upstairs hallway. Mrs. Monroe smiled again at me. I could see her teeth were large and even. She said, "So what do you think?"

"It's a great place. Big, but great." *You sound like an idiot,* I told myself.

Mrs. Monroe had a way of twisting her lips and making an exaggerated face before speaking, as if demonstrating that she was thinking her words over carefully. It reminded me of a pudgy brunette whose name I can't recall who sat across from me at the small round table in Mr. Porto's class. I didn't care much for her—she liked to nibble Cheetos from her purse beneath the table, her fingers orangefying throughout the day.

"Thanks. It's a gift from my husband."

"Your husband?"

"My late husband—he died two years back. He was a stockbroker for Merrill Lynch. I think he worked for the Mob, too, but I'm not sure."

We were down the hall from the bedroom, I realized. Did she realize? I wondered, not contemplating why Mob references and dead husbands weren't a complete turnoff. I could feel my pulse racing. Having started puberty prior to last Christmas, I knew hard-ons and desire and electricity-in-your-teeth yearning.

She directed me into a sparsely furnished office with a long glass table and two leather chairs on rollers. Two Commodore computers ran noisily on one end. Pencil sketches of beautiful elf maidens, broadswords, horse-drawn carts, and scar-faced goblins covered the room like wallpaper. The room smelled faintly of coffee, a scent I knew well since my parents went through three pots of decaf a day.

She tilted one of the computer screens toward me. "What do you think?"

I couldn't speak. My heart rate and respiration shot into the stratosphere. The force of it struck me like a thunderbolt. All outside stimuli other than optical and aural ones melted away. There might as well have been celestial trumpets and cherubs.

It was a WoW-like, Halo-style (a popular science fiction shooter-game franchise with stunning graphics and award-winning music), first-person interface looking out on a fully realized fantasy town right out of a Peter Jackson movie. I don't know how she managed it on such primitive equipment—maybe my memory is skewed and it wasn't much more than boxy figures running around in a three-color block maze. What I recall, though, was magnificent. Intoxicating. Feeling as if the top of my head had blown clean off in surprise and amazement, I drank deeply.

She moved the character around for a few minutes. Then I got a turn. When I stumbled across a pissed-off ogre lurking beneath a bridge, she showed me how to yank out a spear and run it through him. With a whoop of delight, I made that 300-pound monster go down for good, bleeding and squealing until he lay still.

"These trees are alive and will snatch up the unwary traveler," she explained, as my character entered a shadowy forest. "Like evil ents," she added, and the geek in me was pleased by the Tolkien reference to the giant tree creatures. Then she showed me her version of a balrog, a dragon, and even the pint-sized hobbits, which she called halflings. TSR, the company that owned Dungeons & Dragons back then, would've paid piles of cash for this type of immersive experience, I remember thinking. Hell, I would've, too, had I something more than an eight-dollar-a-week allowance. But from what she said, no one had witnessed this gaming miracle yet. It was a virgin game.

"Not until it's ready," she'd repeated to me more than once.

"Cool," I said, wishing I could articulate the awe that shuddered through me.

We played together for fifteen minutes, my breath quickening as I uncovered more of the game that seemed a marvel of strategy, luck, and skill. My character—Mr. Car Wash—wasn't even dying every few moments like at first.

Then her hands started to knead my shoulders, really pressing firmly into my skin. I froze.

"You're a pretty handsome young man," she said, tracing the length of my forehead with her fingertips. My skin tingled as though she gave off sparks.

Still trying to maneuver our character over a narrow bridge so I could reach the Blackfield Dungeon, where she'd said the best treasure was, I swallowed nervously, hoping my voice didn't betray the extreme embarrassment I felt. "I—I don't know what to say. Thanks, I guess."

Range Wars temporarily forgotten, I half-turned from her, trying to hide the huge erection that made the front of my jeans shorts bulge.

Mrs. Monroe waved my awkwardness away with the sureness of one used to getting her way. "You're just being modest. C'mere."

She took my hand again—oh, it was sweaty and clammy, but she didn't complain, a wonder for which I was thankful, still spending all my energy trying to disguise my uncomfortable hard-on. I could've said no. I could've said anything instead of follow her dumbly down the hallway. She hadn't forced me; just the way she had taken my hand without question had shown me she was in charge.

There was something foreign in the way she moved, in the flexing of her fingers, in the way she cocked her head—an accent throughout her body. And then, as if by a magic trick in which you blink and find yourself whisked somewhere else, we stood in the bedroom. In contrast to the extravagant furnishings of the rest of the house, the bedroom was simple: a king-size bed with white sheets, a single oak dresser with a silver-edged mirror, a neon-red abstract painting in a black frame, and that was it.

She cut me a glance. "Do you find me attractive?"

My voice refused to work. I had never seen a woman undress before, a series of stooping postures and strange, awkward stretching. Her clothes lay wrinkled in a pile on the floor. I wanted to see what her body looked like, but all I could do was stare at her face. Think wolfish. Think predatory. Think hungry.

"Well?" she said.

This is it, my brain howled. My chance to run like hell and go be a kid on a bike riding through the neighborhood doing nothing, chucking pinecones at squirrels, or playing Zaxxon alone in my basement. I could just run to the bike on the front porch and tear off now, and it'd be over, an insane dream. She wasn't going to chase me naked.

But I couldn't leave.

"How's this?" she said, tugging on a silky green bra that had frills on it and a gauzy green skirtlike thing that was tight about her waist. Mrs. Monroe stepped toward me slowly, and the movement of her slender leg traveled up her body in a long, sinuous ripple. "Like it?"

I began to peel my shirt off slowly, the movements motorized and stiff. My eyes were fastened on hers and there was no way for me to extract myself. I was awestruck that I even had the ability to move. Some part of me, some flare-up of ego or innocence or self-preservation, still wished for me to break free of her spell. She sensed my confusion and pushed my hand against her breast, tangling my fingers in the silk and green fringe of the bra that felt like angel hair. Her sweat-slick face was lighted with eager expectation.

"I can't do this," I said, pulling away.

Her bright eyes fastened on me, and like a serpent's, they didn't blink or turn away. The air between us hummed with tension. My penis quivered as if in response.

She said, "I'll bet you can." Then she sidled close, pressing her firm, smooth body up against mine and running her hand across my crotch.

I shot hot, wet stickiness into my still-on underwear.

"It's okay," she said, putting her hand on my shoulder as if trying to console a crying child.

This wasn't pleasurable; in fact, I felt as if my insides had shriveled up and were crawling with maggots. I clutched my shirt against my chest, stumbled back into my pants, and ran all the way home, fighting the blistering sting of tears, my bike—and so much more—left behind.

That night, I didn't dream of Mrs. Monroe's naked, curved body or of having my first sex-related orgasm, but of Range Wars, how the twin suns lingered overhead like two silver coins, a pair of lustrous eyes watching me, beckoning.

❖

Maybe I enjoyed the game more than it merited, because it never made it to the market, so on some level it seemed like mine alone. But what self-esteem I had left was hanging by a thread as thin as spider silk, and to think much about my fleeting connection to Mrs. Monroe was to bring scissors into the equation. I wasn't ready for that type of destructive introspection and soul-blinding honesty. Not yet. So all I was left with was my memory of that game, wonderful and bewitching.

❖

I saw Mrs. Monroe again, despite promising myself I'd stay away. It was three times, in fact, before she stopped answering the door, no matter how hard I pounded on it—her and Range Wars and the entire taboo world of adulthood locked within the house that I was no longer allowed inside.

I lingered outside her house for weeks after she rejected me, found excuses to zoom my bike (which I'd snuck back under the cover of darkness to retrieve that first night) up North Saratoga Drive. The shades to her windows were pulled down, as if she didn't want anyone—meaning me—to know what was happening inside. Was she asleep, or perhaps peering out unseen through the security peekhole, watching me watching her? Was she inside doing some final tweaking of Range Wars, adding in weather magic and goblin snipers, as I'd suggested?

One Saturday afternoon, I snaked my way up and down every

street in our neighborhood a few times, from Topanga all the way up to Rohlwing and back, really working up a sweat for no particular reason, and I found myself roaring past her house, hoping against reason that she might be watering the thick-blossoming azaleas beneath her front picture window and would stop to wave me down and apologize, telling me she'd made a terrible, awful mistake in driving me away.

I heard the laughter first, her tittery tee-hee that I suddenly decided was a bit shrill and more than a little fake. My ten-speed's wheels slowed. Then I saw her coming around the side of the house, animatedly speaking into a cordless phone. She was wearing a blue string bikini with mini ruffles that I'd once peeled off her with my teeth, its stretchy terry cloth fuzzy against my tongue as I tugged the top free, then the low-rise bottoms.

I sped up, anger boiling up inside me. I didn't want her to see me. The fury I felt the day she spurned me returned tenfold. If I'd had some X-Man power, I'd have incinerated her right there, blasted her into oblivion. But then I would have used my powers to resurrect her and mind-warp her into loving me again, unconditionally and forever. She never said she didn't want me anymore—she had just said, "We can't see each other like this anymore. We just can't."

The illusion that I was grown up and important wilted in that moment, when she irrevocably became the adult and I was the child again, helpless to do anything except ride the waves and crests of the bitingly cold ocean of my existence.

❖

That summer, I became friends with Brad, a really good drummer my own age. We talked off and on about playing in a band together. We once went camping in his backyard in a brand-new brown tent his father had bought for the two of them to use, but they never did. Brad was a delinquent and had been arrested a few times, so I knew he was the one to approach with my plan. I asked him one June night if he wanted to play a prank on someone.

"Sure," Brad said, an eager wingman for anything stupid.

Near 1:00 AM that night, the first of Mrs. Monroe's windows exploded in an unsatisfying, glittering shower of glass that tinkled for seconds as shrapnel settled on the kitchen linoleum or tile or whatever hard floor the broken glass clicked against.

"That was great," Brad said, grinning. In his hand were two more fist-sized rocks we'd absconded with from a Japanese rock garden at some for-sale ranch house over on Topanga.

What came next was like a video game in which we racked up points with our rapid-fire suburban carnage. Ding, ding, clang! Our scores shot up to the stars. We sent the next rocks, then, a volley of stone that broke glass, cracked door frames, shattered floodlights, and banged all hell into the siding. We spent ten minutes destroying that place. I'll bet 80 percent of the windows were ruined, easy. And no one had come out to scream at us. Was she out of town? Had she moved?

In the distance, a police siren wailed. Closer.

Panting, Brad said, "I'm out of ammo."

I thought of how tenderly Mrs. Monroe had once rubbed my forehead with an icy cloth because I had a headache after playing a long afternoon of Range Wars, and I couldn't bring myself to fling that last stone. I dropped it in the thick green grass that she paid some service $100 a month to keep "low, tight, and bright."

"Me, too," I said.

Then I silently said good-bye to Mrs. Monroe and Range Wars and went home at last.

❖

For the next six years, I played every video game and game system I could, scrambling for the hot "next thing" as though my life depended on it. Yet the games got bigger and better so fast that nothing reigned for long. Gauntlet, 1985's arcade-style dungeon crawl, fell victim to the success of Dragon Warrior, a console role-playing game (RPG) so groundbreaking that nearly every RPG to follow borrowed heavily from it. And 1987 welcomed Maniac Mansion, the first point-and-click interface for an adventure game. Ultima V: Warriors of Destiny appeared in 1988, implementing non-player characters (NPCs) who acted differently depending on the time of day in the game, and it started to make game worlds feel very real. Throw in Tetris, the Legend of Zelda, Leisure Suit Larry in the Land of Lounge Lizards, Castlevania, Contra, the Oregon Trail, the Pool of Radiance, and Mega Man, and the 1980s were an exciting time for gamers.

No one really noticed how much I was gaming, because everyone—my brother, the neighborhood kids, my classmates—were all gaming like crazy, too. The difference was that they were just having fun. Me? I was trying desperately to recapture the fleeting sense of joy I had known years before—the pure delight of being spellbound inside the spirit of a dream that a video game created out of nothing.

Three

NETWORKING AT NORTHERN ILLINOIS UNIVERSITY (NIU)

> Computer games don't affect kids, I mean, if Pac-Man affected us kids, we'd all be running around in darkened rooms, munching pills, and listening to repetitive music.
>
> —GARETH OWEN

My parents finally left.

I sat alone in 1017 Stevenson Towers North of Northern Illinois University (NIU), nearly everything I owned stacked in a heap on one of the army-style mattresses. The smell of pine disinfectant and urinal cakes hung thick in the air—one of the communal bathrooms was just outside my door.

I nearly lost it. On the one hand, the idea of getting away from my hellhole of a high school, where I'd been unpopular and spent two, three, sometimes four hours a night playing Sonic the Hedgehog and

Golden Axe because I had nothing better to do except noodle on the guitar and dream about being famous, was a huge positive. On the other hand, I was eighteen and scared and unhappy to be on my own at a school of 25,000 that none of my high school pals were attending. They'd gone to the University of Illinois, Northwestern, Eastern, Duke, Southern Illinois University (both Carbondale and Edwardsville), Western, Roosevelt, Purdue, and Notre Dame.

Oh, a couple of Palatine High School kids I didn't know well went to NIU, but for most of the students, it was their backup, their backup-backup, or even their backup-backup-backup school, the type of place where they'd wear a paper bag over their heads if they ended up having to choose it. With parents like mine, who said they'd pay $10,000 per year max, I had to pass on the other two schools that accepted me (University of Southern California and Northwestern) and attend NIU. Go, Huskies!

As I was mulling over whether NIU—or college at all, for that matter—was perhaps the biggest error I'd made, in sauntered my roommate, in black biker shorts and a loose tank top that read F.B.I. (FEMALE BODY INSPECTOR).

"Howdy, I'm Steve," he said. We'd spoken on the phone one time a few weeks ago to make sure we didn't each bring a TV, a microwave, all that kind of dorm crap. It was up to me to bring the SEGA video game console—that fool didn't even own one.

So slender that he looked as if something was critically wrong with him, and with hair so light that he might've passed for albino had his eyes not been dining room–table brown, he was nothing like I imagined. He eyed me, too.

"I'm Ryan," I said, and we stiffly shook hands.

In *Blink: The Power of Thinking Without Thinking*, Malcolm Gladwell writes about a concept he calls "thin slicing," in which judgments that are made after minimal amounts of information are often more accurate than judgments that are informed by meticulous research, mental effort, and laborious processes. In short, make a snap judgment—a blink—about something, and go with it. That's the idea. I thin-sliced that Steve and I would get along satisfactorily but wouldn't be friends.

It turned out that a guy from my old high school, Mitch, and a guy from Steve's old high school were roomies just down the hall, so the four of us regularly hung out in their room. Mitch was a kid I didn't know in high school, but I had certainly known *of* him. Everyone from Palatine knew Mitch's story. Some dickweed choir kid drank himself stupid on Jim Beam, then lost control of his van during an erratic drive home and slammed Mitch—a diehard skater—off his totally rad board and into a brick wall, crushing his spine. Surgeons put enough of it together to keep him alive and more or less mobile, but Mitch had some eleven feet of scar tissue that he claimed he'd one day get a tattoo artist to transform into a gigantic Chinese dragon. With the big-time settlement from the lawsuit, he could probably have afforded to get it done in actual twenty-four-carat-gold ink, if he had been so inclined. Mitch walked again, but the nasty limp was too much like Quasimodo for some. I felt sorry for him. He didn't seem too pissed about it all, though. Maybe the seven-figure settlement eased the pain.

Mitch's roommate, Hong, was from Oak Park. Hong—I suppose he had a real name, but no one knew it, and we all called him Hong—and Steve had actually been pretty close in the past, so it seemed only natural for the four of us to team up nightly to play Trivial Pursuit, play Arnold Palmer Tournament Golf on SEGA, or watch MTV while devouring beer nuggets (deep-fried balls of pizza dough, usually dipped in marinara sauce) and cheap pizza. Hong proved to be a chronic depressive, often lapsing so deeply into despair that he'd curl up on his bed and skip classes for two days straight. I liked Hong a lot, and not just because he was into Japanese comics and could do impressions of George W. Bush that brought us to tears. He sported a glistening bald dome that he shaved three times a week.

"Why?" I once asked him.

"Question not the hairless one," he said in his over-the-top imitation Asian voice.

Hong had a strange family. He often shared moments with us, like the time his brother-in-law called at 4:00 AM, yammering into the phone that the secret to financial wealth was to own a 7-Eleven. "They're everywhere, man!" Or how one year on Hong's birthday, his grandmother sent him a pair of thick coffee-table books on the Peloponnesian War.

We drank together, too. Hong was particularly susceptible to alcohol of any type, so one night while watching the first episode of *America's Funniest Home Videos*—we were game enough to watch anything other than the growing news coverage about Operation Desert Shield, which had us worrying about a draft and being shipped to Kuwait to fight—we decided to drink a shot of lemon vodka every time anyone in the audience laughed. Steve, Mitch, and I seemed to understand the game. Put that bottle of Absolut to your lips, blow into it to create air bubbles that mimicked what happened if you really chugged at it, then pass it on, mumbling, "Wow, that burns going down. Woot!"

Hong really drank each time.

By nine o' clock, he couldn't stand. His eyelids must've weighed twenty pounds each, the way they were slugging down. He belched once. I could smell it from the bed across the room where I lounged, my feet up on the mini fridge that was set precariously on the desktop.

"Hey, you okay?" I asked, poking Hong in the stomach with a pool cue that he had walked off with from the billiards room at the student union. Mitch gladly paid Hong five dollars to see him try to hide it down the back of his shirt and pants in order to swipe it. He had to Frankenstein-lurch his way home, taking twenty minutes instead of eight, but he got the five dollars and hung the stick on their wall as a memento.

"I'm terrific," he said untruthfully.

"Sure you are," Steve said, leafing through one of Hong's chemistry books upside-down.

Hong suddenly sat up, then charged from the room with his hand over his mouth. He tripped over the pool cue I'd dropped on the floor. Still, he stumbled on.

"You guys actually drink any of that?" I asked after we'd switched to HBO and watched a decent chunk of *The Terminator*, nodding at the three-quarters-empty one-liter Absolut Citron bottle. I picked up Hong's guitar and played a little snippet from *Deliverance* on it.

No one had.

Arnold Schwarzenegger delivered one of the best lines in all of Hollywood: "I'll be back." We all said it with him, then laughed. I used my second-rate Schwarzenegger impersonation to add the line from *Red Planet*: "You got what you wanted, give the people the air."

We all laughed some more.

Hong didn't return from the bathroom. We had to send Mitch to fetch him, because he'd fallen asleep against a puke-covered toilet. The whole damn place stank of lemons, Mitch said, dragging Hong back by his leg. We helped Hong up onto his bed and tried to tuck him under the covers.

"You fuckers," he kept muttering into the pillow as he lay facedown on the bed. "Fuckin' fuckers."

It seems stupid and pointless now to get someone so blasted, but name me one person who went to a four-year public university who didn't at one time or another make it their mission in life to get someone else—usually a good pal—totally and completed shit-faced. I mean knock-down, drag-out drunk. Pickled their brain. Wasted. Blotto.

It's a rite of passage, and it happened to me, but not because they force-fed me oatmeal cookie shots or slipped me a roofie. I did it to myself plenty of times. Away from my parents, bored by the lousy classes (Intro to This, Intro to That), I had far too much time on my hands. I should've signed up for band after playing trumpet all four years of high school, but my parents and others warned me "how much more difficult college will be than high school. A whole new ball game." They had me really nervous—I didn't want to overcommit and goof up my GPA, which I ended up tanking for other reasons.

So I burned through that time by drinking and wearing out my SEGA controllers. I avoided practicing my guitar, which was stupid since I was a classical guitar performance major. Beer and video games made more sense than bloody calluses and endless scales. A Keystone Light with some cornflakes for breakfast, a beer or two after lunch to take the edge off the classes along with a dozen rounds of Tetris, then a sixer or so after dinner before I went out with Mitch or Steve or Hong or none of them to party, which sometimes lasted until 2:00 AM —which made those 8:00 AM classes pure murder.

I got more than a little obsessed with Tetris during the first few months in the dorm. It became my little electronic drug that gave me a nice high—later, studies showed that playing Tetris increased the consumption rate of glucose in the brain, which is what provided me with that high. What got me, too, was the sense of unfinished action in the game. All those blocks coming down in the wrong patterns needed resolution and order, and with a few button clicks I could put everything in its place. Bam—two or three rows disappear, and it's the most ridiculous burst of satisfaction. So I kept playing. That little devil of a game could keep me going for hours before a series of S and Z blocks (real Tetris fiends call them *snakes*) would ruin it.

That's the thing about Tetris. It's unwinnable, which perhaps was part of its appeal, too. Video game limbo.

My girlfriend then, a high school senior named Amanda, would complain that I always sounded exhausted on the phone when she managed to catch me in my dorm. Soused or nearly so, I'd tell her it was just too much studying, even though the three or four times her mother let her drive up to DeKalb to spend a Friday or Saturday night, I never had any books around. All we did was get tanked together and mess around until we fell asleep, snoring so loud that Steve would sleep on Mitch's floor rather than live with "that type of racket." My buzzsaw snoring was worse than Amanda's intermittent gulping and snorting, but not by much.

We'd been dating for a year, and here are the top three reasons I dated her: She was gorgeous. She was adopted (like me). And she played all heck out of Super Mario Brothers 3.

The best times we had were when her dad was away on a business trip and her mom was pulling a double shift at Cook County Hospital. No, we didn't drink tequila and screw all night—we got amped up on Jolt cola and would win Super Mario Brothers 3 as many times as we could in a single evening. Sex eventually became part of our relationship, but it was gaming that kept us truly linked. We were sad, lonely people who felt profoundly displaced in life. She was as gifted at flute as I was at guitar, yet creating beautiful music wasn't enough to fill the shared emptiness within us. What got us through the eddies and riptides of young love were video games, because the stakes were always lower than in real life, but the rewards felt exponentially higher. We understood the rules. We got better at it quickly. We won a lot.

That type of togetherness was so powerful that I couldn't imagine anyone else would ever understand me as well as she did. I was convinced I'd found my soul mate.

In mid-October of my freshman year, Amanda dumped me. It was with a two-line note that arrived in the mail one Thursday (had there been text messaging back then, she'd have sent me packing with a "w'v 2 breakup. Im sry. its nt u, its me."). The reason? It was just over. The real reason? She started dating a twenty-two-year-old secondary ed student from NIU who was finishing up his student teaching at Palatine High School. I went home the following weekend and heard all about it from a neighbor's younger sister who sat next to Amanda in concert band. She recognized me and was happy to dish, as long as she could jog in place while we talked, since her workout was a timed thing. Between retying her Jennifer Aniston hairdo back in a ponytail and gulping water from a little pink bottle, she confessed that Amanda was dressing more maturely (skankily), acting different (bitchy), and sneaking around in cars (screwing in backseats) with this goatee-wearing idiot.

"I don't like her anymore," my neighbor said. She flipped her sweaty bangs back and scowled, as if for the benefit of an unseen audience. Maybe just for me—I don't know.

Angry at losing Amanda, I started really drinking then—what I mean is, I tried to drown myself in alcohol. In the depths of an Old Milwaukee's Best haze, an idea came to me unbidden. *Revenge.* This asshole had no right being with her. Yes, she could date again, but wasn't it illegal or something for a student teacher to be preying on high school girls? I called the Education Department and told the department chairman, who didn't believe me.

"Do the fucking research," I told him, then hung up. Even a marathon Streets of Rage session on the SEGA wouldn't perk my spirits up, because I kept thinking of how the last time I played it, she had trounced me. She had ridiculous reflexes, and it translated into more than a few high scores that I had no hope of matching.

I was devastated, and a video game was not the salve it once was.

I loved Amanda despite all that had transpired between us, so I even drummed up the courage to call her mom—they were very close, almost best friends—to make sure that Amanda wouldn't get hurt. Her mom, a pediatric nurse, didn't listen to me. She insisted that I stop calling either of them and get some help for myself, meaning psychotherapy and some self-control. As if she knew anything about getting help—she had been sleeping alone upstairs for the past six years while her husband essentially lived in the basement of their house on a foldout cot, spending extra days on the road for work because home wasn't home for him. I understood that kind of agony. When home becomes a minefield, the constant buzz of stress works at you.

Amanda's mom assumed I was making the story up in some elaborate ploy to win Amanda back.

"Are you drinking?" she asked in an accusatory tone.

"Some."

"How much?"

I couldn't help it. The smart-ass in me said, "Not enough."

"If you keep drinking like this and acting out," Amanda's mother warned—and I could just see her wagging her pudgy index finger in the air— "you're in for a boatload of trouble."

It reminds me now of the fictional teacher in J. D. Salinger's *The Catcher in the Rye*, Mr. Antolini, warning Holden Caulfield that he was headed for "some kind of a terrible, terrible fall. . . . This fall I think you're riding for—it's a special kind of fall, a horrible kind. The man falling isn't permitted to feel or hear himself hit bottom. He just keeps falling and falling. The whole arrangement's designed for men who, at some time or other in their lives, were looking for something their own environment couldn't supply them with. Or they thought their own environment couldn't supply them with. So they gave up looking. They gave it up before they ever really even got started."

Amanda's mother was right. My fall was coming, and I rocketed toward it without realizing how fast I was moving because the rest of the world sort of fell away from me, I was so focused. Who the hell's going to listen to the angry mother of an ex-girlfriend who likes to meddle and who has the most screwed-up, dysfunctional marriage ever?

"Sure," I told her. "I'll get all the help I need." Then I hung the phone up, cracked open the last beer from Steve's fridge, and stared at the growing night sky, wondering if there really was something toxic about me as I fired up the Nintendo Entertainment System (NES) I'd bought the week before with the care-package money my mom had sent me. For the next eight days, I lost myself in Nintendo.

❖

Despite the near-constant video gaming on the new Nintendo, which I'd bought to replace the SEGA, and the amazing amount of alcohol I drank freshman year—sometimes two cases of beer a week—I got serious about writing. Maybe it was being dumped by Amanda that made me want to vent, I don't know. But as if someone had flicked a switch in my head, I started writing fantasy stories, which started to connect and grow, and before long, I'd churned out *Eyes of Most Unholy Blue*, a 445-page fantasy adventure novel on the 286 computer my father had sent me at school to do my homework on. It didn't have a single game on it—not Pong, solitaire, blackjack, or anything—or it'd have been commandeered for that purpose, too, most likely. During this time, it never occurred to me to buy games for the computer, thank God. Of course, computer games weren't nearly as complex or graphically interesting as console games at that time, so they didn't have the draw yet that they soon would.

"A computer is a necessity for the smart student," my father told me cornily that July, as we shopped and looked at dot-matrix printers, green-screened monitors, and computer desks. Sometimes my father gets all Polonius on me and spouts doses of wisdom like some Zen Buddhist midwestern salesman half in love with Confucius.

At the time, I didn't much care for having to lug a computer around. But once I started to see my identity shifting from rock star to published author (think Christopher Paolini, the teen who wrote *Eragon*—that's the type of youthful success I invented in my head), it was a godsend.

Confident that my written brilliance would dazzle anyone smart enough to give me a chance, I fired off insanely curt letters of braggadocio to three of the top literary agencies between sessions with Battle Chess and Final Fantasy. Noah Lukeman's successful e-book, *How to Land a Literary Agent*, suggests sending well-researched, polite, careful query letters to fifty agents total, starting with ten at a time. Why did I do only three, then? I didn't think I'd need more than that, and I even thought that three might be too many.

Some young hotshot at Curtis Brown wrote back immediately asking for the full manuscript. And two women from the other top New York agencies followed suit, asking me to send what I had ASAP. If you think of seeking an agent as trying to land a fish, you usually get nibbles, a tug. These were full-on bites that nearly ripped the rod from my hand and broke the twenty-pound line. One might be beginner's luck. All three, though?

I went out to Molly's, a local bar, to celebrate with Hong. Steve and Mitch weren't creative types and wouldn't appreciate this kind of moment, but I invited them anyway since we did damn near everything as a foursome. Hong played guitar—he was far better than I was at it, really—and he had sincere and achievable dreams of being a first-rate studio guitarist in Chicago. If he stayed on his meds and managed to even out the emotional dips, he'd have a shot at it. He'd get what this meant to me, I decided, as I walked over to Lincoln Highway. He understood dreams.

"So cool," he said, toasting my success, his eyes dark and irrepressible, as always.

Steve was typing a paper, but he eventually joined us, too, mostly for the free drinks, since I said I was buying. And why wouldn't I? I imagined quitting school within a year to write full-time from my mansion in Evanston, where I'd be so successful that Amanda and every other girl I'd dated would stalk me, they would now want me again so badly. What a beautiful, tempting dream. A revenge dream. An intoxicating dream of power.

The next day, when I got ready to print out the manuscript to send it to all three agencies, I encountered a problem.

I had never saved *Eyes of Most Unholy Blue* anywhere except on the hard drive. These were the days of 5¼-inch floppy disks, and I didn't keep any around. I never even considered the idea that the hard drive might fail. I didn't even have a printed-out copy for myself; I couldn't afford the reams of paper, since I'd been spending all my money on Keystone Light, cheap vodka, pizza, and video games (my collection of NES games was now up to sixteen). I just did all the writing and revising right there on the green-lit screen, expecting the damn thing to always be there.

The book was gone. The NIU tech people spent two hours with my computer. I paid a local computer repair geek twenty-five dollars to give it a shot, too, in case the NIU techs were stupid interns or just lazy or something (which they weren't—thanks for trying, guys). The millions of zeros and ones in the binary data that made up my 445-page story that top agents eagerly wanted was compromised, scattered into a spill of electrons and energy and, ultimately, emptiness.

My bestselling, million-dollar-advance book was gone.

Years later, I interviewed Terry Goodkind, author of the famous Sword of Truth series, for a piece I did on him for the *Las Vegas Citylife*. He was the first fantasy writer to crack a seven-digit advance for a single book. *Eyes of Most Unholy Blue* would've given me a shot a few years earlier than Goodkind. I stand by this claim—it's the best piece of fiction I'd ever written. It was naive and uninformed, yet it still had the sizzle and snap of pure passion that made every page a winner. In the way that some geezer who never played organized sports in his life can somehow sink a half-court shot for a million dollars at Chicago Stadium, I beat the odds that year with that book. The planets were in alignment. My biorhythms were just so. I had the perfect dose of emotional baggage, thanks to Amanda and everything that had happened earlier. I also had passionate intent.

I don't know why—it just was what it was.

I've tried three times to recapture that text from the faulty grasp of my memory, but all my subsequent training in writing makes me second-guess what I had or should've done, then I tinker and reconsider, and before long it's a whole damn different story. It's just plain lost. Like the draft of a never-to-be-published World War I novel that Ernest Hemingway left in a suitcase that was stolen from his wife in Paris in 1922, my epic fantasy would never know an audience. Brutal.

❖

Sophomore year I joined the marching band. Our director, Mr. Sims, was a notorious chain-smoking, foul-mouthed, Dewar's-swilling womanizer from West Point who regularly had band kids over to his house for pool parties and late-night Trivial Pursuit matches. Sims and I got along great. I couldn't stomach the scotch and water in highball glasses that he tried to foist upon me, but he usually had a twelve-pack or more of decent beer in the fridge, so his smoky split-level was welcome enough for someone of my meager means. I enjoyed the breaks from classes, and as much as I loved gaming, I needed the Nintendo breaks. I'd played guitar so much as a teen that I had blown my nerves and my tendons all to hell. I had given myself carpal tunnel syndrome so bad that I couldn't open a jar of peanut butter most days. All that button mashing took its toll, too. I still managed maybe two hours of gaming at a time, but then I'd need a rest or it'd feel like someone was dragging barbed wire through the inside of my arms.

When it came down to a choice—quit guitar or quit gaming—the decision I made at the end of my undergraduate career was simple. I packed up my Ibanez Roadstar II electric guitar and my Takamine classical guitar in their cases and left them in my parents' basement for the next ten years. Not once did I think I'd made a poor decision.

Thanks to my crazy loneliness and slow-burn anger over the lost manuscript, I passed on living alone to save cash and was rooming with Steve again, along with Peter, a mouse-faced kid one year older. We'd met him through a mutual friend, an allergy-plagued Sigma Epsilon who declared that Peter was "a regular, stand-up guy." Pete, like Steve, was a former gymnast, and that—like Skull & Bones or some other secret society whose members flashed a special sign to one another—made them instant best friends. Me? I thought they were both good for the rent. Peter also had a great collection of Nintendo games that he let me use whenever I wanted.

Steve and Pete air-jammed to Foreigner together and helped each other do the laundry. They had hand-walking contests in the parking lot and did backflips onto the couch. In retrospect, this might have been one of my happier moments, witnessing such carefree whimsy, but an accounting issue over our shared food bill—I'm a writer, video gamer, and sometimes rock star wannabe, not a rocket scientist—and the fact I had my new girlfriend, Kimberly, sleep over a few times a week pissed them off to no end, such that I became unwelcome at our own parties as well as at every other time. Our neighbors didn't like any of us, either, and I used to think that they were the ones who every few days knocked over my blue Honda scooter that I used to ride all over DeKalb because I loved the wind in my face and just riding and riding with nowhere in particular to go. Now you know what I think? It might've been Steve or Peter kicking it onto its side hard enough to shatter the mirrors twice.

I studied their happiness in more detail that anyone else would have. I imagined the late-night gab sessions I barely heard, muffled as they were through the floorboards. I tried to get a sense of what joy really was. My parents kept a respectful, distant relationship. My brother got girls, but he always kept them away from the family and away from me, and he was at a different college downstate, so I rarely saw him. Other than what I knew from books and TV, I never had any model for how successful relationships or even friendships worked. And if you base anything purely on books or TV or video games, you're as doomed as I was to fumble through life, angry and alone.

We had parties at least once a month. Rent parties, we called them. Our two-story on Hillcrest cost $600 a month, so if we had a three-kegger and charged $4 at the door, we could usually cover rent with a single seven- or eight-hour party. The mess was a pain and the noise got excruciating after the third or fourth hour, but rent was rent. The money our parents gave us that was earmarked for rent then became pizza money, movie money, beer money, whatever.

That's how I managed to have such an extensive Nintendo game collection.

Kimberly and I dated for something like seven months. She worked in the basement computer lab over in Daniel Hall, slowly becoming an expert on Macs, which would've given her a career option as a computer techie, but she kept insisting that "it was just a job, like slinging cocktails or handing out towels at the rec center." I visited her often at work and played around with the big-screen computer in her little cubicle, toying with the graphics features, testing out the word processor, noodling away at video poker. On the corner of her desk was a poorly framed, sort of blurry snapshot of me that she had taken when I drove her to the theater up on Hillcrest Drive to see *The Silence of the Lambs*. We both dug scary flicks and both, surprisingly, adored Sno-Caps chocolates. In that picture, I'm almost smiling, a rarity after my father told me at age seven that "you look funny when you smile."

"You like video poker?" she asked, bringing me a Diet Coke to help me wait out the last hour of her shift. Dimpled and blessed with shiny, full lips, she smiled a lot. She reminded me of Jennifer Connelly of *Labyrinth* and *A Beautiful Mind* fame. By that I mean wholesome.

"Not a bad way to pass the time," I said, cracking open the soda, which fizzed a bit onto my hand. I slurped it up and went for a straight flush with a three-card draw. I got nothing and lost my fake-money $200 bet.

"If you like games, we sometimes play games on the networked computers after we shut the place down for the day."

Something impressed me about the idea that all thirty computers worked together, spoke together, operated as one. I'd had a computerized English class in which we sent one another notes, worked on writing together, and could click a button to see what someone else was up to. Really cool stuff. But to play a game with a bunch of other people all at once? At the same time?

Intrigued, I said, "Absolutely."

Even after Kimberly and I broke up—I don't know why it happened, only that one day she moved from the dorm to an apartment and quit her job in the computer lab, not bothering to tell me why or give me her new phone number—I kept playing Tron with her old coworkers in the evening at the computer lab. The only game they had that worked well on the network was the bike game, in which you drove variously colored motorcycles and left a glowing wall behind you that was lethal. Hit an outer wall or one of the thin incandescent trails left by another bike, and boom, you were done. Sounds easy enough, but when you have eight or ten people playing, you were sometimes toast the second you began, your random starting point putting you right into someone else's trail. And even when you made it past the initial lucky die-or-survive moment, you eventually wound up trying to corner inside an ever-diminishing square of your own design, hoping you could keep banking well and not run out of room before your opponents boxed themselves in, a slow race to oblivion.

Great fun, that game. I played it a lot during the last half of my sophomore year. The only reason I didn't play it junior or senior year was that most of the lab people I knew, Kimberly included, were gone. I was also trying to lead a very active social and drinking life, and that took a commitment that precluded gaming for hours in the evening with a bunch of tech people, no matter how much fun it was.

Back then I was a lot less dedicated to any single addiction. Anything to thrust me out of the humdrum crap of my too-normal life would do.

I met Rob a few weeks later in marching band, and as we got to become great friends, I finally tried to explain what it was like playing the Tron game. Rob and I spoke the same language: video game geek. We played the early Bill Walsh football games on SEGA and burned through a pile of sports games on the NES, so if anyone would understand, it'd be my future best friend, our lives bonded by competition, video games, and music.

"It's like your entire body is lit up like a Christmas tree, every nerve firing as the game counts down to the start. You have no idea where you'll appear on the map, so your mind is racing. Do I need to bank left? Shoot? Hit the brakes?" I told him, wringing my hands at the memory of that kind of wild excitement. We had eight people playing the first time. Three went down in the first few moments. The rest lingered for a while, until I got boxed into a corner and finally took out two others before Kimberly eked out a win. "I'd always been competitive, Rob, but playing against other people in the same room like that? It was amazing."

A few years later, Kimberly got arrested in Milwaukee. It was in the papers. She'd been working as a high school track coach and started giving rides home after practice to one of the sprinters, a kid named Hank who lived near her studio apartment. From all accounts, he was a real handsome guy with a flattop and well-muscled arms, probably the type who was really popular in school and would've picked on someone like me endlessly. Kimberly started screwing him and got caught.

She was a really sweet girl; I wish I knew what happened to make her go sideways like that. I'd been an ass to girlfriends before plenty often, but with her? I really liked her. We argued some and had terrific makeup sex, but I basically treated her well and would've done so even if she hadn't introduced me to networking gaming. I even took her to my secret spot in Lake Geneva, Popeye's, and bought her a humongous cheeseburger and a beer to picnic with me there on that wonderfully quiet beach just down the road from where Dungeons & Dragons was invented by Gary Gygax back in 1974.

"I love you," I told her in that moment there on the beach, the moon emerging from the distant treeline over the water.

"I love you, too," she had said.

I think that whatever the reason was that Kimberly left me suddenly, it was all about her, and so was the affair with the kid later, I suppose. People just leave me suddenly. It's happened so often that I don't even register it as odd anymore. Mrs. Monroe. Amanda. Kimberly. My birth mother. Others.

Like breathing, it just occurs.

❖

Junior and senior year blended together in my mind as I moved into a basement-level efficiency way out on Ridge Drive. I had to repaint the window molding every three weeks to keep the walls from being overrun with splotches of Chernobyl green. But it was cheap and that was important—I blew money like crazy on stupid things, and couldn't keep hitting up my parents for more. They were well off, but if you get greedy, you get questions.

I also got dogs. It started with *a* dog. One. Singular. Heidi Beast the Yorkie. Driving home to spend a weekend with my folks in August 1993, I stopped in West Dundee for gas and saw the skinny red sign for Noah's Ark Pets right across the street. For no particular reason, I hustled on foot through the intersection and went into that two-story place that reeked of pine chips and animal food. I liked the neon tetras, the macaw, the gray-faced kitties, and the pair of roll-belly beagles, but what caught my attention was the pile of Yorkie puppies. Five of them. They stirred and rolled and yipped, and when the owner, a fat Irish woman with a brimless Bulls cap, clapped her hands at them, they all spilled out and pawed at her legs. That's when I saw a sixth dog. She'd been buried under the rest, unable to get free because she was so small.

That was Heidi. I like to think I rescued her. In many ways, she rescued me, providing me with the companionship, happiness, and unconditional love that I'd been seeking for years, I realize now. It's sappy and cliché, but I loved that dog fiercely. She was small enough to hold in the palm of my hand, so I took her into the grocery store inside my shirt pocket, I took her to movies, I took her everywhere.

Then I worried that she'd be lonely when I was at class. You know where this is going—before long, I had three dogs: Heidi Beast; Cubbie Monster, another Yorkie, twice Heidi's size but so dumb that she didn't care who was in charge as long as they all just played and barked and slept a lot; and Minnie Ogre the Chihuahua. I got her from a family that owned a funeral parlor in Oak Brook. Weighing in fully grown at a whopping three pounds, she had a snappy disposition that I admired. She could hold her own, even against Cubbie, who was close to ten pounds.

So I had this herd of dogs. Girls from the band learned about them and wanted to ooh and ahh over the puppies, so one terrific side effect of my dogs was the opportunities to get girls I'd otherwise never have a shot with. During the next two years, I had sex with a girl from my philosophy of religion class, one color-guard girl, and more than a few members of the NIU marching band. There were others, too. I just walked the pups past the dorms or in the fields near the student center, and I'd attract a crowd.

It was like playing some shoot-'em-up game on the Super Easy setting, which should've been warning enough to anyone paying attention, but I wasn't. School was a blur of Bs and Cs (plus one F I got in a logic class for telling a grouchy teacher's assistant to "Fuck off!" after he kept at me about a logic problem I didn't understand). Everything was a blur. I barely remember the video games I played the last two years at NIU, but I know that at the time I had incredible dreams about the games in which I was either playing them or was actually in the games as a character.

Sex was something that made me feel better about myself for a few moments, pushing back the guilt I felt over wasting an undergraduate career with half-hearted learning, too much gaming, and way too much drinking. I'd also really started thinking about what it meant to be adopted, to have been surrendered to the world so early in my life by someone who didn't want me. The brief flicker of intimacy and belonging that sex brought was the closest thing to magic I'd ever experienced, and I wanted it again and again.

Just as I'd done with playing guitar, then playing video games, I threw myself into the college casual-sex scene with a recklessness that verged on something truly dangerous.

It was the dogs that suckered the first few girls in, but after that, my own reputation did enough of the work. If you figure out how to make a girl or two really howl—I mean like biblical noise—word gets around. A skinny mellophone player a year older than I was had a dick reputation, too, only his was for thickness versus my length, a fact that a ponytailed girl from Idaho who played piccolo in the band admitted to me as we lay naked on the floor of my room—the dogs snoring on the futon, the radio playing some John Coltrane softly in the background, the Nintendo on in the corner with an MVP Football game paused mid-hike.

"Tell me, Lisa," I said, running my fingertips across her belly where sweat had pooled in her navel. We were taking a break after half an hour of all-out energy burning. "You think Ross Perot's got a shot at being president?"

"He looks like a turd."

That's about the extent of conversation I had with most of them. We watched a lot of *Home Improvement* and a bit of the election stuff, but it was clear that only I was interested in it. We listened to music sometimes, but this was biological, physical. Emotion was mostly absent from any of these couplings, except with Carla, Amanda's former best friend who went to NIU and was fifth chair in the clarinet section. I'd remembered her as an awkward high school girl who lived in the shadow of a very pretty older sister desired by nearly every guy at Palatine High School. Carla wasn't smoking hot in that way; her teeth were a little less uniform, her cheeks weren't smooth enough, and her silhouette didn't suggest enough curves.

But in her peach United Colors of Benetton outfit, with the afternoon sun making her French-braided blond hair come alive with gold, and her smile as she chatted with a friend as if she regularly knew happy moments in life, Carla looked positively impish. This was during a football game in 1989, the year before I left for college. And that's why I dated her on and off throughout the NIU years, toying with the idea of being with a wholesome girl who didn't want me for any reason except that I held her after sex, I told her how devastatingly pretty she was, and I liked to just stare at her, always seeing in my mind's eye that girl in the peach Benetton outfit who didn't know how terrific she looked, how sincerely nice and genuine she was. This wasn't even a line. Carla was terrific.

Here's how much of a jerk I am. When she was diagnosed with type 1 diabetes my senior year, I dumped her. Perhaps *dumped* is a bit strong, since we never officially dated—she called the on-and-off-again thing we had "whatevering," which maybe alleviates some of the I'm-an-asshole guilt I felt over it all. One thing I'm sure of, whatever we termed it: I left her alone to deal with her disease.

Yes, people up and left me. But in an overly aggressive defensive maneuver, I sometimes left them first so they wouldn't have a chance to leave me later. It's ridiculous, I know, but it made sense to me at the time. And realistically, in the larger scheme of screwups, it wasn't even in my top five blunders.

❖

For my twenty-first birthday, I followed through on a pact I'd made with a high school pal, Tim, even though I hadn't talked to him all that much since we'd graduated from Palatine High and he went off to a different university. My plan was to celebrate my May 20 birthday in Florida on the beach. No beach in particular—just Florida, just a beach. With classes freshly out (the University of Illinois, which Tim attended on a ROTC scholarship, was out, too), I picked him up in Urbana-Champaign in my red Nissan Pulsar, and we roared through southern Illinois toward Florida. Cranking 1980s hits such as Steve Winwood's "Valerie" and Amy Grant's "Baby Baby"—songs we both knew well from the radio we played as we worked summers at a Subway making countless cold-cut combos and meatball sandwiches for the folks of Arlington Heights—we drove straight through the night, taking turns at the wheel for an hour or two, trying to get there in one quick stretch.

The rain started up without warning just after dawn. Before long, I-85 had water sluicing off the road in huge amounts, really floodlike stuff. Even if the sun had come out from behind the clouds, this amount of rain in the air made visibility lousy, at best. We made it all the way to Atlanta without incident and were hauling ass south toward Valdosta, Georgia, in weather that would've sent Noah ducking for cover.

"Maybe we should stop," Tim said, putting down the Coke can in his hand. "Just pull over a little while until the rain lets up some."

I agreed and shifted into the left lane to pass a slow-moving Saab before exiting to a dry underpass. A semi came up behind us and flashed its lights. The Saab sped up, too, as if refusing to let me in. The wipers thumped mightily against the constant wet, and I sped up a bit to get out of this logjam. That's when I learned what it meant to hydroplane.

Hydroplane: (v) to ride on a film of water on a wet surface with a resulting decrease in braking and steering effectiveness.

"Oh shit," I said, as we continued south on I-85 at nearly seventy miles per hour, my car rotating on the highway's fluid sheath. In a heartbeat, we were facing backward, looking at the brown semi, snout to snout. We continued to spin, the world revolving around us as we moved and rotated, like one of those Vegas games in which you bet a dollar and spin, trying to win big bucks while avoiding the many "sorry, you lose" sections.

I remember thinking, *Jesus H. Christ, this is the weirdest thing,* as we continued spinning like a top down I-85 on the morning I turned twenty-one. It was like a spinout on V.R. Virtua Racing.

We went down the middle embankment, the tires deeply digging sideways into the mud, throwing slop all over the car as we ground our way some twelve feet into standing water that stank of sewage, seeped into the car from beneath the doors, and filled the floor of the car an inch or so.

"We're going to drown," I said, then realized how stupid that sounded when the water outside was no higher than a foot or so. It'd take hours of rain to even get dangerous. And if it were to continue, we could roll down the windows and swim for it.

A wrecker yanked us out two hours later for fifty bucks, and for another twenty-five it towed us into town, where some Ma and Pa repair place in Podunk, Georgia, straightened my tires and fixed the alignment for $200. One part of me wanted to leave and head home, but Tim wanted to see the ocean, and so did I, really. Besides, we had a plan, and if we hurried we could still make it to Daytona in time to get drunk on my birthday. We did.

I barely remember the DD-breasted waitress who set her nipples on fire, the bald guitar player who sang "Happy Birthday" to me at the Hilton bar (ending with "Happy birthday, dear dude, fuck me, fuck you!" and giving me the finger), or the five free meals I had that day at five different Denny's restaurants just for showing my ID. I barely remember the girl Tim picked up who in a *Gone with the Wind* drawl told us she worked for Hawaiian Tropic and would be touring the country in a swimsuit soon to hawk its products. I barely remember the dozen free shots I got in a dozen places, including one cowboy dump where a fortysomething woman in a fake leather balloon skirt and frilly white top planted a huge, open-mouthed kiss on me, saying, "How's that for a happy damn birthday?" I barely remember finding a pair of old stand-up arcade games in the smokiest corner of some biker bar and dumping twenty dollars of quarters into Gauntlet, laughing as I got mowed down as if my character, Blue Wizard, had a death wish. I barely remember getting a bad case of sun poisoning the following morning from falling asleep on the beach and then sleeping through so many hours of early Florida sun inferno on my skin that I couldn't wear a shirt for two days, the blisters were so huge and pus-filled.

What I remember clearly is how just before the car went into the ditch, one side lifted slightly, as if tempted to let us flip like one of those massive Daytona car-flipping, fiery crashes. I remember nearly going Dale Earnhardt at age twenty-one, with an utterly who-the-hell-cares attitude as Tim and I were a coin flip away from life or death. I was the ultimate apathetic Gen X kid, staring Death in the black void of his face, saying, "Whatever, dude. Just flip."

❖

Rob (my college friend from marching band) once told me this story about the spring of my senior year at NIU. He'd been trying to find me all day so we could go shoot pool together, a new buddy activity we'd been doing two or three times a week for nearly a month. (We used to play Bill Walsh College Football on the SEGA, but we got so good that it wasn't a challenge anymore, since we could score pretty much at will.) He finally decided upon playing the odds for where I'd be, so he just started checking the bars downtown that we regularly haunted. Three stops later he found me: there I was, bellied up to a table in the back of Molly's, with, Rob says, "I shit you not, thirty empty beer bottles around you."

Considering my quiet commitment to destruction, it's believable enough.

"How long you been here?" Rob asked, marveling at the aftermath of my binge drinking. He'd seen me put down a twelve-pack like nobody's business before, but this type of brain cell genocide must've given him pause.

"Damn long time," I answered.

He slid in beside me and ordered a Killian's of his own. When it arrived, the waitress gave us a withering look. Rob ignored it.

"What the hell's going on here?" he asked, his voice low and full of concern.

I said, "I'm on the slow boat to hell."

Thinking about that incident now and considering the period in which Rob is sure it occurred, I can contextualize it. It was just after St. Patrick's Day, 1994. Bill Clinton had been president for fourteen months. Four terrorists had been convicted for their roles in the 1993 World Trade Center bombing, which killed 6 and injured more than 1,000. The Church of England had ordained its first female priests. A

U.S. F-16 had shot down four Serbian fighter planes over Bosnia-Herzegovinia for violating the no-fly zone. Edvard Munch's *The Scream*, my favorite painting, had been stolen from a display for the winter Olympics in Lillehammer, Norway, and left behind was this note: "Thanks for the poor security."

The drinking Rob witnessed was because of the root beer schnapps incident from a few days earlier. It began like this.

After a microwave dinner of spaghetti and meatballs, an old favorite, I walked to the nearest pub, One-Eyed Reilly's, and met up with Peter, my former roommate and still casual friend. It was St. Patty's Day—the place was hopping. I'd been playing Final Fantasy VI for about three days straight, skipping classes to try to win that damn game. I'd stopped caring about grades sometime in my sophomore year when I realized there was little correlation between how much I learned and how well I did—I got a C- in a Bible as Literature course, but I'd never learned so much in my life.

So I just blew off the classes that didn't interest me and focused on what did: video games, girls, and drinking. Final Fantasy was just the latest in what had become my favorite type of game: role-playing. The allure of being a hero—something I absolutely was not, in real life—drew me in completely. I was never going to amount to much, I'd been told often enough, but I could save the girl and win the day with each new game, so I played and savored each victory like it was one more rung on the ladder leading out of the deep, deep pit I'd been living in forever. Sometimes it seemed that I could almost see the top of the pit just ahead. On days like that day, the pit was endless, and no matter which way I went, it was down.

I felt so incredibly zombified that when Peter called me to go out that night, I just mumbled, "Sure," then almost walked out without my wallet.

"Gotta love nickel beer nights," he said when I got there. We ordered two big trays of Dixie cups full of the cheapest beer known to man. It was Natural Light or worse, from the taste of it. Still, inexpensive beer was beer, so we drank for the better part of two hours.

Enter Emily and Yula.

Emily was a slender Korean girl with a wide face and thick, waist-length hair. She had a not-so-secret crush on Peter, who didn't return the affection when he was sober. The other girl, Yula, was known to most as Mrs. Ed, thanks to a massive overbite and a smile that showed so much teeth and gums you had to stare. She outweighed me by thirty pounds, easily, and even there in the doorway in her knee-length swishy silk skirt that was a pretty shade of yellow, you could see the sausages of her leg stretching the fabric, threatening the seams of her brown, thick-heeled boots. Yet she tossed her hair back, her bottle-job blond hair cascading out and behind her wonderfully as if she were on par with Cindy Crawford, a DeKalb native that more than half the NIU guys kept an eye out for. Crawford was rumored to make sudden appearances in local watering holes, but that's probably just an NIU urban legend, like the corn man who stole farmer's children or the mole people who hid in the sewers beneath the student center.

Peter waved his hand to the pair; he was nice to a fault, especially when tanked. "Have a seat, ladies."

They did, and soon we were chugging through platters and trays of beer—they had the green-dyed stuff out now, the color of Area 51 alien blood. Emily lit up a Virginia Slims with one hand, puffing away while downing cups of beer with the other hand, talking all the while in ADHD fashion. She shared her cigarette with Peter, who didn't smoke but was the type to do anything if a pretty girl asked him to. The dark purple lipstick on the tip of her slender cigarette left marks on his mouth.

Through the growing cloud of menthol smoke and the constant buzz of chatter, I kept staring at Yula, her solid torso and massive breasts that stretched her wide-collared blouse from button to button so that there were little arcs where you could just make out her skin, which was nearly the same shade as her Oxydol-white blouse. The boots had me, too. Their leather looked soft enough to make a pillow. Wrinkled like the face of a pug, they tempted me. How soft were they? I reached out under the table and touched the closest boot. Call it a cliché, but it felt like butter.

"Yummy," I said dully.

She leaned over the edge of the table to look me in the eye. "What are you doing?" she asked, not really upset by my constant attention. Half hidden by the table edge and having downed ten bucks' worth of nickel beers, we kissed. I want to blame her, to say that this girl who was only a 4 out of 10 on her best day (maybe 5½, with significant dental work) came on to me. But she didn't. At least, I don't think she did. I think something about her boots, the girth of her breasts, and the pretty swishy skirt urged me onward.

The air between us grew electric. Did anyone notice? In the crowd of Irish wannabes, including Peter and Emily, who each had a cigarette now, no one did. I could probably have hoisted up Yula's skirt, pushed her down on the table, and mounted her like a million-dollar bull right then and there, and few would've paid attention, much less cared. That's the beauty of alcohol, I suppose. It not only squelches your inhibitions, it also dulls all your senses to the stupidity around you—and your own stupidity, I suppose.

Emily blew smoke from her nostrils and laughed, a big fake titter that had Peter beaming. He apparently had told a joke, but I didn't catch it. The crowd was noisy, and my focus never veered from the smiling, skirted girl across from me.

"And that's why I got a B in chem," Emily was saying, nodding at me as if I should laugh because yes, it's funny, funny stuff. She insisted on being the center of attention. I offered her a weak smile.

"I'm tired of this horse piss," said Yula, never ripping her eyes off me. "I've got some root beer schnapps back at my place. Anyone game?"

I'd gotten pretty good at hookup code, and this was a clear wanna-come-fuck moment.

She was not beautiful. I did not love her. In most ways, I wasn't even attracted to her. Although academically brilliant—really, really gifted in book smarts—Yula was an emotional train wreck, glomming onto any bit of affection she could, which meant that she would think she had a boyfriend just because some frat boy had had sex with her on Hog Night (a fraternity contest whose utterly cruel, and possibly criminal, details I will spare you). I know that she had been with plenty of guys who one-nighted her, many from the band. Yula was simply not someone I'd ever want anyone to know that I had dated, had sex with, or hung out with except in large groups where it was clear we weren't together in any way.

Emily said she'd stay and have another tray of beer with Peter, who appeared ready to slump asleep right on the sticky tabletop if the rate of nicotine ingestion slowed down.

"Suit yourself," Yula said, standing quickly. She steadied herself by holding on to the back of her chair. A trio of girls behind us burst into some Britney Spears song, belting it out really horribly.

"I'll walk you home," I told her, leaving a ten-dollar bill on the table to cover our share.

I went with Yula back to her house, a two-story she shared with three other girls. I'll blame it on the alcohol, but I'm sure I did what I did for a host of other reasons, most of them because I hated myself, and so did she. I mean that she hated herself, but maybe she hated me as much as I hated her in that moment, both of us on a conveyor belt to a destination neither of us wanted but were unable to avoid. It was a collision of sad, desperate planets that wouldn't even end in a satisfying boom, just a muffled thump.

"Keep it quiet, they're probably asleep," she whispered as we entered through the kitchen door.

Stumbling more than a little, she detached herself from me—we'd made it the six blocks only by pressing against each other, groping a little, guffawing loud enough the whole time to draw stares—and went for the schnapps in the cabinet. I hated schnapps. Too sweet, too syrupy. But I didn't come back to Yula's place for the schnapps, which maybe she didn't realize, since she unearthed two highball glasses from a drawer of clutter and poured two drinks for us there on the coffee table in the pink living room, which we'd managed our way into.

"Why pink?" I said, sipping at the awful-tasting schnapps as I surveyed the room with my eyes. Once I sank into the futon couch, I couldn't get off it to really look around, as I liked to do in new places. She joined me with an impact that moved me like a waterbed wave. She yawned, a big toothy yawn that made me think of a hippo. "Nancy did it. I don't know why. Just one day, there it was."

With her booted feet up on the coffee table's edge, we burned through maybe half of that bottle while watching John Candy in *The Great Outdoors* on HBO, the tension between us rising until her hand slipped down the front of my pants and began moving fast. She might've been named after a TV talking horse, but even drunk, her root-beery breath reeking, the stink of secondhand smoke clinging to us both, her hands knew their business. She jerked and pulled with just enough speed and strength and tightness to have my full attention, giving me the type of erection that takes over all brain functions with the command *sex sex sex*. I eventually stopped moaning enough to think of her and her own pleasure, so I worked at the apparently really tricky zipper on the side of her skirt, like smooth liquid silk in my awkward hands. Giving up on the zipper (which was either a gag like trick candles or made by some antisex scientists to be a kind of chastity belt), I caressed her thighs through the skirt's fabric, kneading at her buttocks a bit, which made her groan and press into me with her body as if trying to meld our forms together. Her weight took my breath away.

I continued working at her as the sounds came from her pink-lipsticked mouth—smudged a bit, thanks to so much kissing—showing me that we were well past the point of no return. I wondered if she were already regretting things, too, wishing she'd gone home alone to watch *Oprah* on tape or play computer solitaire instead of hooking up with a trumpet player from marching band who had never once given her an ounce of attention prior to this night. This wasn't making love, not even a close shadow of it—plain and simple, this was screwing.

"You need a condom," she said, pushing my hand off her skirt, which half fell from her waist now that she had helped with the zipper. The room looked ghoulishly yellow, thanks to the only light coming from the TV, but even in that dim glow I could make out the top of lacy black panties. I kissed her hard, then pawed between her legs where she was damp and incredibly warm, even through her panties, which I tugged aside to push my fingers slowly up into her. The motion made the breath catch in her throat.

"Condom," she sputtered, trying to guide my hand away from her crotch but not hard enough to say she really meant it. Had she stopped kissing me or massaging my penis, I might've believed her. This is the classic mixed signal, which every red-blooded American male reads as *go go go go go* and which every feminist reads as "*No* means *no*, even when no one actually says *no*."

Yula breathed hot on my ear, her fingers tangled in my hair as she whispered, "Please. In my nightstand upstairs. A box."

My pants unzipped, I levered myself to my feet and looked down at her on the couch, the great basketball of her body there, too leaden from the cheap beer and schnapps to get moving, let alone with enough steadiness and energy to navigate a flight of stairs. I didn't like to have sex without condoms, and the idea of little Mrs. Edlings horrified me, so I needed that condom even though I savored the flesh-on-flesh contact, the penetrating heat that coursed through us both as we tested, furthered, and committed to a joint rhythm that proved seismic and oh so satisfying.

"I'll be back," I said, without thinking of Schwarzenegger but rather how I would negotiate the stairs in the dark myself when all the blood in my body was inside my painfully stiff penis. My brain firing at forty watts, I simply went ahead. Not even thinking of zipping my pants, I simply held them up in one hand and used the other to pull myself up the stairs by the handle. One step. Another. Deep breath. Another step.

There were three rooms on the top floor of their decidedly cat-smelling apartment. Which was hers?

I tried the semi-open door of the first room I came to and heard snoring. The second room seemed empty, but then I decided that the snoring I'd heard had originated there instead, so I returned to the first room and began to wend my way through dark shapes—clothes on the floor? school books?—to find that nightstand. Near the dead center of the room, something brushed against my thigh. I nearly dropped my pants in surprise. It wasn't me brushing against something; it was something brushing against me. I paused, sure I'd stumbled into the wrong room and awoken someone who was about to scream "Rape!" I cringed.

Then my pants were slowly lowered to the floor, and a pair of soft, gentle hands took control of my penis. In utter blackness—the windows were taped with cardboard—I stood half-naked, wondering if I'd fallen and cracked my head open just enough to give me a bizarre sex dream. I touched my forehead. There were no bumps, no bruises, no bloody gashes. My mind wheeled with the excitement of this unknown lover who was toying with me. Then she took my penis in her mouth and began giving me the most amazing oral sex I'd ever had.

I completely forgot Yula downstairs. She was probably asleep on the couch where I'd left her.

"Oh my God," I said as I came, nearly falling backward with sudden limpness throughout every muscle in my body. I felt fluidless and weak. I felt eleven years old.

She finally pulled away. I waited to see if she'd say anything, but she didn't. A playful swat on my ass was all that occurred between us after that. I heard a rustling, then the creak of bed springs as she got back into her bed, I suppose. That was my cue to leave. I didn't want to. I wanted to lie beside her and wait until I was ready to go again. But I wondered: Which roomie was this? Pink-loving Nancy? Carrie the thick-boned Denny's waitress who allegedly was a foot-fetish model? The other girl, the ninety-pound blonde whose name I didn't know but who looked killer in a crimson two-piece swimsuit when she sunned in the grass out front? Maybe even a houseguest spending the night?

For the first time in a very long time, I knew that those movies in which people managed to make love six or seven times a day weren't bullshit. Feeling as euphoric as I did there in the dark, my pants still around my ankles, I would've had sex with this girl three times a day for the rest of my life. And I didn't even know what she looked like, nor did I care. Chemistry like this you couldn't find if you tried.

I left and found Yula's room at the end of the hall. I was worn out sexually, but I still fished through the drawers of her nightstand, combing through the books and magazines and even looking behind the dildo. Finally, there in the back of the bottom drawer were the condoms. I took out a single condom from the Sam's Club–sized box, the foil crinkling in my hand.

"What are you doing?" I asked myself. I actually said it out loud, as if perhaps expecting an answer.

Still weak, I sat on the edge of her bed. I might've dozed. I finally went back downstairs to find Yula on the futon, her chest rising and falling in the steady rhythm of deep sleep. I put the wrapped condom down on the table and thought about leaving. I'd had enough insane sex for the evening. *This is your cue to go,* I told myself.

She woke up just then and shucked the blanket, revealing that her clothes had all vanished. Taking charge in the way that only a really big girl can, she had me on my back. Some HBO light porn flick was on now, muted, showing a pair of limber blondes kissing on a park bench. I watched as Yula mounted me, my waist feeling the weight of her.

"I want you," she said, as if that point were in question.

Bone-tired and less interested in sex than I'd been in hours, my eyes were more on the TV than on her, but I managed to perform. Suddenly she grimaced and jumped off me.

"You okay?" I said, propping myself up on an elbow.

"It hurts," she said. I'd heard that before. Two options: really get back to foreplay or get some lubricant.

I didn't have the energy to really get all her cylinders firing again, so I told her to relax and lie on her stomach over the coffee table. I kneaded her back muscles, digging deep with my fingers, really working the skin. Meanwhile, I was still thinking about the mysterious upstairs woman—Gretta, I named that faceless sexual dynamo.

Yula and I finally did have sex, then we collapsed onto the floor, and maybe we both slept. Around 5:00 AM, I realized she was snoring, and I couldn't sleep. Certainly I didn't want anyone—especially the angel from upstairs—to see me there naked against her, so I gathered my clothes, dressed quickly, pulled a blanket over her, and left, careful not to yank the door shut so hard that the noise would wake anyone.

I never spoke to Yula again. Three or four days later, I was wracked with guilt of a type that settled deep into my bones, and I was determined to drown myself into a stupor. That's when Rob found me at Molly's. No Nintendo session would wipe this from my memory—it was burned too deeply. So I slapped my credit card down on the bar and told the slack-eyed bartender, "Keep 'em coming until the world ends."

I'm sure that at the time I never knew the two events were connected.

❖

I left DeKalb quite suddenly in December 1994, my first and final semester of graduate school at NIU. I was committed by now to being a writer, since being a musician meant I'd be surrounded by drugs and booze and skanky women, which would combine into a cocktail I'd surely down enough of to kill me. However, the only serious writing professor at NIU retired suddenly due to a tough bout with throat cancer. So in January 1995, I kissed my girlfriend, Jane, goodbye, got in my red Nissan Pulsar NX with my Nintendo and a pile of clothes, skipped out on my apartment's lease, loaded up the dogs, and drove south, stopping at whatever prospective colleges and universities caught my fancy. I didn't know where I'd end up, but I was sure it wasn't going to be NIU, where I'd half-killed myself instead of getting an education. I needed to go somewhere serious.

This is how things worked with me. I overdid something to the point of near insanity, then I was forced to make a decision: quit or completely surrender. I wanted some quiet in my life, and with all the disasters I'd created in DeKalb, I knew I'd never find it there. So I left with every intention of remaking my life, taking charge, and becoming something closer to a fully functioning adult male.

At least, that was the honest plan.

My hope for a revolution of mind and heart was what graduate school at Florida State University (FSU) in Tallahassee seemed to promise.

WHY I REALLY LEFT NIU

All that is necessary for the triumph of evil is for good men to do nothing.

—EDMUND BURKE

Part of what I liked about Super Mario was that every game culminated in the rescue of Princess Peach (formerly called Princess Toadstool in the United States, but she was always Princess Peach in Japan) from Bowser. Now, I'm not going to try to marry her, like "Sal9000," who got hitched to his Nintendo DS Love Plus girlfriend, Nene Anegasaki, in a real wedding in November 2009, but Peach is pretty damn cool.

Apparently I'm not the only one who thinks she's someone to be reckoned with. In 2008, her estimated fortune of $1 billion got her featured on *Forbes* magazine's "Wealthiest Fictional People" list. The little blond dynamo is also ranked in *Electronic Gaming Monthly*'s list of the top ten video game politicians, as well as being listed on many website and blog rankings of hottest video game women. Although I had two posters of her in my bedroom throughout college, it wasn't so much her intriguing "come and get me" gaze as what she represented. Those designers have her so innocent, so doe-eyed and helpless, that you don't dare turn off any of the Mario spin-off games that feature her unless she's safe at last.

Hell, even the *New York Times* claimed that Princess Peach had "grit as well as grace." Who couldn't appreciate that combination in an ideal woman?

So I saved her again and again, always secretly hoping that somehow, in the act of rescuing the damsel in distress (or saving the world on the brink of destruction, or finding the downed Air Force soldier) in whatever game I was overplaying, I'd be rescuing myself. Once you put a few years on and step back from a situation, though, you start to see things for what they are. I needed rescuing, for sure, only I had a hard time admitting it to myself. All I knew then was that I enjoyed the hell out of those games. It gave me a need-a-cigarette-after satisfaction.

That brings me to the real reason I wanted to leave NIU. I pushed the reason out of my mind again and again until it felt about as real as the Easter Bunny, but my wife always kept at me to be open and honest with her, and eventually the walls I'd put up about my past began to crack. Just as my graduate student career at FSU was ending, the two most traumatic events I'd witnessed back in DeKalb flooded back, and with them came so much of my repressed past, including Mrs. Monroe, which reduced me to blubbering.

My first year in DeKalb provided two real-world opportunities to truly make a difference in the lives of others, and those kinds of stakes (and my responses to them) alarmed me. Even without consciously thinking about what happened during those times (which I didn't allow myself to do), the Mrs. Ed incident a few years later clobbered me with the understanding that it was emotionally yoked to Amanda, Mrs. Monroe, and so many other screwups from my past. Hopelessly out of control, I was anything but a hero. The persona I'd created for myself was both reckless and weak. He was a live grenade without a pin.

I needed to roll a new toon (i.e., create a new character) for myself in real life before it was too late. That's why I left.

❖

Date rape number one took place in the late fall of my freshman year at NIU.

Steve brought home a red-haired girl in a tube top from a pledge party—he was after Sigma Epsilon—and he went at it with her for forty minutes in the bed beside me, the mattress and cheap bed-frame springs really howling. I was half asleep when they arrived, stumbling in after 3:00 AM, so I ignored the commotion, which wasn't all that irregular. My bed was propped atop two dressers in a loft position over our mini fridge and microwave, whereas his was properly on the ground against the other wall.

Though not exactly a player, Steve still had action in that bed across from me perhaps once a week, so this type of business wasn't headline news. But that didn't mean I enjoyed listening to it. If I knew a night of wall-socket sex was coming, I slept on Hong's futon. If I were already in bed, I just shut up and tried to remain quiet, praying to drift away on the currents of sleep, and if that didn't work, I'd get out the earphones and play Game Boy until I dozed off. I'll bet that half the time, Steve's partner never even knew I was there, or if she did, she sure the hell didn't care. I did, but what are you going to do?

When his noisy lovemaking—he was a chronic moaner who yipped like a stepped-on puppy when he finally ejaculated—grew too much for me to sleep through, I stared at the glow-in-the-dark moons and stars we'd pasted all across the ceiling and thought about standing on stage at the Rosemont Horizon, playing guitar for 8,000 screaming fans. I still fancied a career as a musician then, because I hadn't quit guitar yet, and Steve's hoots and breathy howls were easier to transform into the cheers of groupies than to try to shut out with a pillow over my face. Trust me, I tried earplugs, too.

I thought he was sleeping with Rachel, the ex that he on-and-off-again loved. They'd done it not nine days ago. I never looked to confirm, because the roommate code of conduct in a situation like this demanded that I not watch. I didn't need to witness any of it. The existential proximity was enough to give me the willies. I could feel the psychological damage occurring without the visual.

It wasn't Rachel. I'm 100 percent sure, because I got up to hit the bathroom at about 6:00 AM, and as I returned to our room, a red-haired girl stumbled out, her pants on backwards, eyes streaming tears, and stinking of piss. She had these wide, open eyes, I recall, and Bambi-style eyelashes.

"Where am I?"

I thought she was screwing with me, plus I was tired, so I said, "Planet Earth."

She seemed to have a hard time swallowing. Finally, she asked, "What building?"

Something in the tone of her voice—still soaked with rum, if the stench was any indication—caught me. I stopped messing with her.

"Stevenson North."

"How'd I get here?"

"I don't know," I said. I was going to ask her name, but she put her hand over her mouth and looked ready to puke. I'd been puked on once before—by Steve, of all people, who had climbed up into my loft in the middle of the night for some unknown reason and let it fly all over me. Mostly it ruined the sheets, but the hot wet of his innards coated my bare arm and chest, too. I nearly insisted he move out after that fiasco, but he'd promised to shape up, and he really had been a bit calmer with his drinking after that night, which had been some kind of kill-them-with-shots evening for pledges. It also helped that he gave me his copy of the Skate or Die 2: The Search for Double Trouble game I'd been eyeing on his shelf but that he'd been refusing to share.

Maybe I should let people puke on me more often, I remember thinking.

"Oh my God, oh my God, oh my God," the red-headed girl machine-gunned, running for the elevators. She punched the button and soon was gone.

Steve was dead asleep on the floor, the mattress and sheets of his bed drenched in urine. I grabbed a blanket and slept in the common room down the hall, which, admittedly, didn't smell all that much better than our trashed room. When Steve cleaned things up the next morning, we found her pee-soaked strawberry print panties on the windowsill. She'd been so drunk that she had peed on herself in the midst of sex, I realized. Steve didn't remember her or her name—he wasn't even convinced that he'd had sex, even after I guaranteed him that I'd overheard plenty of evidence.

"Do you think she'll come back?" he asked me after lunch that day.

Unsure whether he figured he'd get another bout with her if she did or he felt bad and wanted to talk to her about it, I simply said, "I doubt it." He nodded, as if expecting that answer.

I never saw that girl again. I'm guessing he didn't, either.

❖

Date rape number two happened in spring 1991, a few weeks after spring break. Our floor, an all-guys' floor, had a party with floor six, an all-girls' floor. By 2:00 AM, things were winding down. Most of the girls had stumbled downstairs to their own rooms, but a stalwart few were playing quarters with the sophomores from 1018, one of the big corner rooms that roomed three guys instead of two. These guys were a tight-knit group; they had decided to live in the dorms an extra year and save money instead of sharing an apartment or a house somewhere in DeKalb, as most did after suffering through freshman year in "the Towers," as the eight pillars of Stevenson and Grant were called.

Steve was off smoking cigars with Hong somewhere, and most of our floor had either trickled off to bed or gone out for some after-hours drinking up on Hillcrest Drive. I stayed home and worked on a new book—yes, still wasting my time trying to resurrect *Eyes of Most Unholy Blue*—while pounding back the last of our Keystone Lights from the mini fridge. Frustrated at not getting the epic fight scene right, I put the manuscript aside and started my first fantasy short story (which would later appear in Marion Zimmer Bradley's *Fantasy Magazine*), thinking that if the damn computer ate my story, it'd be only a few thousand words instead of 150,000. I saved every eight or nine seconds now, just to be safe, and also backed things up on a floppy religiously. Yeah, I learned my damn lesson.

I gave up after an hour or two and fiddled with Railroad Tycoon, the second of many games I had bought for my computer. This was well before I'd discovered Tron and networked gaming, yet on some level I understood that the future of gaming was computers, not console systems. These machines seemed godlike in their power even then. What couldn't they do? And it wasn't as if Kings Quest V, Apache Strike, and Advanced Dungeons & Dragons Limited Collector's Edition were awful. Ultima VI: The False Prophet, in particular, is the reason I got a C versus a B in Core Competency in Math. How could I go to class when I was so close to finding the Vortex Cube and saving the world?

Suddenly there was a commotion. I knew what a party sounded like, and I knew what screwing around sounded like. This was something different. I pulled on a big Metallica "Ride the Lightning" T-shirt over my boxers and stepped into my flip-flops before heading out of my dorm. I gamed in the dark more often than not, so the harsh yellow light of the overhead hall fixtures had me squinting.

Lenny, a big sophomore with Wild West banker-style glasses and three chins, bounded down the hall at me. "Oh man, oh man, you gotta see this!"

The way he sported one of those Cheshire cat grins, I got excited. What the hell was happening on our floor? I imagined that a few of the drunken girls had started making out or that perhaps someone was getting an impromptu lap dance. This was worth postponing Railroad Tycoon for, for sure.

I hurried after him.

We turned the corner to the back hallway just as T-Bone—a kid I didn't know well but whose real name was Tom, I think—stepped from a room that wasn't his. T-Bone retied the strings on his gray sweatpants, then walked barefoot back to his room without giving us more than a curt nod.

Lenny stopped outside the room that T-Bone had just exited.

"This is it," he said, then he threw back his head and cackled like a mad scientist, really hamming it up. "C'mon. You gotta see this."

College is an easy place to get porn. Internet, magazine, video—it's everywhere. There's garden-variety porn with everyday, plain girls who are fine with doing it for money in front of cameras, and then there's terrific porn, in which the girls are so achingly beautiful that a guy could just stand there gaping and fire a load off in his pants. What I saw in that room was terrific-porn quality. I mean grade A.

The girl on the bed, half undressed, lay there as though she'd been posed by a director for maximum sexiness. Her little white blouse was mostly open, revealing a cream-colored bra that might've been size D. The jeans shorts and lacy blue thong panties were yanked down far enough to show pubic hair three shades darker than her messy perm. She had a tiny blue tattoo of a flower on one arm.

"Wow," I said, as much because of how stunning this girl's face and body were than that she was comatose on the bed—James's bed, I realized, figuring out whose room I was in by all the Black Sabbath posters. James had said bye to me an hour earlier, heading off to throw darts at AmEx. *Did he leave her behind?* I wondered, but then common sense came to me. No one would leave a girl like this behind. She must've wandered into the room on her own afterward.

"WWF style!" Lenny howled, then threw himself into the air. His 280-pound bulk landed atop her torso hard enough to make her arms and legs pop up. Really, it was like what happens when doctors use those paddles to revive someone. Her whole body lurched. The impact was enough for his glasses to come off. He put them back on, pushed them into position on his nose with a fat finger, then reset his body and prepared to launch himself again.

"Timber!" he hollered, then jumped on her again. He lay there too long, grinding her into the mattress as if hoping to fuse their atoms together.

"Your turn," he said when he finally got off her. To this day, I don't know whether he meant that I should just jump on her or actually rape her.

When I didn't respond, Lenny said, "Oh. You're shy. Okay, I'll give you and Ms. Pretty Pretty some privacy." He bent over and gave her a sloppy kiss, then he jerked his head onto her breasts. Lenny shook his head and growled, then finally released her and said, "Okay, okay. Your turn."

Then he left, shutting the door behind me. I was alone with the most beautiful girl I'd seen since coming to NIU. Hell, this was the most beautiful girl I'd ever been two feet from. My body reacted to her proximity in ways that can only be described as primal. Encoded in my DNA was a prime directive to procreate with someone who looked like this.

There are moments when you truly stand on the precipice. You usually don't know quite how you got there, but the way back looks as rocky and difficult to maneuver as the way forward seems. Ahead is a giant, gaping hole, and your body tenses to jump. It's what a cliff diver must feel, I decided, going against instinct and trusting what he knows to be right.

I knew I'd never have sex with someone that good looking—really, I mean on a scale of one to ten, she was like thirty-six, no joke—yet this was a chance. Maybe someone slipped her a roofie, or maybe she just couldn't handle the Everclear-powered jungle punch the guys down the hall made by the pailfull. Maybe she just got too tired and passed out, or maybe she had narcolepsy and dropped into a snooze for no particular reason. Whatever the cause, she was inches away from me, completely at my mercy. I could jump on her. I could do anything I wanted to do with her.

The front of my boxers burst open. I rebuttoned them and tried to use my head to think this through. A girl like this was built for sex—God doesn't give someone a body like that without realizing that every man within fifty feet would respond physically. It was difficult to stay focused. It was late, too, and I'd been drinking off and on for hours.

Who knew how long she'd been in this room? And if T-Bone's actions were any indication, she'd been taken advantage of in ways that repulsed me. Did I see stains on her panties? Was I just imagining that?

I thought of Steve's redhead last semester and the stink of her pee-soaked panties. I thought of the horror in her eyes the next morning. I thought of the horror in my own eyes that I would see if I looked at myself in the bathroom mirror the next morning.

My breath came from me in gasps.

I scooped her up, carrying her as a fireman would, and headed out. First I thought of spiriting her off to my room, but I imagined the scene of her waking, feeling the friction burns between her thighs from what others had done and then her seeing me there, holding her, and how she'd sic the police on me. So I quickly took her over to Mike and Doug's room. They kept losing their keys, so they taped the lock in such a way that it wouldn't ever engage. I knew they were over in Dundee, fishing for a few days, so it was as safe a place as any on this increasingly dangerous floor of eighteen- and nineteen-year-old males.

I pushed their door open with my foot. I laid the snoozing girl down on a bed and tried to adjust a blanket and a pillow for her.

If you've ever seen a horror movie, you know that there's usually a fake-out scene in which the vicious serial-killing monster seems dead. The heroes slump to the floor and cry, exhausted from the battle and drained of all energy. Then in a moment of dramatic irony, the killer sits back up for one last attack, making the audience howl with unexpected terror. It's always the same. Even now.

She sat up, eyes wide upon me.

"What the—?!" she mumbled.

I'd hiked her panties and shorts up some in an attempt at decency, but she surely knew the situation she was in. Stranger. Strange room. Clothes askew. She snarled at me and spit—a big, sticky gobbet that got me in the eye. Then she fell forward onto her face on the bed, and I heard what might be snoring.

I didn't move again for twenty seconds; my heart thundered at seeing her up and running like that. I thought of Jimi Hendrix dying in his own puke, so I turned her onto her side. Finally I eased out of the room, pulled the door shut behind me, and hit the bathroom to scrub her spit off my face. I used a huge amount of industrial yellow soap from the wall dispensers to scour my cheeks clean, but it felt like that stuff never quite came off. I rubbed and worked paper towels over my cheeks so much that the skin burned.

At least you can look at yourself in the mirror, I decided, tired and buzzed and a little afraid at how close I'd come to making a decision that would forever change who I'd be in life. I headed back to bed.

Lenny ran through the halls, whooping like a faux Indian in a bad John Wayne movie. He squeezed past me, moving fast for his bulk. I went back to my room and locked the door, not even caring if Steve had his key with him or not. I couldn't slow my breathing. I used my albuterol inhaler four times and put some Ben-Gay on my aching wrists. I never got back to my game. I crawled up into my loft bed and lay there, panting, sure I was going to jail for something I didn't do. I did the right thing, and God was about to screw me. She'd remember my face. She'd remember a strobe-light sense of memories, little snippets in which my face played prominently in what happened prior to my entering that room. I could see it. I could feel the cold steel bars of a jail cell in my fists as I wondered just who the hell to phone with my one and only phone call.

No charges were filed. No one was asked about that night by the resident assistant or the university police—no one. And so date rape number two just up and disappeared, too. I asked Sasha, a girl from my Spanish 102 class who lived on the sixth floor, if she knew the other girl. She sort of scrunched up her forehead, showcasing her well-tweaked eyebrows. "What's she look like?"

I told her, trying to keep my interest sounding casual. Cindy

Crawford's face. J-Lo's ass. Hair like Angelina Jolie. Smile like Julia Roberts.

"Oh, I don't think she's from our floor."

"Really?" I said. "I thought I saw her during our floor party the other night."

She nodded. "A couple of girls from an apartment by Stadium Club came with us, and they had a few friends, too. I don't remember the girl you're talking about, but she must've come with one of those groups. It was a crazy night."

"Oh," I said, and that was the end of it.

No wonder real life terrifies me so much that I retreat to the far safer worlds of video games and simulations. I see those poor girls in my dreams still, and there's no reset button to push to start things over and get another shot at saving them. There are hundreds of Princess Peaches out there, far more than I can ever truly fathom, I suspect. At least in video games there's usually only one princess to save, and even on the hardest level, the designers built in the possibility for eventual success. In real life, it too often seems as if the concept of winning isn't part of the intrinsic equation. There are just simply degrees of losing, not black or white, but a million shades of gray.

Still I try, because what else am I going to do? Leap?

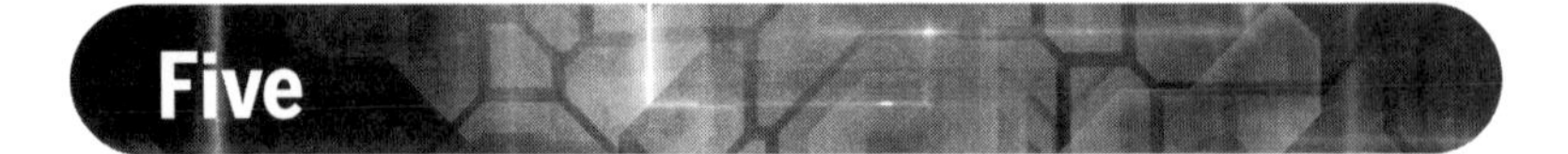

MEA CULPA

Life is a video game.
You always get zapped in the end.

—ANONYMOUS

Thank God that I started dating the woman who would become my wife while I was in Tallahassee instead of in DeKalb, where we had met in marching band. I had known about Victoria earlier, since she played clarinet in the marching band, but had we met prior to 1994, I'd have slept with her once or twice and then ruined any potential future with my after-scam standoffishness.

My current girlfriend, Jane, the color-guard captain from NIU (a long-distance disaster relationship in which we'd get so angry that we'd hang up on each other and fume), wanted to skip Rob's wedding. We both knew Rob well, and I'd no sooner skip his wedding than poke a freshly sharpened number two pencil into my eye, because he was without a doubt the best friend I'd ever had. Jane was part of an adult volunteer color-guard group and had a gig in St. Charles, Illinois, the same weekend as Rob's wedding. I pleaded with her to be sensible—she was Rob's friend, too—but she never came around, so I dumped her even though we had been together for nearly a year.

I really liked her, but couldn't see the sense of not valuing a friendship over a volunteer group. My father would call this kind of thing "the difference between some lightning and a lightning bug," meaning vast. So although we meshed in 90 percent of the possible ways, we differed in crucial ones—like video games, which she didn't enjoy and once admitted "were a colossal waste of time."

Small wonder I used a dumb excuse to part ways.

My diabetic pal Carla knew Rob, too, so she and I decided to go together as friends, even though she was still ticked off at me. We hadn't spoken in months, when suddenly she called me in Tallahassee and said, "Well, shall we whatever to Rob's wedding, or what?"

I think Carla's plan was to convince me that evening that we were destined to be together, regardless of any reservations I had about her diabetes, our physical chemistry, or any of the other dozen stupid ways I'd kept her at arm's length whenever we started to get close. We've talked about it some since then, and although she's elusive, it's clear that she thought this was a turning point in our relationship. In a way, it was.

Rob's wedding proved a blast. Despite starting graduate school weeks earlier that summer and getting semiserious about my education, at last—meaning that I was playing less than two hours a day of games, mostly chess simulations and baseball games on the computer—I'd never really whooped it up at a big event like a wedding, so I sucked down too many Heinekens in the limo between the church and the basement reception hall of some fancy St. Charles restaurant. Being back in Illinois among so many people who were part of my undergraduate years of debauchery made it oh so easy to slip into that mode. Without intending to, I was *that person* again: an epic drinker who chased skirts, all the while loathing being *that person* and wishing I could hide in a dark bedroom and do something safe, like playing Super Mario.

The carafes of red wine at the tables didn't help, nor did the open bar where a straw-haired girl with a silver nose stud made magnificent kamikaze shots, green as a leprechaun's silken jacket, with just enough lime to make you pucker a few times after you slammed one down. I had had maybe twelve or thirteen before dinner was served. Then another trumpet line guy, Jimmy, a gorilla-hairy kid with a weight problem (who later would become, of all things, an emergency medical technician) gave me another kamikaze.

"My treat," he said, smiling in such a way that had I been anything but sloshed, I might've recognized it as malicious. The drink wasn't green like the dozen prior ones, it was golden: piss yellow. He later confessed it was a shot called the Three Wise Men: Jose Cuervo, Jim Beam, and Jack Daniels.

Feeling tough enough to chew steel, I downed it and remembered nothing more. All I remember of that evening beyond that moment are a few seconds-long snippets and what I later pieced together of the missing six hours from accounts by astonished friends, strangers, and a squat, sweating photographer who told me, "I'd never seen *anyone* dance like that before." I can't dance worth a damn, but from what this guy said, you'd think I'd have won *So You Think You Can Dance?* or something.

Memory fragment number one: Mashing with a heavyset brunette who used to work with Rob at McDonald's in DeKalb, her tongue stuffed into my right ear canal as we shuffled together to the words of "My Sharona."

Memory fragment number two: Seeing Rob at the bottom of the stairs in the downstairs reception hall of the restaurant. I'd gone up to the main floor, apparently, to take a leak. Returning to the basement party, I'd stopped halfway down and recognized the groom. I squinted at him then waved.

"Whatcha doing, Ryan?" he asked, as if he were talking to a three-year-old. I said, "Gimme a hug, groomy!" And misjudging the fifteen feet and eight stairs between us as perhaps one-eighth that, I reached out to grab him and went head-over-feet down and landed in his arms as he caught me with an *oooof*!

"Man, you reek of liquor!" he said, trying to keep me on my feet, but then I was gone. I was awake and off doing God knew what, but the black box in my brain had shut down. Nothing was recorded for later analysis or posterity.

I shook my booty atop tables. I did the Chicken Dance to an Elton John song. I told Carla that I "loved her, loved her, loved her." I told Rob that I "loved him, loved him, loved him." I told the bride that I "loved her, loved her, loved her." I told a skinny serving girl whose thick eyebrows and faint green eyeshadow reminded me of Jane (who was off doing her volunteer color-guard thing), that "I loved her, loved her, loved her." I bumped into Victoria, who'd come with a friend from band—yes, the idiot who had Three Wise Men–ed me—and told her that "I loved her, loved her, loved her," too. I stuck some of the centerpiece flowers in the front of my pants and asked people to "smell my luxurious odor." I've got a picture someone snapped of me doing a really bendy thing with my arms and my head, of David Letterman's "Stupid Human Tricks" quality, that I cannot replicate. I gave two toasts, one to Rob and his new wife and one to the NIU trumpet line, "who could blast with the best of them," which was not a compliment, but everyone still cheered and drank, I hear.

The reception lasted for five and a half hours. I remember maybe ninety seconds total, after that yellow shot brought me oblivion. When my memory actually kicked back up it was well after 2:00 AM in a Holiday Inn room with half a dozen NIUers sprawled on the beds, the floor, and the pastel purple couch. I lurched toward the bathroom, thinking I might throw up a dinosaur, my stomach rumbled so much. I nearly did. After ten minutes of the type of heaving that makes you curl your toes so hard that your nails cut through your socks, I was spent.

McDonald's girl (from memory fragment number one) had decided to keep me like a lost pet, I guess, because she'd taken me with her and her friends to that hotel. Carla found me only because she asked Jimmy (the guy who gave me the drink), who knew that I had left with McDonald's girl, because on my way out of the reception, I stuck my head through his open car window and bit him on the chest, clamping down not in joking shadow-punch fashion, but really giving him an ouchie as a thanks for the liquor blackout, I guess. He claims I nearly took his nipple off, but he's prone to exaggeration.

Carla arrived at the hotel maybe fifteen minutes after my third and final barf session. She retrieved me from the bed, where I snuggled alongside McDonald's girl, who I think might've molested me, since my underwear was on backward, but that could've just been the result of wedding shenanigans or God-knows-what I did in the bathroom.

Carla didn't say a word, but just drove me home in my mother's car—a Honda Accord I'd driven to Carla's house to pick her up in the previous afternoon, when her dad had beamed and snapped pictures of us "looking all spiffy." She dropped herself off, muttering, "Thanks for nothing!" before storming inside. Still questionably buzzed, I sat in her driveway, my head on the steering wheel for a long, long time, feeling as if I'd just run through an all-nighter on SEGA and now had to show up for an 8:00 AM final in British literature that I'd forgotten to study for.

I tried to recall any of the many ways I might've wronged Carla at the wedding. Thinking about it now, I realize that she probably just didn't like me mashing with other women. This could've been her night. Our night. One of those magical Disney moments in which I spun her in a crowded room beneath a crystal ball, the cumulative breath of everyone withheld as I dipped her, the pink dress whirling about her like a thousand small butterflies as I said, "Carla? I've been such a fool. I love you. Please do me the honor of marrying me, and I'll spend the rest of my life trying to make you the happiest woman in the whole damn world. Even if you do have diabetes."

She could've been my Princess Peach.

I like Disney as much as the next fool, but real life is just far messier than those crystalline movie moments.

When the world stopped moving and I felt halfway human, I exited her driveway and carefully drove the last three miles to my parents' house. I ambled into the guest room and fell asleep.

Through the haze of the most incredible hangover I've ever suffered in my life, another memory had surfaced: slow dancing with Victoria right before the Three Wise Men incident. I didn't care about Carla or Jane or McDonald's girl. Victoria was on my mind and in my heart. I'd wanted to date her before I left NIU, but the timing wasn't right. I knew I had to see her immediately, before my inner critic convinced me I would never be good enough for someone like her, someone undamaged and with solid self-esteem. She had been dating someone nearly the entire time we were in marching band together, and this was the first time I could recall that she was unattached.

So I called, jackhammer dwarves destroying my brain be damned. I told her I'd like to take her to lunch, the words like sawdust on my parched tongue.

"Sounds great," she said. "But aren't you up in the 'burbs?"

I was. I hadn't worked the details out yet through the fogginess of my brain. DeKalb, where I used to live when I went to NIU, was sixty miles away. I groaned at the effort of making sense of the mayhem in my mind.

"I'm heading to Northern in an hour for some stuff," I said. "I can just swing by and pick you up then." I wondered what kind of stuff I was talking about and hoped that she wouldn't ask. She didn't.

So we lunched at a little farmhouse diner in Sycamore in mid-afternoon, less concerned with the gristly cube steak sandwiches than our growing interest in each other. Shame pinked my features as she told me some of her memories of my wedding antics, and not having anything to compare them to, I couldn't defend myself. I tried to look cute and innocent. Think "lost puppy," I told myself more than once. People can't resist lost puppies—even ones who dry-humped a chair and yelled, "Wahoo!" the evening before while Johnny Cash blared.

"Survive the ride home?" Victoria asked, seeing how I couldn't stop sweating from the migraine I couldn't shake.

"Of course," I said, though probably not as smoothly as I liked.

But for once in my life, I didn't blow this moment. I didn't freak out, get scared, or turn off the internal editor of my brain and blurt out something stupid. I managed to be something resembling a marginally clever, fun-loving, normal human being. Although every ounce of reason I had suggested that another long-distance relationship was a poor idea—the one with Jane didn't make it eight months—it was what I had to do. So I did the most impulsive thing ever. I invited her to come visit me in Florida. Right then.

Miracle of miracles, she agreed.

❖

The long-distance thing fell into place nicely. I'd go to class in the morning, play video games most of the afternoon, walk the dogs a couple of times, talk for an hour on the phone each night with Victoria, and then read Charles Bukowski poetry (or sometimes game some more) until I passed out around midnight. I mostly played Myst, a seemingly endless mystery game, but I also discovered Warcraft II: Tides of Darkness. This was more of a battle simulator than the first-person MMOG World of Warcraft was, but I still got hooked by its ability to play other people online, which was like my old Tron days, only better and more graphically cool. In the fall of 1995 alone, I must've logged 100 hours of game time on Warcraft II. At the time, I remember being pretty impressed by that figure.

Victoria never knew how much I was gaming, mostly because she didn't care. Video games held no draw for her. She was all about movies, TV shows, and hanging out with friends. She was the yin to my yang. Despite dumping Jane because she wasn't like me, I suddenly felt quite sure that being with someone like Victoria, different as she was from me, would help to make me be a better person. I don't mean not gaming, but rather being at peace with myself, being happy and healthy. Those things glimmered at me like distant jewels I needed a turbo boost to reach.

We got engaged the following fall, when I drove back to DeKalb to surprise her on the front stoop of her apartment, all three dogs in my lap as I got on one knee and said, "Will you marry us?"

We married on June 15, 1997.

Had I not gotten so drunk that I pissed Carla off the night of Rob's wedding, I might've ended up marrying her. Victoria and I both knew that I loved Carla. My wife has pointed that out on more than one occasion. Yes, if Carla hadn't had a scary disease like diabetes—scary, at least, to someone who is desperate for safety and couldn't risk losing a loved one—things might've worked out differently. You just never know.

I was in a place where it was either go it alone into the dark tunnel my life was fast becoming and see whether I'd make it to thirty, or try to establish some security, some stability, a sense of warmth and belonging and love. In short, I was ready for commitment. For the right type of partner, I was ideal. *Right type* meant, of course, someone strong enough to handle all the finances, cope with my neurotic behavior, deal with my manic sex drive, insist that I stop drinking so much, love dogs, love me unconditionally, and ignore the many physical flaws I had (weight, "mild but resistant acne," omnipresent nose hair, and no butt, to name just a few).

My wife is probably right. I loved Carla. But things happen for a reason, you've got to believe, and I'm not complaining about how it all finally shook out.

❖

While Victoria and I were engaged, 1995–1997, I lived alone in a two-bedroom apartment in Tallahassee and started really playing computer games. *Start* is the wrong word. *Restarted* might be more accurate, since I'd always played some on my computer and had even gone on Dungeons & Dragons benders back in 1988, when the original 3¼-inch disk version of the Pool of Radiance came out, which had you basically walking six party members first-person style (where you "see" the game as if looking through the eyes of the characters rather than through a camera following them, like a movie) through a heavily pixellated maze, where you'd encounter a group of Orcs and you'd have the option to "act haughty, meek, nice, or abusive." Then you'd kick ass or befriend them, depending on your choices. The game was buggy and froze up a lot, but it was Dungeons & Dragons, which I remembered fondly from my early days in Wisconsin.

In high school I had done three things: play video games, chase girls (unsuccessfully), and play guitar. I'm not sure which was most important to me. Back then I would've said guitar. A few years later, I'd have confessed that it was girls. These days, being as honest with myself as I'm capable of, I'd have to say video games, hands down: Wizardry, Zork, Doom, Populous, Bard's Tale, Wing Commander. God, I can recall so many of those games, every moment, every wrong turn, every victory, every setback. The girls I dated? The songs I played? The bands I jammed with? It's like I have Alzheimer's with those categories. With games, however, my neurons fire full blast, making my trigger finger itchy, my palms sweaty, and the hairs on the back of my neck standing at attention.

My games of choice in grad school, when I was living solo at FSU, were Empire II (very similar to the board game Axis and Allies), Warcraft II: Tides of Darkness (a real-time strategy game set in a medieval fantasy world), Star Wars: Dark Forces (a spacey, George Lucas–inspired first-person shooter), and Heroes of Might and Magic, one of the big daddies of turn-based strategy games.

I got accepted into FSU in January when I moved there, but I didn't work out registration properly, which meant that classes didn't start for me until summer. So I had a lot of time, which my dad was kind enough to pay for, covering my rent and general expenses all the way through my master's program, which ended in May 1997, just before my wedding. Purportedly, I was to be working on my writing, which I did, to some extent. I wrote partial drafts of three different supernatural thrillers, all deeply flawed works that weren't much more than Stephen King knockoffs. I spent far too much time at I. C. Flicks, a nearby movie theater where they'd ripped out every other row of seats to put in small tables. They served beer, popcorn, pizza, hot dogs, and lots of deep-fried mushrooms and mozzarella sticks. I spent maybe thirty bucks a week there, drinking thirty-two-ounce Miller Lites and eating pepperoni pizza while watching such flicks as *Ace Ventura: When Nature Calls*, *Outbreak*, *Congo*, *While You Were Sleeping*, *Braveheart*, *Waterworld*, *Get Shorty*, *Seven*, *Twister*, *The Birdcage*, and *Jingle All the Way*. All these movies were better on a sixty-foot screen and accompanied by super-salty popcorn and a big tub of suds, I've decided since seeing them all again on my own tiny TV screen.

I'd come home after seeing two or three movies, then fire up a microwave burrito meal and play computer games until I was too tired to stay up. I didn't watch TV. I didn't really go out, except to the movies, I talked to my fiancée on the phone maybe twice a day, and I played all hell out of those video games, sometimes well past 2:00 AM, before walking my dogs one final time in the chill of the Tallahassee dark and shutting down the computer.

My little two-bedroom apartment on Ocala Road stood on the edge of St. Mark's National Wildlife Refuge, 68,000 acres of pure Florida jungle that began not thirty feet from my front door. You'd think I'd have considered that critters might come into my yard, but for two months I was blissfully oblivious. Then came the five-foot black racer snake that paused on my porch before slipping through the chain link fence and disappearing into the underbrush like a thick black mobile rope.

After the snake incident, whenever I absolutely had to leave, I'd check the pavement first, get my keys ready, then run out to my Accord (which had belonged to my mom and was given to me by my dad after my Pulsar died in Dothan, Alabama). I really laid tracks out of that wildlife-infested area. I also kept a nine-iron in the car at all times, just in case that snake lay in wait for me on the steps. I was terrified, but I'd bash its snake brains in if it didn't get the hell out of my way.

The units were all duplexes, and the other apartment in my little green building went through about six different people before remaining empty for good. My favorite tenants were the married cop couple who parked their cruisers next to my Honda—I have never felt safer. I also liked Sharonda, an African-American ROTC student at FSU who had a knack for casseroles. Her recipes were for a family, not a single slender girl who looked incapable of consuming even a single-serving plate of anything, so she regularly brought me plastic-wrapped portions of cheesy pasta casseroles, broccoli-noodle parmesan bake, layered tamale pie, and chicken spaghetti. I know she wanted more from me than an occasional "Hey, Shar!" through the front screen door as I saw her lugging groceries.

I was engaged and scared of relapsing back to my NIU mentality, which was self-gratification rather than self-esteem. I hid inside my house for weeks, just feeling lousy about being so afraid of talking to someone. Enter MMOGs. I could finally interact safely with others; being mediated through screens and games left me open to pretending to be anyone I wanted to be. This included someone who wasn't tormented by a nagging sense of not being fully in control of his life.

❖

The three-bedroom orange brick rental house on Beaumont Drive that my wife I and moved into soon after she moved to Tallahassee was the first real house I'd ever lived in as an adult. Summering with my parents back in Palatine, Illinois, didn't count. In some ways, it was stupid to have a house, since it required yard work, housework, and other obligations that a smaller, less expensive apartment would not have required. But we were too much for the two-bedroom apartment I'd been in for the last two years, and having a house rather than an apartment seemed to make the marriage more legitimate, so we dove into it.

Actually, the biggest reason I wanted to leave the Ocala place was that snake, which I'd seen only twice in two years but which I imagined lurking about in the dark almost every night. Snakes terrified me. I live in constant fear of their sneaky slickness, the way they can come at you out of nowhere. One attacked me when I was a boy in Wisconsin. Like a heat-seeking serpent missile, it came at me out of some bushes at the woods' edge of the park my brother and I always went to. From then on, snakes and I had a very tentative uneasy truce, which I always worried they'd break by plunging their venom-dripping fangs deep into my thigh.

Wanting to kick off our newly married status and new home right, we held a housewarming party and invited all my grad school buddies. Maybe *buddies* isn't the right word, but if you go drinking often enough with your classmates, you get to know one another well enough to obligate them to come to your parties. I did have a few I genuinely liked and hung out with more regularly. There was Nick, from Searcy, Arkansas, who studied poetry with Rita Dove at the University of Virginia prior to the FSU program. Then there was JT, the eternal grad student, who had one master's degree from Oregon State University and another from the University of California at Irvine (where he was classmates and poker pals with Pulitzer Prize–winner Michael Chabon, author of *The Mysteries of Pittsburgh* and *The Amazing Adventures of Kavalier & Clay*, two books I've taught before and deeply, deeply admire). JT was on the slow boat to a Ph.D., taking his time to write a lot of novels before being spit into the real world. He started his Ph.D. program the same time I started my master's program, and even though I finished my own Ph.D. in 2001, he didn't finish his until 2003. Another friend was Oliver, an enigmatic, loves-to-hug-everyone son of a Tampa firefighter and McDonald's magnate who was with me in Wisconsin later, when we got robbed. Finally, there was Chad. I called him "Belly" after hearing about his

Big Mac exploits as an elementary school soccer star.

I invited all my professors to the housewarming party, too, and much to my surprise, a few came. Dr. K showed up for maybe twenty minutes and brought me a small potted fern. The Cuban-American writer Virgil Suárez came, too, a cigar as thick as a sausage clamped between his teeth.

"Trouble's here, ladies. What shall we break first?" he said, then cackled like a mad scientist. He loved to make a production out of his well-crafted "I'm loco! Watch me eat paint!" persona that served him so well at book signings and in the classroom, where kids would line up just to witness the spectacle. During one fiction workshop I had with him in 1997, he told a wide-eyed kid from Texas, "Your story is crazy. Really crazy. I mean, I don't get the plot. It's almost as if you want to say to the reader, 'Hey, to hell with plot. Let's all be crazy!'" And then Virgil fell to the ground and did the Curly (of Larry, Moe, and Curly fame) spin, running in place with one shoulder to the ground, hollering, "*Whoop! Whoop! Whoop! Whoop!*"

After more than half of our guests had finally left—the beer ran out by 11:00 PM, so we were down to cheap vodka and some second-rate rum mixed with Diet Coke now—Virgil began to explore. My wife was a little nervous about this strange bearded man roaming through our house. Despite taking two of his classes, I'd never had more than a few words of private conversation with him, so I decided that this might be the moment. I needed some guidance in my writing career, a mentor. Dr. K was an option, to be sure, with his scholarly books and proper academic career, but Virgil was pure energy and vibrant with life. He published a lot. He had a presence, and that presence was addictive. Call it Cuban charisma. (He blamed it on the three shots of Cuban coffee he took every day.)

Virgil peeked into the master bedroom and nodded as if everything there was as he expected. Then he stopped at the bathroom, examined himself in the mirror, licked his fingers, and combed his eyebrows up in what he later admitted was his homage to Salvador Dalí. He was mesmerizing in his strangeness. He sang quietly to himself as he walked, some sort of Cuban gangsta rap music, I think, if my eighth-grade Spanish served me well.

I followed Virgil wordlessly—call it stunned silence—as he literally hopped into the last bedroom, recently transformed into my office. I had three big plywood shelving units with all my reference books, school stuff, and copies of the magazines and literary journals in which my writing had appeared. I'd been pretty active in sending my work out since I had come to Florida, so the collection was sizable by late 1997—perhaps four shelves' worth, by this point. I especially liked small journals, the type of venues that got back to you fast and really appreciated the crap out of any decent submission: *The Back Porch. Fell Swoop. Melting Trees Review. Lilliput Review. FEH!. The Poet's Attic.*

Virgil ignored the stacks of video games near the little TV I'd set up in the corner and let his gaze rest upon the rows upon rows of saddle-stapled literary journals, the many names of which he wouldn't recognize. No professor would. These were small, one-man-in-the-garage desktop deals, most being little more than a few sheets of colored paper stapled together. Many weren't much better than a Kinko's packet or church pamphlet. Some were barely a menu in size and length.

"*Dios mío,*" he said.

I wondered if it were a mistake to let him see this. *You should've redirected him to the back porch and offered to smoke with him,* I thought angrily. Too late. Always too late.

Reboot! my mind howled. *Reboot!*

Then Virgil turned to me and threw his arms around me in a sweaty, smoky hug, saying, "It's the most beautiful thing I've ever seen."

We've been fast friends ever since, including coauthoring a poetry collection and coediting four poetry anthologies for the University of Iowa Press. He's an amazing man, which is why I'm ashamed to admit that he's on the list of people I have wronged. Hell, it'd be easier to count off everyone I *haven't* wronged (best guess: zero), which somehow never bothered me until I began to write this book. Does writing this book mean I'm taking responsibility for it at last? Does it mean I'm working against my impulse to never look bad? Does it mean I'm finally owning up to my own shit?

Virgil gets a lot of flak in the academic world for his antics, his tendency to overpublish (sometimes even the same poem many, many times), his unorthodox style of teaching, his suspiciously friendly behavior at school, which other academics take to mean he's hiding some terrible dark secret—which he isn't, other than that he's a child at heart and, as such, collects model cars, reads comic books, paints fantasy figurines, and sometimes listens to his daughter's teeny-bopper music when no one's around. I think he big-man dances to that cotton-candy boy-band music, too, although I can't confirm that.

In addition to having a big house in north Tallahassee, where he often held late-night powwows with favorite students and friends on the screened-in porch, he owned a nice condo in Key Biscayne, where he still summers and spends all of December. He had a reading at the Miami International Book Fair that November, so he brought JT and me along for company.

It's easy to take advantage of a guy who wants to cultivate a "Look at me, I'm *crazy*!" image, so we ushered him to the Bayside Market Place outdoor mall to watch the Rock Bottom Remainders (Stephen King's and Dave Barry's band) while slurping down strawberry Jell-O shots that Virgil famously said "didn't have enough kick to get an African pygmy drunk."

That kind of crack, to grad students, is a challenge.

Five shots and a thirty-two-ounce Banana Banshee each later (I might've gone my own way and had a Dirt Monkey, too—I can't be sure), the three of us stumbled our way to one of the after-event parties at the nearby Hilton, thrown by Oprah author "Betty." She'd ordered a case or two of good beer, and more than a few people brought their own bottles of harder stuff. A grad student, I usually wasn't given access to a party of this caliber—not the quality of the snack food (sausage pizza rolls, steamed mushroom caps, and organic tortilla chips), but the quality of people. National Book Award winner Tim O'Brien was there. Guggenheim winner Fred Busch was, too, and a host of others whose work I knew, taught, and admired. This was a world I envied and deeply desired to be part of. It was like a very young Bill Clinton—high school age—being introduced to then-President John F. Kennedy and his entire staff. Eyes wide with wonder stuff.

This was one of the few times the real world exceeded anything I'd ever accomplished in a video game. No high score could equal the rush I felt that night thinking *these are my people.*

Fortified by the pizza rolls and a bottle of Harp's, I eventually cornered O'Brien by ignoring the irritated looks of the two expensively attired blondes who were speaking with him and leaning close to say, "You know, I'm Lieutenant Jimmy Cross. I read that book and I'm like, *wow*, that's me!"

He adjusted his baseball cap and eyed me, answering, "You know, sometimes I feel that way, too."

Overly confident by an ocean of beer, I worked to convince O'Brien to stay and tell me in painstaking detail about the process of writing *The Things They Carried.* "What a fan-friggin'-tastic book!" I exclaimed, but the two women hurried him off, saying he had a plane to catch at

5:00 AM. He said in earnest (I hope), "I wish I could stay. This party looks like it's really getting underway now," as he left, motioning at Virgil, who had gotten so drunk that he had taken the covers off the bed in the center of the room, climbed in, and was now fast asleep, despite the clamor of twenty-five people in a fairly small suite. A pair of female grad students sat on the edge, poking at him, seeing if he was pretending to sleep as some kind of strange only-Virgil-might-get-it joke that he'd laugh about for months after, to everyone's confusion.

I don't remember doing it, but sources tell me I poured beer on your pants, Virgil, to give the impression that you'd peed on yourself. For this, I am sorry. I did not, however, write "Hi, my name is Virgil!" on your arm with a black Sharpie. That was those two drunk brunettes—poets, I think, from Florida International, who poked you and tried to braid your unruly eyebrows. They claimed they were tired of explaining who you were to everyone who came in and asked what that big lump was under the sheets. They also drew the stars on your forehead and blackened the Snidely Whiplash mustache on your face. That was not me. Not any of that.

So I apologize. Once again, drinking made me do something regrettable, although at the time I suspect I thought it was mostly your fault for trying to sleep on a bed during a gut-thumping, crowded hotel room party where your two buddies were networking and having a great time. Still, JT and I should've extricated you long before that. We knew better. For my own part, I am truly sorry.

I am sorry, too, that I spoke with Fred Busch, asking him something about his novel *Absent Friends*. He cut me a look, then said, "I think I've heard about you."

The way he said it? Christ. What was I doing to myself? My reputation? That high I had? Fizzling fast.

❖

My days in the Ph.D. program at FSU mostly consisted of reading fantasy books, ignoring my wife, and playing cards online (Hearts, occasionally, but mostly Spades and low-stakes poker with pretend cash). Victoria was out of the house a lot, because while she was studying for her master's degree in education, she was also working nearly full-time at Dillard's at Governor's Square Mall and was teaching in various capacities in Tallahassee: adult ed at the community center, third-grade at Caroline Brevard Elementary School, and substitute teaching all over the city, at one point or another. She was a warhorse with a workload to match, for which I never thanked her. I simply got my share of the finances handled by taking out student loans. A ton of them.

That's how a gamer handles something: put things off until tomorrow so you can enjoy the enjoyment of the now. Tomorrow can bring whatever reckoning it chooses. And who knows? With a little luck, maybe the trouble would just dwindle away on its own.

My $40,000 in student loans, however, did not dwindle away, although it gave me plenty of time to write a lot of poems and play video games more and more and more. At one point, I recall playing from Friday night until Tuesday morning with no break for sleep. I don't even know which game—maybe Warcraft II? Maybe Age of Empires: The Rise of Rome? My carpal tunnel syndrome was back, and it felt like lava in my veins, but I kept playing. I persevered.

All my friends played video games. It was just another thing we did, like go to class, eat dinner, play cards, and sleep. I didn't think there was anything odd about it.

No wonder my wife and I fought a lot. I had created a responsibility-free zone where I had friends and finally fit in. Grad school gave me that. She didn't understand, and she knew that accumulating debt wasn't a solution to anything, even when what it bought me was the illusion of comfort and security—two things that being adopted had made me painfully shortchanged in.

"I'm busting my ass here," she said.

"What am I doing, picking my nose?"

"Great. Just great. You do that."

I sneered. "Thanks. I will."

That's how we fought: sarcasm mixed with insults tempered with disgust. It was really toxic stuff that might have given John Gray (the Mars-and-Venus guy) fits.

I did feel bad about the arrangement, but we both knew that I had to get that Ph.D. It would allow us a lifestyle we both wanted. Without it, I couldn't get anything more than slave-wage adjunct work or perhaps a lousy high school job, which I didn't want because, as I told everyone, "I'm afraid of being shot." I had zero marketable skills and probably couldn't have landed a job at Wal-Mart if I had tried, if things got that desperate. It was all about the Ph.D.

To augment my money contribution, I played a hell of a lot of cards. That was stupid, I know, but I was trying. You give a guy a good IQ, and he thinks he's Kenny Rogers's "The Gambler." Good thing I didn't know about the World Series of Poker, or I'd have really been in trouble.

I was a so-so poker player, and during one of my fabulous losing sessions, when I was down maybe thirty dollars in perhaps fifteen minutes, I eyed my friend Nick, a gentle soul you couldn't look at without wanting to throw your arms around his big chest and hug the stuffing right out of him (think the Caucasian version of Ruben Studdard of *American Idol* fame), and I told him, "Jesus H. Christ, you are the luckiest person I know. Do you really want to burn so much luck drawing a winner from a near-dead deck? Someday you're going to be on a plane somewhere, and you'll wish you'd stored up a little of that luck you're wasting now."

Good-spirited and generally happy, Nick didn't explode even though he had every right to. He smiled at me and said, "I wish you wouldn't say things like that."

I shut up and continued to lose hand after hand, until I finally excused myself and went home, wondering what defect in my makeup allowed me to act like that. I suppose it was the same defect that allowed me to argue with my wife, who worked a full-time, crappy mall job while getting her master's degree. The same defect that made me think it was perfectly okay to play video games for six hours straight and then be indignant that dinner wasn't hot on the table the moment I realized I needed a break. *Defect* was the right word, because I did indeed feel broken most of the time. I was like a car with improperly inflated wheels that always pulled to the left. That kind of thing.

I don't know why I do it. Sometimes I simply say dumb things—like that gaffe with O'Brien, in which I must've come off as mentally challenged. Or the time during a writing conference that I vodka-ed myself stupid with a few FSU pals and a trio of girls from Nebraska's creative writing program. Stumbling out of the door after a big steak dinner and too many after-dinner fuzzy navels, I threw my arm around the oldest, Lisa, and boozily announced, "I love writing. One day, I'm going to do something great with it."

Lisa kind of pushed me off, saying, "We all love writing. That's why we're all in grad school."

"Yeah," I said, my common sense asleep at the wheel again, or, more likely, snoring away all that liquor I'd rivered past it. I rubbed at a sudden crink in my neck and added, to everyone present, "But I want it more than the rest of you. I mean, I *really* want it."

To this day, Lisa avoids me at conferences and tells people that I am an asshole. Yes, I am an asshole sometimes. All selfish people are assholes. But I don't worry so much about an alcohol-exacerbated moment in which I simply spoke without tact and apparently disparaged the self-esteem or value of every writer in the room by playing up my own self-worth as a writer. Plenty of writers have an overinflated sense of themselves and their own literary and existential importance. It just sucks that I voiced mine aloud, but it happened, and I can live with it. What bothers me is when I tell my good friend Nick, right smack in his face before our all our friends, including his childhood-sweetheart wife, that he deserves to be in a plane crash because he's too lucky at cards. Who the hell does a thing like that?

I suck at apologies. I've never apologized to Nick for this, because I've been too ashamed to have said something so foolish, so unfriendly. He's a terrific guy, and we've remained friends throughout the years. Still, I owe him one in a big way that I might never be able to offer.

A good apology has two parts, I've decided. The first part is the obvious one: to admit being sorry for what has happened. Most people, albeit too often insincerely, manage this one well enough. But the second part is one that I honestly cannot recall anyone in my life ever doing to me. It's some version of the sentence "What can I do to make things right?"

That's the most important component. Regret and/or shame is fine. But if you're truly remorseful, you want to do whatever you can to make amends, and asking for help in figuring that out is the best way to do it.

Nick, I am sorry for saying such a shitty thing to you, especially in front of your wife and our friends. No hand of poker, regardless of how much or how little money was at stake, is worth saying such a thing. I apologize. And if there's anything I can do to make things right, please let me know. I will do it.

Same goes with you, Virgil, my pal. I miss how close we once were. What can I do to make things right?

One last thing about the Nick story. After the plane-crash crack, Nick bought a lovely new twenty-five-inch TV and jokingly said that his friends had paid for it with their poker losings. The universe loves a good joke, so for the next few months, Nick steadily lost more and more until all the money he'd vacuumed out of our wallets with his stunningly good luck all went away. There's a lesson here somewhere, I imagine.

❖

The thing about addiction is that those who suffer most aren't the addicts, it's the people who love them. I will never be able to apologize enough to my family for all the crap I've put them through. This book is a start.

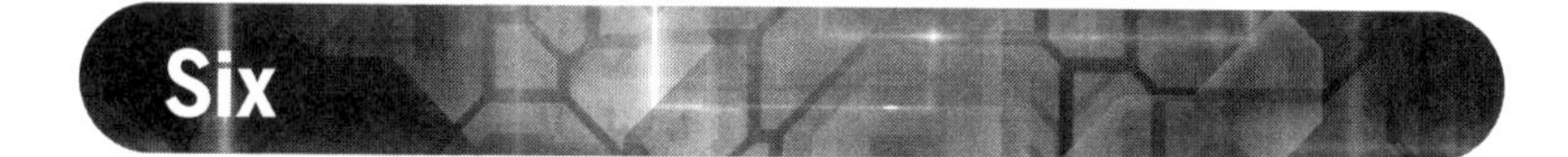

CONNECTING AT LAST

From now on, I'll connect
the dots my own way.

—BILL WATTERSON

Three creative writing fellowships in this country are worth doing just about anything to get: the Stegner Fellowship at Stanford University, a fellowship at the Fine Arts Work Center in Provincetown (Massachusetts), and the Institute of Creative Writing fellowships at the University of Wisconsin–Madison. When Dr. Casey, codirector of the institute, phoned me down in Tallahassee in April 2000 to invite me to become the Anastasia C. Hoffman Poetry Fellow for the coming year, I told her something calm and poolside-cool, like "yes, yes, yes, yes, yes!"—without asking my wife first.

"Are you sure you don't need to talk this over with anyone?" Dr. Casey asked, the concern in her voice quite evident even over the radio I had on in the room, which blared Creed's "Higher," a song that never hit number one but stayed on the Billboard Hot 100 for more than a year. (After I had quit playing guitar, I still listened to a lot of music and made up for that void in my life by remembering stupid facts about songs and bands, like that Scott Stapp and Mark Tremonti both were FSU guys like me.)

I turned the radio off so I could hear Dr. Casey better.

"You kidding me? I love Wisconsin. I was born in Wisconsin. I grew up there. I'm coming," I said, swinging my arms around in my patented "I Rule" dance. Having visited Madison a few times in my youth, I was already picturing myself lounging on a chair outside the Rathskellar, sipping Pabsts with my feet up on a table as I watched Lake Mendota fill with the distant triangles of sailboats. I was nibbling cheese curds so fresh they squeaked against my teeth. I was riding the carousel outside Ella's Deli, the strange Disneylike ice cream and sandwich shop on the east side of town. I was eating a brat burger from a sidewalk vendor on State Street.

I thanked Dr. Casey far too much, then babbled inappropriately about how much I thought the state of Wisconsin had better writers than Florida and how I planned to visit Mukwonago's Elegant Farmer (a huge grocery story and bakery where the raspberry muffins were nearly as big as your head), then hung up, wondering if I should've asked my wife first about accepting the offer. My hindsight is better than 20/20, but my in-the-moment vision can be atrocious, she reminds me regularly. It's not untrue.

Fortunately, Victoria had had enough of Tallahassee and was game to move, despite liking the little one-story starter home on Grey Fox Run we'd bought a year ago with student loan money and what little savings we had. The wacko in the house behind us continued to "raise my land up" by piling leaves eighteen inches high around his house because "the damn builders didn't deliver with the fill they'd promised," and the Japanese lady next door continued to wander naked through our yard at night, peeking in our windows with her pie-pan face, her eyes unblinking and cold. The home-owner's association, too, kept leaving anonymous notes on our porch to "please abide by the rules and take down that ghastly fence." The dog fencing I'd put up in our backyard—completely out of sight from the front of the house and the unused road there—was simply some waist-high farm-quality stuff secured by six-foot metal posts I'd driven into the ground about every ten feet or so.

Leaving suddenly seemed a more viable option. The house sold quickly to a bachelor accountant who worked for the state of Florida, and the school year wrapped itself up nicely, classwise, and we were ready to move come May.

❖

I love Wisconsin, and not just because I was born in Neenah. I love the lakes, the people, the overabundance of cows, the cheese curds, the farmers' markets, the back roads, the laid-back folks, the Wisconsin Dells, the Green Bay Packers, Door County, Culver's butter burgers, the Nicolet National Forest, the Friday fish boils, the honey museum in Ashippun, Johnsonville brats, Pabst Blue Ribbon, supper clubs, the House on the Rock, Woodman's Markets, Summerfest, the Oshkosh Airshow, the carved trolls of Mount Horeb, Miller Park, and white-tailed deer, to name just a few of the many things that make Wisconsin great.

My wife was substitute-teaching all over Madison. I taught three hours a week at the University of Wisconsin and made good money, so I had plenty of time to dive deep into Everquest, my new gaming vice. Computer games had made massive leaps in the graphics department, but what really captured me was what I called the Tolkien Effect: the ability to drop you into a rich, developed world that you could explore endlessly. If you've ever read *The Silmarillion*, you know what I'm talking about. Tolkien actually invented an elf language to make the book seem more authentic. I spent weeks just walking around Norrath and marveling at the range of playable races. There were Lizard people, Cat people, and Dragon people. The game also allowed role-playing, dueling with other players, and joining guilds. It was Dungeons & Dragons come to life at last. In my mind, Madison is synonymous with my entry into the world of MMORPG. I love them both.

I was sad to go on the job market in the fall of 2000, which meant leaving Madison. I'd have stayed there forever. My job search that year wasn't as successful as I'd hoped: I was candidate choice number two at three different schools, all of which landed their top person. Not a total surprise, since most creative writing jobs at the university level had hundreds of candidates for a single position. When you figure that most writers who land a job tend to stay for a very long time, you can see why the dozens of newly minted grads from creative writing programs end up waiting tables, driving taxis, tossing pizzas, and painting houses instead of teaching at a university, a sobering fact few programs tell you, since it would most likely hurt enrollment.

I did get one opportunity that came unexpectedly. The University of Wisconsin–Green Bay (UWGB) needed a fiction writer, and I knew the city well, since my parents had Packers season tickets—I'd been up there dozens of times, and I love the area. They needed someone at the very last minute, so they called around to every other University of Wisconsin school, including Madison, which is how I found out about it.

I drove up one Wednesday to interview and settled in as the third choice for the one-year visiting assistant professor of humanistic studies position. University types like to torpedo job candidates so often that it's not at all unheard of for someone fairly far down the pecking order to get the job—when I was a grad student at FSU, the guy they finally hired to run the department was thirteenth on the list. By comparison, third choice was pretty high. High enough, anyway.

The move from Madison to Green Bay was eventful, as so many things seemed to be that year. The fourteen-foot U-Haul I drove out of Madison leaked, and a torrential downpour soaked half of our stuff, ruining the TV, stereo, and a lot of books. Thank God I had misunderstood the sleepy Asian kid running the desk at the U-Haul and had actually bought the insurance rather than declining it, as I usually did. Twenty-one hundred dollars later, we replaced the electronics' water-fried guts and kept the rest of the cash, tossing the sloppy paperbacks and poetry books (including forty copies of *Say Hello*, my first collection) into the trash.

Hindsight is 20/20, as I noted above, but with four dogs (my wife had added one to the mix), it was damn hard finding a house to rent in Green Bay, so we just took the only option we had. We'd spent three entire days looking before finding a little two-story in Tank Park. Mostly a Hispanic and a Hmong community, Tank Park had a reputation for being a bit rough. My wife and I thought we could deal with it, however. We were young. We were pleasant. How bad could it be?

Within five weeks—the day before 9/11—I was on a *Cops* episode. Literally. The three-story next door, which housed maybe sixteen Mexicans from at least three different families, was a madhouse. People screamed and fought, and even in the moments of domestic calm, we'd get the occasional 2:00 AM blast of electronica while a couple of Spanish-speaking neighbors drank homemade wine coolers on their sagging porch. They got raided one Wednesday evening by a Green Bay SWAT team: helicopters, drug dogs, machine guns, flak jackets, the works. I heard the racket and stumbled out onto our back deck in my T-shirt and leopard print boxers. I rubbed at my eyes, watching a dozen black-garbed, heavily armed men smash through their rear door. One stopped and pointed a finger at me.

"Get back inside! Get the hell back!"

When you witness something like that, you figure the cops are clearing out all the baddies. It's ugly to see, but the neighborhood would be safer for it all, you think. Wrong.

A few weeks later, just after the first real cold front swept in and left two inches of powder on everything, we were burglarized. It was during, of all things, a poetry reading I hosted at UWGB on a Tuesday night. I'd brought in an old grad school pal, Oliver, to read from his new poetry collection on campus. My wife normally skips literary readings, but she thought Oliver was cute ("like a Smurf," she once admitted), plus she hadn't had a good piña colada in a long time, so she tagged along more for the after-reading festivities than anything. We stayed out at a nearby bar to welcome Oliver to Wisconsin until maybe 11:30 PM, then we returned to find my four-hundred-watt stereo speakers gone—along with the TV, the collection of DVDs and CDs, and my computer printer. The back door was off its hinges on the floor, kicked in.

All four dogs happily bounced up at our knees, licking us. On the kitchen table was an empty bag of Snausages.

"Jesus F-ing Christ," I said, knowing that the bag had come from the top shelf above the sink. "They busted in, fed the pups doggie snacks, and robbed us blind."

My wife called the cops while I grabbed one of my curlicued golf clubs and searched the house for stragglers. The home invaders had vandalized as much as they had stolen, putting my Hewlett-Packard laptop in the washing machine, then turning it on to make a sudsy

$1,000 mess, and stealing my $150 Cort bass guitar while snapping the neck of the $3,000 Les Paul custom I'd bought a few months ago from Mars Music in Houston. They took my Playstation 2 and the three dozen games I'd accumulated for it. They took my crappy old Super Nintendo. They took every computer game, even the old junk on floppy disks. They'd rooted through our clothes and drawers upstairs, even taking the time to pose my wife's stuffed animals in a sixty-nine position on her knickknack shelves. My desktop computer was kicked over, the screen smashed, the printer missing, my books scattered all around. They'd even gone through and emptied my asthma medicine bottles; the tiny white pills had been ground into the carpet, and a few were floating in the toilet like miniature white turds.

The cops wouldn't let us stay there, since the back door wouldn't shut and lock, so we talked, around 1:00 AM, to a sleepy State Farm agent who told us that our insurance would spring for two hotel rooms (one for Oliver, who was supposed to be staying with us).

Statistically speaking, only 2.1 percent of U.S. homes were burglarized in 2001, so we had felt safe. But that statistic doesn't take into account that certain areas—like Tank Park—have a much higher incidence than, for instance, the well-manicured area my parents lived in down in Illinois. We thought that would be the end of our run-ins with bad people.

No one was ever arrested for the crime, despite the most valiant attempts by the Green Bay police investigators. I mean, how could they figure out who did it? It's not as if it had been snowy and there were deep boot prints going from the recently SWAT-raided house next door and over the fence and onto our back porch where the door was kicked in. (There were.) It wasn't as if they had chucked beer bottles into our yard every week and kicked over our trash and shouted drunkenly one evening, "You su-u-u-uck!" (They did.)

My wife insisted I put new locks on everything, which the

landlords refused to pay for since we "probably were asking for it"; after all, they'd lived there for a few years without incident. That was probably just because our landlords dressed like white trash, complete with big 1980s hair and ripped-up, stonewashed jeans, so our burglars didn't think they had much worth stealing, at least compared to a young professional couple. So I handled the locks myself. Neither of us felt that safe, regardless. Clearly the dogs weren't a deterrent, despite what law officers say about a noisy dog being the best home protection. Every creak of the house settling, every neighborhood dog bark, and every tree snap against the window from the wind had us awake, wondering.

With both of us working, this was the most money we'd ever made in our lives, but since I was making maybe $15,000 per year less than a regular (not visiting) assistant professor would make, we felt poor—meaning we didn't think we had much opportunity to move. And that's not even considering how difficult it'd been originally to find a rental place that would allow us to keep four dogs, who seemed decidedly nonchalant about the current affairs. They continued to sniff through the yard, eat the dandelions, chew on my sneakers, and sleep 90 percent of the time as if everything was hunky-dory.

❖

After a few months of paperwork and phoning, and we'd finally been paid for all the damage and had replaced the most important items, we had a fire. The house was small, and most of our stuff was still in the two-car garage in boxes. So when the fire burst to life in that garage one January morning, it might as well have torched the entire house, we lost so much of our lives. I'd guess that 80 percent of what we had was ruined, including most of the things we'd just replaced from the burglary.

I was smearing some peanut butter on wheat toast when I smelled the smoke. Through the sliding glass window, I could see plumes of smoke boiling out from under the garage door—thick, oily smoke that reeked of burned plastic. We had six crates of collectibles—Star Wars figures, McDonald's Happy Meal toys, bobble-head dolls—that were oozing into a soupy, worthless mess. We had boxes of summer clothes, old poetry manuscripts, an extra VCR, all sorts of things in boxes. Not two days earlier, I'd added a new replacement Playstation 2 and six brand-new games, including Dark Cloud, Twisted Metal: Black, NCAA Football 2002, and Resident Evil Code Veronica X. We had everything in there.

"Wake up! Fire!" I hollered, grabbing up as many dogs as I could as I ran upstairs and kicked my wife awake. Yes, I actually kicked her shins as hard as I could, because she was (prior to having kids) a heavy sleeper. We could've had flames licking the heels of her feet, and she might've continued dreaming of a quiet life on an island somewhere without yappy dogs, a brooding husband, endless video games, and lousy-paying teaching jobs in places where the snow was two feet deep.

We took our dogs, grabbed our wallets, and ran out to the car in our pajamas. We always left the car in the driveway, since the garage was our giant closet. Today it was parked far out in the street, a good ways from the flames, which looked ready to make the two-foot leap from the garage roof to the house roof. The neighbors quickly emerged from their houses, all crowding, despite the fact that it was 7:00 AM, to watch as the garage really lit up, the smoke thickening the air like a tire fire in a country lot. The fire department finally showed up and managed to save the house. Our stuff in the garage was a total loss. If it wasn't burned, it was smoke-damaged and soaking wet.

The Green Bay police department did its usual bang-up job, even going as far as to remove the jimmied-open garage window—the point of entry, one rookie cop observed with great delight at being able to contribute—that had dirty fingerprints on the cobwebbed glass. We all suspected arson. The Mexicans from next door were part of the crowd that lingered in the street, smoking cheap cigarettes, maybe Bucks, and lurking about.

"So you think we'll nab them?" I said, pointing at the evidence.

"I'll do my best," a Gomer Pyle–like officer assured me, placing the entire window inside a big plastic Piggly Wiggly sack. "But I've never done fingerprinting before."

I felt a sinking sensation in my chest, my faith in law enforcement diminishing by the second. The neighbors were never charged with either the arson or the burglary. But justice was sort of served: two of them were later arrested for a home break-in a block away. I hear both got two years in prison for it, which the newspapers said "surprised" their friends and family members. Really—I mean, how dumb do you have to be to break into the house next door, try to burn it down, and then continue to burglarize houses in your neighborhood? You're just begging to get caught.

My wife says that maybe they didn't do it.

Yeah. Maybe.

❖

We moved two days later, having found a place down by Lambeau Field in De Pere, where we lived up until I got a job offer at Clemson University in South Carolina. But even that wasn't without incident. A flood drain burst and sent 100 gallons of muddy rainwater into our basement, where some of our newly boxed stuff was stored. The real problem, though, was our landlord, a contractor who decided to keep our security deposit after we left for no reason other than that he was an unorganized, mean-spirited prick. We had to sue him nearly a year later to finally get it back, and I hate, hate, hate dealing with lawyers. I wouldn't even watch *Ally McBeal* with my wife, I detest lawyers so much. I vaguely remember a pair of them from my childhood, how they had so much power over me as an adoptee: where I could live, who could see me, who could hold me. I remember.

It wasn't right, and even just thinking of the legal profession still kicks my heart rate up to near 200—real red-eyed anger stuff, where the world melts away and you focus intensely on what's setting you off.

❖

After 9/11, the university job market went kablooey. More than half of the jobs I applied for in fall 2001 disappeared, the funding having vanished as administrators huddled for cover, fearing statewide cutbacks, mass hysteria, God knew what. The jobs were just gone. Two search committee chairpersons admitted I was their top choice, but they'd been hamstrung by the finance people, so the searches were canceled.

I was out of work.

I couldn't get a job anywhere, even when I started looking in Green Bay for nonteaching employment. Anything, really. The idea of having a Ph.D. and no job was unthinkable. I should've been able to keep the job at Green Bay, since the inside candidate wins something like 90 percent of the time, but the other two people they brought in prior to me in 2000 were women. The others they brought in while I was there? Women, too. What a surprise that they hired a woman to offset their male-dominated department, despite my good evaluations and hard work in every task they'd assigned. I even went to every department meeting despite not being required to. I liked that job a lot and really understood those kids: 80 percent grew up within a 150-mile radius of Green Bay, and more than 50 percent were the first ones in their families to go to college. I was born in Neenah, not forty miles from Green Bay. I knew this type of person and could speak his language. I was a midwesterner through and through, and someone who loved Wisconsin.

To be fair, I missed a class because of the burglary and two more because of the fire. And being forced into the job market, as sad as it was, kept me from quite a few more classes that spring. Maybe that all played into it, I don't know. All I know is that the interim chairman shook my hand, told me thanks for doing what I had done the past year, and wished me better luck elsewhere.

"You bet," I told him, boring holes through his ovalish skull with my eyes.

So instead of becoming the regular full-time assistant professor at UWGB, I was filling out applications at Arby's, Blimpie, the Wizard's Lair comic book store, Just Tires, Sam's Club, Target, and Wal-Mart, all to no avail. It made some kind of strange sense for the twenty-three-year-old manager at McDonald's who stank of cigarette smoke to explain, "Pal, I'd hire you, but with your credentials, you'd be out of here in two weeks for a better job, and then I'd have to go out and hire someone else. Why waste that kind of time for either of us?" But when the manager of one of Green Bay's finer bookstores (Barnes & Noble) told me I was "overqualified" for the job, I'd had enough.

Yes, I was the author of three books at this point: a single-author poetry collection and two coedited poetry anthologies. Yes, I had a Ph.D. in American Literature from Florida State University. Yes, I'd worked as a professor at the local university. But I needed a job, I was willing to do anything, and I knew a hell of a lot about books.

I said, "Isn't part of the problem with the big chain bookstores that when someone asks a question about an author or title, the salespeople have to rely on the computer system because they don't know

Dennis McKiernan from Dennis Rodman? I know books. I love books. I'm happy to help get others excited about books, whether it's buying them or just reading them here while they knock back five-dollar drinks from the café. I shop at B&N all the time. I know this store. I know how to help, and I'm happy to do it."

He frowned and gave me a look as though he were eyeing a red-tailed guppy in the tank at Wal-Mart and debating whether it'd die before he brought it home to give to his zitty, fat son.

"Yeah," he said slowly, as if testing the words on his tongue. "That all sounds good, but I don't know. I'll have to get back to you."

He never did. Even when I called and left three messages over the next two weeks, I never heard back.

So I was one of those Ph.D. disaster stories. The joke at FSU was that Tallahassee had more pizza delivery guys with Ph.D.s per capita than anywhere else in the country. I don't know if that was true, but it sure seemed true when the barrage of rejections continued. Being a writer, I was used to rejection. I had boxes of slips rejecting my poems, my stories, my essays, my books. But this was personal. They were saying no to me, not to something I'd written. This hurt.

I finally had a good lead, though. The manager of a video rental place near Lambeau Field invited me in for an interview, which apparently was not an interview where they Q & A you but rather a thirty-minute sit-down with a number two pencil and a math quiz work sheet. I'm not a wonder with numbers, but there were questions like this: "If a customer owes you $3.52, and then pays with a five-dollar bill, how much change would you give back?"

Or: 134 + 53 – 2 = ?

I didn't get the job.

I later learned it went to an employee's cousin who was fresh out of rehab for her crack habit. The former gangbanger stole from the cash box and took movies off the shelves for her personal collection. As a result of her theft and her selling cocaine at work, which got the cops involved, the place eventually had to close.

You couldn't make up a story that pathetic.

❖

I'd met Roger at a bar the year before in Madison; he was a lumpy, balding kid in grad school there who had gone to MIT for his undergraduate work. If you've read Ben Mezrich's *Bringing Down the House: The Inside Story of Six MIT Students Who Took Vegas for Millions* or *Busting Vegas: The MIT Whiz Kid Who Brought the Casinos to Their Knees*, then you know the type I'm talking about. He palled around, he claimed, with a group of MIT gamblers who had ways to hit it big.

"I'm talking six figures a haul," he said, chuckling with a full belly laugh even though I'm not sure what was funny about it.

"Good stuff," I said.

We hit it off because Roger was a big Packers fan—"Brett Favre is *bad ass*, man, I swear, *bad ass*," he kept saying—and he was lonely in Madison and wanted a drinking partner who had an IQ "above room temperature." Madison had plenty of smart people, so God knows why he wanted to hang with me, but I sensed that we had similar childhoods as well, so it was easy to develop camaraderie. Broken people have a sense about others that way.

"Look," he said one Thursday afternoon, shuffling a deck of Bicycle playing cards that he tugged from his backpack. We sat in the outdoor café part of State Street Brats, drinking Killian's in twenty-three-ounce glasses. It was busy with the late lunch crowd, but a nice breeze from off the lake kept us cool. "It's really not that difficult. You start with hi-lo. You simply assign a value of minus one to every ten, face card, and ace. The middle cards are zilch. The lows, two through six, are plus one. When you have a high positive count, you bet bigger."

His chin was scarred from acne of the type you see on those scary information cards at the dermatologist's office, but his hands could manipulate cards like a magician's. The cards absolutely danced between his fingers. He shuffled and sorted with blinding speed. It was impressive, even though I fancied myself a fairly good card player. I'd tinkered some with poker at FSU, but mostly I enjoyed cribbage, a game my father and mother sometimes played. Blackjack had no real appeal, at least not until I was broke and out of work. I had computer game versions of both and toyed around with them on occasion whenever I got burned out on action games or MMOGs.

"If you've got these moves down pat, then why don't you hit Monte Carlo or Vegas and make a fortune?" I finally asked, when his talking about the techniques bordered on bragging. The way he said it, you'd think he could clear ten grand an hour.

"My pal got the backroom treatment at Harrah's," he said, then chuckled inappropriately again. He laughed too loud at all the wrong things.

"C'mon," I said, not buying it.

He licked his lips and eyed me. "Are you calling me a liar?"

The way his voice rose at the end came close to hysteria.

"Sure, you've got some techniques," I said, drinking more Killian's before it got too warm. "But really. If it's that easy, why isn't everyone out there kicking Vegas's ass?"

Roger ignored what I'd said. "You calling me a liar?"

"Take it easy, man," I said. We'd hung out maybe only five times, and he was cagey. I had a knack for getting along with cagey people, though, so it didn't really bother me—until now. I didn't like being forced into a corner.

"Screw you," he finally spat, then got up fast enough to bump the table with his sizable belly, sending my drink onto the cement, where the glass shattered and beer sprayed my shoes and pants. A girl in a blue miniskirt and Sigma Sigma Sigma blouse nearby got some on her bare legs. Her two girlfriends glared at me.

Roger gave me the middle finger, then turned his fist and used that finger like a pointer, jabbing at me as he said, "*Screw you.*"

When my grad school buddy JT told me in late 2001 that he'd been gambling online for months, making good money by maximizing the bonus first-timer offers, I started to piece together Roger's conversations—call them lectures—on how to turn the blackjack odds in your favor. Wanting something to do, wanting to help out financially, wanting to kill the achingly empty hours while my wife was at work, wanting to be able to afford to stay home forever and stop having to interact with people face-to-face, I started playing blackjack. I played online as JT did, taking those 200 percent one-time bonuses and playing for hours with minimum bets, trying to protect the free money that I had to run completely through six or eight or ten times before they'd let me cash out.

You know where this is going. I started hitting up the Indian casinos. Hell, Oneida Bingo & Casino was six minutes from my place in Green Bay. The techniques sort of worked. I made a few hundred here and there. But the big-breasted UWGB girls who hoisted drinks around to make tuition were told to comp me freebies, and I started drinking Jack Daniels because I couldn't afford to drink it at home. Drinking and driving is certainly stupid, but drinking and gambling?

Talk about a recipe for a massacre.

One Monday, I was down $3,000 dollars after forty minutes of play. I was making well under $300 a week through unemployment and maybe another $150 from gambling, so this loss represented a big chunk of cash to me. Fearing the tongue-lashing my wife was sure to give me when I confessed that I'd been gambling at all—no, I didn't tell her—I got scared enough to say a prayer and throw my last $600 onto the table despite the count not being that much in my favor. The dealer gave me a jack, then an ace. Thinking that for once in my godforsaken life, things were in my favor, I let it ride. My nineteen beat the dealer's eighteen. Then I pressed my luck. Hard.

The count was only plus three, but I didn't care anymore. It was luck now or nothing. Really, what did I have to lose?

My breath was tight in my lungs; I didn't dare to breathe, I eyed the yawning dealer, who absently picked at a scar on the back of his left hand. Then I left $2,000 on the table and said, "Go."

The casino boss, a barrel-chested guy who might've once played for the Packers, rumbled over and glared at me. I wasn't cheating, but the way he was looking at me, I suddenly wondered about Roger's friend who got the backroom treatment. I imagined knuckles crushed in a vice. I imagined a razor blade sliding across my belly. I imagined pins pushed into my eyes, or a rattlesnake removed from a dark jar and dangled in front of my nose.

When I hit blackjack, I took my winnings and got the hell away as if the place were about to be struck by a Hollywood-sized meteor and not even Bruce Willis could save the day. I never played blackjack again.

❖

I'd known darkness before, but this was a very bad time for me. I stewed alone at home for hours in the basement, staring at the cement wall as if I might burn holes through it with my eyes. We'd been there fifteen months. My wife still had the same job she got when we first moved to Green Bay, but I was getting $212.46 a week for unemployment, a situation that looked unlikely to improve anytime soon, since I was terrified of gambling (which I eventually confessed, to my wife's disgust, although I downplayed it significantly).

"Never again," she warned, not needing to threaten divorce. I knew how hard she worked for the $29,000 she earned at that Catholic elementary school. No joke.

All I had to do was sit on my ass and waste my time applying for two jobs a week to keep getting my shitty, lazy life subsidized by the U.S. government. Some of my writer friends were jealous.

"Man, I'd love to have all day to just bum around and write!" said a novelist with two books out.

"Yeah," I told him, tossing a deep-out pattern pass with Brett Favre in Madden NFL 2002 on the Playstation. My receiver dropped it. "It's terrific."

I wrote maybe twenty minutes a day for the eleven months I was unemployed. I read comic books. I listened to Nickelback's "How You Remind Me" maybe eight million times. I watched a hell of a lot of HBO. I played every Playstation game I owned and started renting more from the local Video Mart before it shut down. I also played Diablo II, a fantasy shoot-'em-up game that could go on forever, your character becoming increasingly more powerful with magic and weaponry. You could play it online, too, which I did, and I really enjoyed it. Then there was Unreal Tournament, which I played far too much of, as well. I put in at least forty hours a week on the Playstation 2, the computer, and the Game Boy. On some days I'd dig out the old Super Nintendo system I'd picked up at a garage sale and have at Zombies Ate My Neighbors and Contra III: The Alien Wars.

Money started to run out, and to keep from thinking about Roger and gambling again, I started mulling over any way to make cash. I mean anything. I looked into selling my plasma, my sperm, anything. If there'd been a guy on a corner with a sandwich board sign saying, "Will buy kidneys for cash!" I might've gone for it.

So it came to me one afternoon that I didn't really need the boxes of books that had somehow survived the U-Haul water damage, the burglary, and the garage fire. I was barely reading anymore, and the idea of lugging those heavy boxes during the next move, whenever it came, made my back muscles quake in fear. I used to buy books on the last day of a library sale, when you could fill a grocery sack for like five bucks. I used to pick up ten sacks at a time, thinking I'd devour them all in my university-sponsored literary life. Now each of those unread titles felt like bricks piled atop my chest.

I listed a few on Amazon.com as a third-party seller, and they sold. So I listed more. Then more. Before long, our online bookselling business (Vancleavebooks) became a nice little cottage industry to augment my wife's crappy private school salary—which was perfect, since unemployment ran out. It wasn't big bucks, but it was enough to scrape by for just the two of us (and four dogs, which aren't as cheap as you might think). It wasn't a good life, especially with me fuming about the house all day, feeling worthless and unappreciated, but it was a life.

To call what I felt each day "depression" is to call a Hurricane Katrina a "weather event." It doesn't come close. Hope was dimming, desperation was growing fast, and the misery lay in my heart and mind until I thought I couldn't bear it.

I'd worked for years to position myself well in the academic world, had even passed my Ph.D. oral exam with distinction (which I'd been told that less than 5 percent did at FSU), and had three books with my name on the spine. People like that don't become unemployed. You screw a student and get caught, fine. You punch out a colleague, okay. You don't show up to teach, or you skip out on mandatory university meetings, of course. But I did what I was told and did it well. I couldn't get my head around this idea of unemployment. The Ryan who was unemployed was a Ryan I didn't know. He ate too many potato chips and lay around all day staring at screens—not writing, not doing much of anything. He didn't put on a shirt most days. He played Nine Inch Nails's *Pretty Hate Machine* in repeat mode, letting the thick bass and drums pound awake the unfocused resentment inside him. And he played video games endlessly, as if setting enough high scores would translate into an accomplishment in the real world.

The literary equivalent of Unemployed Ryan is Bartleby, or Rip Van Winkle. A sluggard. A layabout. A loser.

I hated him, and yet he was living my life.

Then the chairman from Clemson University called to offer me the job. I didn't quibble about money. I didn't bitch them out for offering it to me in late July. I didn't even remember to breathe, so I nearly passed out while holding the phone.

The universe had thrown me a lifeline at last.

"I can't wait to get there," I gasped, meaning it.

Seven

THE WAR AT WORK

> University politics are vicious precisely because the stakes are so small.
>
> —HENRY KISSINGER

I'd been out of work for nearly a year when I got the Clemson job offer. It came late—near the end of July 2003, which was problematic from a stress standpoint, since my on-campus interview had been all the way back in February 2003—but my wife and I were eager for me to finally slide into a tenure-track position after two one-year deals and another year of hardscrabble unemployment. Tenure-track meant a future, security, and belonging.

South Carolina was lousy for K–12 education (my wife's work), and we had less than a month to find a house and move there before school started, but tenure was the goal. Tenure was the distant buoy luring my wife and me (no kids yet) onward. Tenure made my wife quit her very fine job at Holy Family Elementary School in Green Bay, which gave an education so good that Brett Favre's kids went there. Tenure took us 1,000 miles south to a state that neither of us had ever been in before. Prior to my moving there, if you had given me a map of the United States and told me to point to South Carolina, I'd have waved my hand vaguely at the bottom right, hoping I was correct.

Things started with a clang the first weekend. I had just returned to our new house from Chicago, where I'd picked up a truckload of stuff that my parents had jammed in their basement for the three years that my wife and I had bumped around Wisconsin in tiny rental places. Victoria was asleep upstairs in the rocker, an ugly green afghan her grandmother had given us half across her legs. The TV croaked away on some infomercial for hair-growth products, that's how late it was. I clicked the tube off, then tucked her in a little better and thought about how impossible it'd have been to unload the U-Haul without a partner who could dead-lift sixty pounds over her head.

Since our job offer came so late, we had moved in a rush and weren't able to finagle help at either end. It took more than twelve hours to unload the twenty-four-foot U-Haul truck and the twelve-foot trailer at our new two-story in the fancy subdivision of—no joke here—Camelot. Yes, we had moved from Green Bay, Wisconsin, to the Camelot area of Clemson, South Carolina, where we owned our first real house and indeed felt regal about it, despite the fact that the exterior was Barbie Corvette pink.

I eased down our creaky stairs to the Ken blazer-blue kitchen for some tea, my mind still hustling over the change of geography and the mounting work responsibilities. I'd already met a few of my students-to-be when I swung by my sixth-floor office to test out my key, and even those few had struck me as better than most of the ones I'd worked with elsewhere.

After chatting with them for only a few minutes, I could see that they knew William Butler Yeats and Allen Ginsberg and appreciated the hell out of L=A=N=G=U=A=G=E poetry. I have to confess, I was a little intimidated to teach these diehards, who clearly knew the difference between a dactyl and a spondee, between synecdoche and metonymy, yet I was kind of excited, too, so I knew I wouldn't be able to sleep. Thanks to video games, I hadn't had eight hours of sleep in one night for nearly two decades. At least being wound up about being off unemployment and teaching full-time again was a good reason to bypass some solid sleep, for once.

Jazzed to be starting work in two days, I put on the tinny-sounding pocket radio speakers in the garage, unloaded the Camry, and listened to a 1980s station that was playing a marathon of the Australian rock band INXS. I was working up the kind of sweat that makes the back of your shirt slurp tight against your skin. Even when I was through, the car as empty as ever and much of our stuff stacked neatly against the walls of the oversized two-car garage, I wasn't ready for bed. My wristwatch said it wasn't yet 11:30 PM, so I turned off the radio, threw on a tan guayavera shirt, and headed to downtown Clemson (which is almost an oxymoron, since the buildings were no higher than two stories and the main drag went for only about three blocks).

Clemson Boulevard was packed with loud kids, almost as if a movie were being shot there and some Hollywood suits were offering fifty bucks a head to any and all who'd stand around and provide a good crowd. The kids might've been ready to get rolling with a new academic year on Wednesday, but for now they appeared content to margarita and tap beer themselves into oblivion, which didn't sound like a half-bad idea to me, then, either, I was so worn out. I wondered if they had Leinenkugel beer. I'd developed a real taste for it at NIU and during my years in Wisconsin.

Someone waved at me from half a block away. I rolled down my window and waved back, then realized it wasn't any of the kids I'd met before. What was I thinking? I barely knew anyone here. But I had a face like that—from a distance, I seemed like someone you might know. From time to time, people mistook me for a pal.

I lucked into a just-opened parking slot near Nick's, a smoky dive that professors often visited, but it wasn't crowded enough. I wanted juice, energy, a little kinetic pick-me-up to counteract my weary muscles and my tired mind. I decided to hit a place called Tiger Town Tavern instead. It was all about students, and I wanted to feel the thrum of 100 eighteen-year-olds banging together at the arms and the hips while listening to "Crazy in Love" by Beyoncé and Jay-Z.

I hadn't heard of iTunes yet, or most likely I'd have stayed home and played Silent Hill 3 (which had just came out on August 6) on the Playstation 2 while blasting Nickelback's "How You Remind Me" and Linkin Park's "Crawling" through headphones off my laptop. I liked a college mob scene as much as the next junior professor, but my Playstation was packed away somewhere, and we didn't have the computers hooked up yet, so the options for entertainment were limited.

I ordered a twenty-ounce Killian's Irish Red and some chili fries—South Carolina has apparently never heard of Leinenkugel—then bellied up to the bar. A leggy brunette in white camel-toe shorts summoned a cloud of smoke off her Newport while chatting up two Sigma Epsilons who both weren't listening but were openly staring at her chest. She either didn't notice or didn't care. At age nineteen, maybe it doesn't matter. I watched Sportscenter on the big screen across the room and wondered how many of these noisy, sweaty students would be in my classes in two days, trying to brownnose their way into my heart.

Having not met any students beyond the three from my lit class (who, I was beginning to suspect, were less smart than I thought; maybe I'd simply been taken aback by their eagerness to impress me), I imagined teaching a handful of these eighty-watt kids around me who were killing brain cells by the millions. One shaven-headed kid in a SLUT T-shirt near the Golden Tee machine drank two gorilla farts (that's a drink) in five seconds, to the great delight of his three friends, then he hurried to the john to undoubtedly hurl. A girl tried to play the Simpsons pinball game while holding a half-full highball glass in her mouth, but she spilled the drink all over the machine and on her shirt. Two guys who were shooting pool kept purposely bumping the rears of their sticks into the rears of nearby girls. When a redhead turned and said, "What the shit?" one of those guys shrugged and said, "Whazup?!"

Watching the chaos around me unfold, I realized that teaching these particular kids would be like digging ditches in the rain. That's why so many teachers burn out—frustration. Better to pound your skull against a brick wall than try to instill sense and knowledge into members of Gen Y, or whatever moniker the twenty-and-under crowd holds. Still, I was here in Clemson and ready to try. That's what educators do. Try, try, try.

There's an important distinction here. If you're an educator, teaching defines you. If you're a teacher, it's just a job. I couldn't help it—I was an educator, even if I was a lousy husband, a second-rate student, and a video game "enthusiast" who couldn't get his mind around the idea of addiction yet.

After a year of unemployment, I was willing to try my ass off. Take away a man's ability to make a living for his family, and you learn what agony really is. Agony is motivation. And motivation is what makes the American Dream a possibility versus a pipe dream. Forget talent. Screw training. Give me someone who is properly motivated, and you'll see someone who gets results. Like Gatsby, I was ready to turn back time if that's what it took.

I've got a freelance writer friend I've known since grad school whose work was always so-so compared to that of a few powerhouse classmates whose prose absolutely soared. This friend knocks out the rent, drives a Beamer, and has hundreds of publishing credits, thanks to his refusal to fail and the constant fear of bankruptcy. Meanwhile, the über-talented classmates with all that God-given word wizardry are nearly all operating off the map, in cubicles or worse.

My fries were drenched in cheese and Tabasco-hot chili with big, dark beans. All I'd eaten in the last ten hours were a couple of candy bars and a lukewarm McChicken sandwich, so I ignored the heat and downed those dripping fries. The beer helped cool off my insides. Chili fries and beer so cold that a sheen of ice forms over its surface are a magical combination, which I'd learned to appreciate as an undergraduate.

"Need another?" one of the bartenders asked, cupping his ear to hear me over Staind's "So Far Away," a song I'd come to enjoy, though not as much as their previous hit, "It's Been Awhile," which stayed number one on the Mainstream Rock Chart for sixteen weeks. I sometimes forget the name of Yeats's poem that ends with "And what rough beast, its hour come round at last, / Slouches towards Bethlehem to be born?", but I remember that the Legend of Zelda: The Wind Walker was released in North America in March 2003 and that 50 Cent's "In Da Club" stayed number one on the Billboard charts the same year for nine weeks straight. My mind's a strange dumping ground for information, try as I might not to remember ephemeral, pop-culture stuff. My wife says I should try out for *Jeopardy* and win us $50,000. I suck at Final Jeopardy, though, and would lose it all trying to double my meager winnings on the last question.

Just then, I saw a woman two booths away: "Administrator Sally." I recognized her from my campus visit so many months back. She had the sluggish, glassy-eyed look of someone who'd drank both too much and too long, and the evidence of empty glasses on the table furthered the image of a middle-aged academic type trying to recapture youth by overindulging and basically making a fool of herself. Worse, she was doing it alone.

Nearly six months since I'd met her in her office on my campus visit, I figured—as most people with self-esteem issues do—that she wouldn't remember me. I imagined myself as largely forgettable.

My Killian's was gone, and I figured this was as good a time as any to head home. Maybe I could dig up the Playstation if I poked through enough boxes. It was late, I was tired, and I needed to start getting my syllabus together beyond the hurried book order I had put in three days ago over my cell phone. Moving from Wisconsin to South Carolina, all that packing and organizing, had sucked up nearly every moment for the past two weeks. It was time now to get ready to teach for real.

Of course, the Playstation marathon idea grew more compelling by the second. When it came to actual work or gaming, gaming won, more often than not. It's the ultimate procrastination tool.

Then I realized that Sally was not sitting alone. A young woman of perhaps twenty-four perched on a stool nearby, but not close enough for me to have realized that they were talking together in low voices. I'd later meet Anne, a graduate student in the College of Arts and Sciences, who intended to study corporate law when she was through with Clemson. Petite and blond, she wasn't unduly attractive, although her refusal to wear makeup or put more time into her hair than it took to work a tight ponytail into shape would've made me like her instantly, had I not seen her at Tiger Town this night. Call her beauty au naturale.

Despite my years of thundering-volumed amplifiers in half a dozen rock bands and rim-shaking radio blastings in my mom's 1973 orange Chevy Caprice station wagon, I still had decent hearing. These days, I'm no longer any good at the cocktail party effect, in which a crowd is chattering away and one is supposed to be able to discern individual conversations from the cacophony. It's how two people manage to communicate in a noisy airport or pub.

That night, though, I heard every word between Sally and Anne through the racket, the din, the shouts, and the clinking of empty margarita pitchers. There was no way to call it anything other than what it was: a lover's quarrel.

"Stop it," Anne said, pushing Sally from her.

Sally, who was married and still lived with her husband and her kids, reached her arm across Anne's back and tried to nestle her head against Anne's cheek. Anne had what some would call porcelain skin: not a freckle in sight next to the spaghetti straps on her top. Like everyone in this body-packed room, she glistened with a thin coating of sweat.

"You *always* do this to me," Anne said, pushing her again. "I don't like it when you embarrass me."

"I don't embarrass you. You embarrass yourself when you act like this."

College bars are strange places. You'd think a scene like this would've drawn looks, or at least eavesdroppers. But spats, over-the-top PDAs, yo-mama one-upmanship shouting matches, and "Michael Jordan is way better than Kobe" debates are so commonplace, no one really cares unless they're directly involved or implicated in the flare-up.

Anne appeared ready to cry. In her dark camisole top and flare-bottom jeans, she could've passed for any of 100 other kids who were out that night to shoot pool, get loaded, get laid, or dance. Only they weren't there with a thickly lipsticked woman twice their age. They weren't being pawed in public, apparently enjoying it despite the protests.

"C'mon," Sally said, pressing close to console her.

"No," Anne said. "Not here."

They got up and readied their purses. I was between them and the door. To leave Tiger Town Tavern, they'd have to sidle right past me through the thick of people.

In moments such as these, my brain seizes. Were this a Halo match, I'd have entered the fight-or-flight reflex immediately and at least done something. Were I a soldier in Desert Storm, I'd have fired my M-16 or phoned for backup, reporting a potential unfriendly closing in. But this was real life, and in real life I'm an idiot who doesn't think on his feet fast enough, nor do I appreciate enough how mean-spirited and angry some people are.

I did the worst thing possible—I sat there staring, listening as they approached. I at least kind of lowered my head into the crook of my arm to disguise my face.

"Don't see me, don't see me," I muttered like some drunk talking to Jesus or his dead Aunt Martha through his wristwatch. It was a bit too much like the Son of Sam, now that I think about it.

I whispered it again, "Don't see me."

Sally brushed so close I imagined static electricity firing between us. Did she really not notice me? I wondered, watching as she merged with the crowd near the door. Then she paused and turned. The smoldering disapproval in my eyes over a married teacher–single student relationship was impossible to hide. Recognition flooded Sally's face. For three full, painful seconds, we played chicken with our eyes, daring the other to veer off. She clicked her tongue, then took hold of Anne's shoulder and directed her out into the night, as if dismissing me entirely.

I left a ten on the counter for my food and beer, then followed, thinking maybe it wasn't that big of a deal. Classes hadn't even started yet. It wasn't as though I had actually done anything, I tried to convince myself, moving into the live-wire dark of this August night in Clemson.

To say my teaching career went downhill from that moment would be like saying Michael Jordan was familiar with the game of basketball. This was the beginning of the end of my days at Clemson, though of course I didn't know it, and classes hadn't even begun yet.

❖

Echo came to me. The name is so pretentious that I would've written off her and her hand-me-down Birkenstocks immediately, except for the early assignment I had given in a poetry-writing class during my first weeks of teaching at Clemson: Use a simile to describe your relationship to writing poems.

Most kids come up with something like this: Writing a poem is like going to the dentist for a root canal. Or: Writing a poem is like flying an airplane in a thunderstorm. Or: Writing a poem is like surfing a big wave off a beach in Honolulu.

Her answer: Writing a poem is like cutting grass. Then sewing it back together.

My relationship with my students was like looking at the moon a thousand times and seeing a moon, then one day seeing an alabaster bowl brimming with soul-shaking brightness. I began to cultivate an appetite for working with strong students. I'd had a few in Green Bay, Madison, and Tallahassee, kids with a little linguistic sizzle and pop to them, but Echo was something new. A student like this was a growling bass line to go with the alligator-shoe two-step of my teaching.

If you're reading this as sexual, you're be wrong. I was intellectually aroused for one of the first times in my life. Go ahead and think "mentally erect" if you want—this was an exciting time for me, to be sure, especially after languishing in the mental morass of unemployment and the seemingly eternal numbness of gaming. As a graduate student, I thought a little about teaching, which is to say I thought a lot more about myself. In my thirties now, I'd been thinking more about students and what they each brought to the academic table: Their coffee-dream excitement. Their heavenward hopes. The unpruned contours of the things they thought were poems.

"I liked your answer," I told Echo after class that day as we headed out.

She didn't respond but just smoothed her shoulder-length Princess Peach platinum hair. Despite us being twenty feet from the doors leading outside Daniel Hall, she lit up a Marlboro red, which managed not to kill the scent of her perfume (lavender). She didn't smile, either—still, I sensed that my appreciation stirred something within her.

Bold in her writing from the first assignment, she wrote throughout the semester about the snag of a dress zipper opening, the late-night noir flick of her life, the geometry of empty rooms, the blue midnight ceiling of her unfathomed love, the melancholy tune she'd been taught so well.

And there was Luke, a frail kid whose rainbow belt wrapped twice about his waist. His staccato alto was a sax played right, as though everything that emerged was positively vaporous. And Miles with the forked goatee. And Charleston Kevin, whose gaze bordered on hypnotic. And the foxfire voice of Becky, a hospice nurse from Columbus, Ohio, who testified every chance she could that her husband came at her with a circular saw, swinging it so fast that the blur of teeth sang through the air. She'd "cunt" and "dogpiss" and "faggot" her way in poems, past the meth head in her skull forever testing the circuitry.

These were students I could work with. I knew a couple of them were gamers, especially Miles, who had a Halo patch sewn into his jeans jacket, but the subject simply never came up. Teaching had become my safe zone, where video games had no part. We talked about pure black magnolias, Hitler's jackboots, high school rodeo queens, the yank at your eyes from a stranger's glass of dark booze. Students in this type of volume and need announced the presence of a teacher. They conspired to make me who I wanted to be.

All my life, I'd wanted to be a teacher. And now a teacher was needed. They needed and wanted me, which was hard for me to fathom but joyous for me to accept.

Clemson became home.

❖

This was the fall of 2003, just prior to my discovering World of Warcraft and my wife finding out she was pregnant. I kept my office hours religiously, even though it usually meant leafing through out-of-date poetry anthologies left by the previous occupant of 615 Strode Tower. My little gray boom box regularly spewed Mozart—mostly because my mental picture of a university professor included a classical music soundtrack like the Neville Marriner *Amadeus* score, more than anything else—and I chewed on the eraser of a pencil I used to jot down ideas in my notebook as I read. I did have a Game Boy in the desk drawer, too, just in case.

When Echo appeared at my door like a ghost one Thursday, unseen for God knows how long before I noticed, I stood up too quickly and nearly fell out of my roller chair.

"Hi," I said, steadying myself on the edge of my circa 1970s desk. It had "AC/DC rulez" carved in its faux-walnut face. A crudely scratched penis with a smiley face lay hidden in the corner near my sliver of a window.

She sighed, then said, "Hi."

I'd never heard her voice. Even during the first-day get-to-know-you icebreaker, she hadn't spoken. That "use a simile about your relationship with writing poems" exercise in which she'd had a terrific answer? I forgot to mention that it was written. They each tore off a square of paper and jotted down an answer or two, then I collected them in a hat and read them aloud, writing them on the board, too. Hers was the only one I saved—it was taped to my wall right next to the shelf full of plastic alien figures from one of my favorite video games (made by the same company that was, at the moment, months away from launching the World of Warcraft). This was the same game that a twenty-eight-year-old Korean man was playing in an Internet café fifty or more hours before he dropped dead in August 2005, according to a BBC news report.

"Hi," she repeated, as if unsure whether I'd heard her the first time.

I recently read a biography of Vladimir Nabokov and discovered that he suffered from synesthesia, a neurological condition in which one sensory pathway stimulates a different one so that you hear color or see music. It's fairly rare, but poets call on it frequently because it is interesting, if nothing else.

Echo's voice: lemony.

"C'mon in," I said, turning off the boom box and gesturing at the hard plastic chair next to my desk. Industrial orange, of course. It was an absolute affront to my eyes, but it was the only chair that had been forgotten in the halls when I moved in, and I was told by a colleague to "snag whatever furniture I could from wherever I could." I had hoped that this meant I could break into some senior professor's office at 2:00 AM and make off with his or her sparkling new Office Depot equipment, but I decided that it probably meant I should just root through the junk that had been left in the halls for the supply guys to eventually load onto a flatbed and haul off to storage.

We sat in silence for an uncomfortably long time. If this had been a classroom full of students in which eight or ten seconds of dead silence had elapsed after I'd asked a question, I would have told them about a Stanford study on group dynamics in which a body of people larger than ten cannot cope with a silence of more than fifteen seconds (give or take a few). Someone will ultimately blurt out something, I would tell them, anything to stop the quiet. I can't recall now if that was an apocryphal story, but it always worked. With Echo, I didn't want to guilt-trip or bully her into speaking. I sensed that this silence was important.

"I was writing a poem last night," she started, then caught herself and stopped again for a moment. She pursed her lips and watched two squirrels scamper atop the roof of the MacAdams Building across the road. Echo was easily sidetracked.

"My father's dead," she finally admitted.

"That's a terrible thing."

Maybe it's the photos of me with long rock 'n' roll hair they've seen in my office. Maybe it's that I'm a guy who writes poetry. Maybe it's because my office shelves contain a makeshift army of figurines from half a dozen video games in addition to Starcraft (Warcraft, Halo, and House of the Dead, to name just three). Maybe it's because I emanate (as my wife suggests) a vibe that attracts broken, damaged women. Maybe any teacher would've been in this same spot.

Nick Carraway, the narrator of F. Scott Fitzgerald's *The Great Gatsby*, complains on page one, "I was privy to the secret griefs of wild, unknown men. Most of the confidences were unsought—frequently I have feigned sleep, preoccupation or a hostile levity when I sensed that an intimate revelation was quivering on the horizon." I know what he means, because these people come to me too, people with unasked-for declarations of guilt and pent-up sorrows. I do not want them, but damn it, there they always are. Students tell me things as if they want me to play amateur psychologist with them. They come clean. They unburden. They admit things to me that I suspect no one else knows, as if my office is some kind of confessional booth. It happened at Florida State and at both Wisconsin universities, too.

As my parents have said on many occasions, "Our son is a doctor, but not the kind that helps people"—meaning I'm not a medical doctor. Well, I'm no shrink, either. But I do feel an obligation to help, which often means listening and sometimes sharing stories of my own that might inform the problems the students are suffering through. I rarely tell them what to do—I don't want that type of responsibility. That's too much like real life to me. All I'm okay with is being their sounding board and the occasional anecdote machine. Anything more is terrifying, and since I don't understand life too well, it feels irresponsible to pretend that I do.

Echo cut me a look.

"Why don't I feel sorry about it? I mean, I should be all tears and stuff, but I'm not. I'm glad he's dead. It's a relief, really. I mean, he's my father and all, but the fact that he's gone doesn't make me feel like I'm supposed to. What's wrong with a daughter who doesn't cry at a time like this?"

Thinking back over the many poems I've seen of hers, the reading journal responses, the free writing, and the mind map exercises, I decided that it's quite likely she was abused as a child. The disconnects were there, as well as the oddly attached emotional significance to things most kids would've ignored: a glittering chandelier in the foyer, a black vase holding fake roses, churned-up earth in the garden, the distant chatter of night birds, always-dirty sheets with ripped pillows.

I didn't know exactly what was wrong, but she needed someone to listen. I could listen.

"I don't know why I'm telling you this," she said, her eyes brimming with tears that refused to fall.

"We speak the same language, I guess," I said, sensing that she would think I meant poetry. I meant death, however; I was trying hard not to think about Mrs. Ed and my yearlong Wisconsin depression in that cold, dark climate that still lingered in this new but promising land. Still, you don't shake that kind of dysfunction, and in that moment I slipped backward into myself until I was behind my eyes, watching me watch this sad, beautiful girl. I was almost a bystander in my own life. I knew this detached feeling well—it happened a lot when I gamed. I kind of just disappeared.

Echo finally cried. Afterward, we talked about how it was a good idea for her to share this with people. "But not just me," I told her, and I suggested she go to Redfern, the campus health center, which provided free psychological help for staff and students. Echo wore a thick row of bangles on her wrist. When she moved her hand to gesticulate as she explained the imagined flight of a hawk at night, which was a line from one of her recent poems that she was using to avoid talking more about her dad, I noticed the cuts. Clearly in a state deeper than suicidal infatuation, Echo was in trouble. This girl knew despair.

I asked, "Would you like me to walk you there?"

And we went right then, despite the whirling rainstorm that left me shivering, since I'd forgotten my umbrella. Echo took a medical withdrawal a few days later and never returned to Clemson. I got an e-mail months later that simply said:

Dr. VC—

Thanks,

E.

It didn't say much, but it said enough. I'd been having dreams in which my students were disappearing one by one, killing themselves while giving no outward signs of their pain. This worry was somewhat informed by my wife's offhand story about her Chicago all-girls' high school (the same one Jenna McCarthy attended—I've looked her up in the yearbook), where girls kept getting pregnant in droves. Still, it wasn't as bad as the public high school just down the street where a very popular girl stood up in third period class, pressed a revolver to her head, and committed suicide right there in Algebra II.

"Surprised the hell out of everybody," my wife said, shaking her head at the memory of it. "She was very popular. Well liked."

It's amazing how people miss all the warning signs.

I never wondered what the warning signs were for someone who played video games as if his life depended on it.

❖

My wife was pregnant, three months along. It was unplanned, and the sudden idea of us having kids was a shocker and even a bit unwanted. It's not that we didn't want kids, but the plan was to have her work for a year so we could stockpile cash like a pair of South Carolina Rockefellers. All the big things in my life happen at the wrong time—this had become one of the great themes of my life. Even the three-month ultrasound happened this way. We arrived late to it because I'd gotten wrapped up in a Madden football slugfest and stopped noticing the clock until my wife woke up from her nap and howled that we were fifteen minutes late already.

"It could be worse," I told her after a tech person squeezed the clear gel over my wife's tummy and ran the ultrasound device there, the *whup-whup-whup* filling the small medical room.

"How?"

"It could be twins," I said. Twins ran in her family. With no hard evidence to support it, I had the unshakable feeling that they ran in mine, too.

The tech lady, all business in her brown lab coat and no-nonsense hair bun, said, "There. That's your baby," and pointed to a teensy black-and-white peanut on the screen.

"Where?" I asked, not seeing a miniature person lounging there in the blur and the fuzz. What did I expect? A party hat and a smiling face? Teensy hands waving at me?

She tapped the screen a few times as if she were pointing out an elephant in an empty room. "Right there."

"Boy or girl?" Victoria asked. We'd agreed to let it be a surprise, but in that moment I wanted to know, too. My wife wanted to start shopping for the right clothes. I just wanted to know whether I needed to start planning my I've-got-a-shotgun-and-a-shovel-and-I-don't-think-anyone's-gonna-miss-you glare for future teenage boys who would be slinking around my house, wanting to deflower my little princess angel.

"Girl. Of course," the tech said, as if we were blind. Of course.

This was Valerie. Valerie the little peanut. Valerie the little hug muffin. This was our Valerie. We argued the name until late March, because my wife was still stuck on "Jessica" but was unwilling to use it since her college roommate had already given it to her daughter. I wanted "Bram Stoker Demosthenes Van Cleave" (no joke—even for a girl—I'm bonkers for *Dracula*, and I had a thing for Demosthenes the Laughing Philosopher, perhaps the greatest orator ever), but my wife pretended I wasn't speaking every time I brought it up. So my daughter got "Valerie Lynn" instead.

Even taking it easy, Victoria got sick. Really sick. One of those bad bird flu strains raged through South Carolina starting in December, so from finals week—about December 10 or so—until two days after Christmas, we both (yes, I got it, too, like a good husband) hunched over the toilet and lay on the floor, moaning. We were so sick we couldn't drive. A kindhearted neighborhood friend, Lucy, the forever-single dog groomer, brought us a Sam's Club–sized bottle of Tylenol and some microwave soups.

"Need anything else?" she asked, standing there at the front door, her gum snapping between her purple-painted lips.

"Thanks, no," I groaned, then crawled back to the living room, where we continued our *Sopranos* marathon on DVD. We watched the first three seasons in a row, pausing only to slurp down Campbell's chicken soup or hit the bathroom for a puke session that left us shaking. I didn't touch a video game for nearly ten days, I was so sick. Just watching TV wiped me out.

Tim, my old high school pal who now works in the air force, tells me that biochemists call their business "bugs and gas." As lousy as we felt, I had to wonder if we'd been nailed with both ends of their industry. We'd never been so sick in our lives, and it lasted two weeks. Thank God it didn't affect the pregnancy in any way.

❖

The first two students I referred to the campus health services for immediate intervention were in sad shape, to be sure. I recognized the signs of depression. I can see now that I did so because I knew them firsthand, intimately. Then, however, I'd have just called it teacher's intuition.

The third student who came to me was going to kill herself. Not like Echo, who was borderline. Not like Joe, who had repressed his homosexuality for so long that the self-loathing, guilt, and shame were making him violently sick to the point that he was missing class a week at a time and his corn-silk hair was starting to fall out.

Andrea was committed to dying. She wouldn't make it through the week. Every sign was there. Her 300-pound body radiated a dull sense of gloom, an almost palpable aura of surrender. No one would even sit by her in class anymore. She was just that miserable. Everything about her was toxic.

I saved her life, I believe.

When this heavyset brunette came up to me after class and blurted, "I don't have the paper. Just give me the F. I don't care," most teachers would've failed her and moved on, secretly being happy they had one less paper to read and grade. I, however, took her outside on that beautiful Tuesday morning, and we spoke in front of the Cooper Library while watching the fountain cast sprays of water into the air like a giant liquid umbrella. Half an hour later, I walked her to the doors of Redfern, right where I'd left Echo a few semesters earlier. But this time, I went inside with her. She was sobbing and shaking, and her entire world collapsed right in that moment. This was a feeling I knew, because I felt it every time I chose to power up the Xbox or launch a computer game rather than be a father, a husband, or a human being. Of course I understood. My own cliff was just ahead, looming.

People stared at the two of us leaning on each other as we moved across campus. One shaven-headed Kappa Sigma guy with his arm in a sling snickered, and I could've killed him.

I helped Andrea to the receptionist's desk. The student worker there insisted we make an appointment.

"Young man," I told him, summoning every bit of my Stern Professor Voice. "You go back and find someone right this second. This is the most important thing anyone's asked of you this month. Go right now."

He did. Within thirty seconds, some wizened woman with close-set eyes and thinning gray hair pulled back in a French braid took Andrea by the arm and led her away. Andrea was hysterical now, shrieking, "I can't watch my sister's kids. I can't go to work. I can't, I can't, I can't. I just can't find any more of myself to give. I can't, I can't."

You don't get credit for saving a kid's life this way.

You do get credit for what your wife didn't say at a faculty party but what some half-drunk colleague's wife misremembered and then told her husband, who then told an administrator, who then brought you in for a disciplinary meeting to discuss how your wife was "leading the insurrection" at your school.

You do get credit for being a bad colleague because, as one self-described curmudgeon told me, you throw too many parties.

You do get credit for writing a rhyming diddy about a colleague's wife's breasts on the bathroom wall at the local dive bar, even if you didn't do it.

You do get credit for being academically dishonest by having more than one version of your résumé because you've published so much that you've outperformed half of the senior professors and you're being warned to "slow it wa-a-ay down."

Clemson was not my home, I'd come to realize. I'd casually been on the job market the entire time I'd lived in South Carolina, which is what most academics do until they receive tenure. At this point, I started actively looking to leave. I'd even accept a lesser job. This was quickly becoming a very bad fit, and that sadness encouraged me to find some escape, which made World of Warcraft an even bigger part of my life than the twenty hours a week it had already begun to consume.

❖

From February to October 2006, my last full calendar year at Clemson, all four of my dogs died.

I'd had them for years: two Yorkies and two Chihuahuas. The oldest, Heidi Beast the Yorkie, was fourteen. The youngest, Charlie Ogre, was only eight.

Cubbie Monster the Yorkie, the second oldest and Heidi's best friend, went first. I was in Los Angeles on a job interview—yes, even someone as blind as I was could sense that I needed to start seriously pursuing other options at this juncture, especially with Administator Sally now openly assembling a litany of complaints about me that would ultimately oust me from my job. I was sitting one evening in an In-N-Out Burger joint just outside Long Beach, playing WoW on my laptop while sipping a chocolate shake, when Victoria called.

"I have some bad news, but I don't want to tell you, since you're on an interview."

I hearthed (that is, I used a magical "hearthstone" to teleport my character back to a safe city) and snapped the laptop shut. The tone of her voice worried me. She liked to just bonk you on the skull with bad news. This kind of slow windup had me really guessing.

"Just fire away," I said. "If you don't tell me now, I'll probably think it's something worse than it is."

My wife's voice broke. "We lost Cubbie."

I didn't expect this. Prior to my heading to the airport, we had taken Cubbie to the vet, where she had to spend the night for observation because she kept throwing up and seemed "a little dehydrated." From a touch of doggy flu to being dead, though?

My wife added, "She had some seizures and they couldn't help her."

At ten pounds, Cubbie was the brute of the bunch. She weighed as much as any two of the others put together. She'd often lie on her back in the middle of the living room and bark at the other three to "Come attack me," which they'd do. They'd all roll around and flail at one another with their paws like lightweight boxers, stopping immediately if anyone let out a genuine squeak of pain. Cubbie was a bundle of love. Cubbie was everyone's favorite, a big dumb monster who'd lovingly lick the skin off your arm if you let her.

I couldn't imagine never seeing her again.

Worse, the job interview went well, so I began to wonder if God was giving with one hand while taking away with the other. I didn't find it a fair trade to get a job in L.A. if it cost me Cubbie, who liked to sleep in the crook of my arm while I worked on poems at the computer (or, more and more likely, played WoW).

Worse still, I didn't land the job.

The second dog to go was Minnie, a three-pound Chihuahua, who one day just teetered and plopped onto the floor next to the pantry. Like the Imperial walkers on Hoth in *The Empire Strikes Back*, who, after having their legs roped by snow speeders so they couldn't move and they simply toppled to their sides, Minnie went down on our wooden floor in the kitchen, her head smacking hard. I saw it happen from two feet away as I was making a meatball sandwich in the microwave.

We rushed her to the vet, who said it was a seizure. I understood what that meant from the Cubbie disaster. Cubbie had suffered a few seizures right near the end. Seizures meant great danger for a dog of Minnie's years. The vet tucked her in a little brown blanket and put her inside a glass cage that worked like a giant oxygen mask—pure oxygen was pumped into it nonstop.

Half sitting up, her eyes drippy, Minnie looked miserable, punch-drunk like Muhammad Ali at the end of his career.

The vet called about six-thirty that night, saying that he didn't keep anyone on staff overnight and everyone would be going home soon. He wanted me to take Minnie to one of the emergency hospitals in Anderson, which had round-the-clock care.

"It's best to be safe, to have someone with her all night long," he told us.

So we went back to the vet and carefully took our wheezing Chihuahua in her favorite blanket, an ugly red and white sleeping bag we'd remembered to bring this time, and we got in our Ford Windstar and drove for Anderson, maybe twenty-five minutes away. My wife held Minnie in the basket of her arms in the backseat, talking to her, rubbing her little brown and white belly with a fingertip. Minnie liked being nestled tight and seemed okay with the attention, though a little winded and somewhat weak.

Valerie sat in her car seat playing with a rattle. She loved the dogs and knew all their names. She sometimes asked, "Where's Cub?" (she couldn't yet say "Cubbie"), to which we said, "She's sleeping." What the hell do you say to a not-quite two-year-old about death, especially that of a beloved dog?

Video games might've taught me a lot about hand-to-eye coordination, puzzle solving, and excitement, but it taught me very little in the way of interacting better with my family. I was unequipped for disasters.

Fifteen minutes from our destination, Minnie started gasping. Then came the blood. If this were an early *ER* episode, George Clooney would have yelled, "She's bleeding out!" and begun heroic measures that would involve defibrillator paddles, an epinephrine shot, and CPR. Then a CT scan, chem-7, and blood gas, too, most likely. We had none of those options in the car. I called the vet on my cell phone and said blood was hosing out of my dog's nose, all over my wife's hands and legs now.

"She's not breathing," my wife moaned. I couldn't see Minnie in the rearview mirror, cradled as she was into my wife's chest, but blood and dog snot and other fluids—including piss, which I could smell and knew signaled a very bad turn in events—were everywhere.

It looked as if my wife's stomach had ejected a creature like in *Aliens*, all slime and goo and yuck and blood.

"She's not breathing," I hollered through the cell phone to the vet.

"Okay, okay. Bring her back. Can you do CPR?"

"On a dog?"

"Yes. Put her on her back in your lap. Hold her nose while you keep the mouth closed. Cup your hand over the nose and blow slowly into it, twelve to twenty breaths a minute. Then around the fourth to sixth rib, maybe one-third of the way up from the bottom, press down gently on her chest a few times with your hands. Then stop and check for breathing."

My wife followed the instructions while I drove tremendously fast and relayed the information. I could hear something happening behind me, sputtering, maybe. Valerie sobbed.

"It's not working," my wife said, which I parroted back to the vet.

"Do what you can and get her here as fast as you're able to," he said, then hung up to get ready.

My wife turned her body so Valerie couldn't watch, but our daughter was howling, which made my wife more upset, and pretty soon everyone was crying and Minnie wasn't breathing, although the blood and mucus was still leaking out.

When I was seven, our class had a hamster that a kid dropped from his desk while he was pretending to throw it like a football. Herbert the Hamster curled into a ball and stopped breathing right there on the linoleum, where he'd hit. Mr. Jackson, a hip twentysomething who refused to wear long-sleeved shirts and ties, fetched a straw from his desk and put it in Herbert's mouth and blew into it. We saw Herbert's chest rise and fall, rise and fall. It was magical.

Breath, the stuff of life.

Herbert didn't make it. His spine had snapped upon impact.

Minnie didn't make it, either.

I called back three minutes later, telling the vet that Minnie didn't seem to be breathing any longer. The vet didn't seem surprised, but he said he was sorry and to bring her body back so he could check and make sure. When we arrived, her little body in my wife's arms, he pressed the stethoscope to her chest. She was gone.

The third to go was Heidi, the oldest.

In many ways, this was the worst, not just because she was my favorite and had been with me for nearly a decade and a half, but because her body gave out bit by bit, like a grandparent who clings to life despite renal failure, glaucoma, heart issues, melanoma, and Parkinson's, the type of degeneration that a grandchild might look at and cry. With each new problem, you had to ask: Is this the last straw, or should we let her suffer a bit more because we're not ready to let her go yet?

We ran up $2,000 of medical bills in three months. Tests. Blood work. Cortizone shots. Pills. Ointments. Drops. We had emergency 2:00 AM visits to the big vet clinic in Anderson—the one we tried to take Minnie to, I couldn't help but think each time we hurried Heidi there. Both times she stayed three days and was sent home only because they couldn't do much more for her and it was getting expensive.

My wife, suffering too, chose to spend all her time with Valerie, relocating joy through a child's play. I played WoW for three days straight at one point just so I wouldn't think about how much suffering my little dog knew. I drowned myself in gaming. At one point, I stopped eating for two days and didn't shower for a week. I remained outside myself, a watcher, horrified that I was no longer able to clink minds with anyone on a human level. All of my meaningful interactions were mediated through screens that yanks things out of the real fabric of our lives and turns them into a performance. The person I played was a spliced-together figure who, if you stripped away all the movies and television programs, games and books, clichés and contradictions, wouldn't even exist.

I wasn't a person driving fast through a bank of fog at night to an unknown destination—I was the fog itself, ephermal and meandering.

"Do you want to come and pick her up this afternoon?" my regular vet asked when I dropped Heidi off on Saturday morning to be monitored for her breathing, which, if it worsened, might signal the end. Heidi was a trouper. Her breathing stayed just good enough, as did her heart rate. So they hooked her up to tubes and fed her intravenously, trying to summon a bit more of her flagging strength.

On the back porch, I sat shirtless—God knows why I was shirtless, but I remember that well, the sun through the bug-screened windows so warm on my chest, my laptop still running WoW there on the porch swing—and I watched the koi snip at water bugs on the surface of our little fish pond that I struggled and struggled to keep free of algae but just never could. I didn't have the knack for it, or something.

"No," I answered the vet, regretting it but knowing that I couldn't go and see her face-to-face. We had a nearly psychic connection, and I couldn't bear her pain anymore. "No, I won't be coming in."

"Are you sure about this?" he asked. We'd talked about the various scenarios before. Leaving her there meant euthanasia.

I managed a yes.

I dialed the vet back six times but never let it ring. I wanted to scream, "No! Don't let her die! Do anything, anything you can!" But I knew her quality of life was too poor. She wasn't eating. She had constant seizures. She limped. She yelped in pain when you picked her up. She had diarrhea. She was constantly dehydrated and lethargic. She didn't have the strength to stand on her own.

I paid the vet to kill her, and with it, something vital in me, too.

The last dog, Charlie, ran scared for a few weeks, since one by one her buddies all vanished. She clung to us, as though an amazing show of affection on her part would enable her to stay with us forever and not disappear like her sisters. Charlie was young and jumpy, and it seemed that she would be with us for many, many years.

After my Wednesday evening graduate poetry class, I came home and walked Charlie, hugged Valerie, said hi to Victoria, then grabbed a Diet Coke and a Twix bar and headed upstairs to play WoW with Rob. I'd been playing WoW for quite a few months now, and everyone knew I was a bear to deal with if I didn't get in half an hour of the game the second I came home from anywhere. Rob and I were gaming together nearly every night now as a result.

Halfway through a deliver-an-item-here quest in Feralas, I typed to Rob, "Hold on, I gotta check something," then hurried downstairs without even bothering to hearth my guy to safety or even parking him behind a tree or a big rock. I had suddenly noticed there was no barking, nor was there Charlie's warmth near my socked feet. She liked to snuggle beneath my computer desk upstairs, and I had been so distracted by wanting to finish up the Missing Courier series of quests that I hadn't noticed her absence right off.

"Charlie?" I called from the back porch.

"Where is she?" my wife asked, getting up from her *E!* channel show.

I didn't remember having brought Charlie back inside. Usually I brought her in after I grabbed a quick snack, but WoW had my full attention, so I think I might've just gone upstairs and left her outside. It's happened before. Also, Valerie liked to walk Charlie and would sometimes yank the door open and let her out. The problem was, she wouldn't warn me that she had done that, so sometimes Charlie would be loose for a good while in the backyard before we heard her barking at the frogs or dragonflies or nothing at all.

It was dark now, so I found flashlights for everyone, and the three of us (Valerie was now two years old) went out looking for her. Charlie didn't always bark in response when you called, and she was nearly all black, so you really had to look close with the light. We walked all over and aimed the flashlights beneath bushes, into the pond water, and behind the rosebushes.

"Charlie!" Valerie called, struggling to keep her Dora the Explorer flashlight pointed straight up at the tops of the eighty-foot pines behind our house.

"Charlie!" I called, heading toward the front of our house. We had a small backyard that was virtually hemmed in on all sides by hedges and trees. If you followed the driveway out, you would see two other levels of long, green grass before a row of trees separated our yard from Issaqueena Trail, a thirty-five-mile-per-hour road that high school kids liked to do sixty on. I checked the shed. I checked the crawl space under the house. I checked the ditch beside the road. I checked our neighbors' yards on both sides. Across the street was a huge wooded area big enough for three Wal-Mart Supercenters.

I walked up and down it for fifteen minutes, peering into shadows with my high-powered halogen beam, calling for the dog we'd bought for my wife when we got married. The other dogs were all mine, and she regularly complained, "Your damn dogs did so-and-so," and I wanted to make it "Our damn dogs did so-and-so" to spread the blame around. So we bought Charlie from a breeder in Florida. The runt of the litter, she was a feisty dog with attention-deficit disorder who loved my wife dearly. And even though my wife had pulled away emotionally from Charlie over the past year or so in order to focus on

Valerie's well-being, I know that Victoria still loved that little dog with a tenderness I couldn't even recall if she had ever had for me, our relationship had been strained for so long.

Charlie was our only pet now, and we all loved her.

I got everyone back inside and told them to stay put while I got in the car and started checking the roads in Camelot, the subdivision of maybe 1,200 houses behind us. There were many roads, so it'd take a while, but I had to find Charlie. She was our last dog, and Valerie was already crying, calling "Chahwee! Chahwee dog!" inside the house, checking in cabinets, under tables, and behind the fridge.

I put down the Windstar's window and drove slowly away from the house, thinking that I might be out all night, the area here was so big. Charlie liked to chase, too, so any raccoon or squirrel or neighborhood cat could've led her a quarter-mile from the house, where she would find herself completely disoriented, scared, and alone. I phoned my wife and warned her, "This might take some time." Then I saw her.

Not five houses up the road, right there in the middle of the two-lane road that was Issaqueena Trail, I pulled into the nearest driveway and hurried to what was left of her. She'd been hit by a car. Run over, actually. You could see the tread marks over her head. Her skull was flattened and one of the eyes was missing.

Two decades of heavy-duty video game violence had desensitized me to a lot. I could watch the goriest reality doctor shows or horror movies without flinching. This, though? My Twix bar came up and I doubled over near the bushes on the side of the road, my stomach a massive, clutching knot.

When a Volvo came roaring up the hill at me, its headlights turning to bright to warn me off, I moved to the side. Then the driver of that Volvo saw the dark mass in the road and swerved—not to miss it, but to hit it. That asshole ran over Charlie's body on purpose. I felt rage thunder through my body, and I almost got into my car to run the jerk down, slam into the rear bumper, and drive the Volvo into the trees on the side of the road, hoping that Hollywood had it right and cars did explode 99 percent of the time, leaving that horrible person a burned, stinking corpse there in the dark—dead, dead, dead.

I couldn't let my wife see. I didn't want her final memory of this wonderful dog she loved so much to be a mangled, bloody mess of fur and shattered bone and brain matter. I got a black garbage bag from the shed and returned to pick up as much of Charlie as I could. Then I hid her by the garage, went inside, called Rob, and told him that I wouldn't be finishing the WoW quest chain we'd started together that evening, asking him, "What the hell am I supposed to tell my daughter, who is standing on the back porch with her flashlight calling for a dog who's never going to come?"

He swallowed thickly—I could hear it—then he said, "I don't know, man."

Sometimes there is no answer.

I quickly explained to my wife what had happened, then I retrieved a shovel from the garage and went across the street with the garbage bag and commenced digging. I cut hard into the earth, tearing through old roots and weeds. I dug and dug, making a hole big enough for a pair of mastiffs. Then I opened the bag and foolishly took one last look at Charlie, who didn't resemble the happy, bouncy dog I once hoped would help solidify the marriage that my video gaming had constantly worked to tear apart.

I buried her there, at the base of the same mulberry tree I'd backed into the first time I ever pulled out of our driveway. The gouge is still there to this day in the bark, about knee-high and half an inch deep. From the right angle, it looks kind of like a smiley face.

Since this book is about truth and accuracy in reporting every foolish thing I did, here's what really happened. I didn't bury Charlie. In a fit of anger, pure darkness, and utter contempt for all that is good in this world, I put the garbage bag inside the can we'd set outside for the next day's trash, and I left her there to be buried in some anonymous landfill. The act reminded me of Holden Caulfield, who hated Ossenburger, the Pencey Prep alum who'd made his fortune in the funeral business, and so said of him, "You should see old Ossenburger. He probably just shoves them in a sack and dumps them in the river."

It was a horrible thing to do, but I did it. I Ossenburgered Charlie's body.

For the next few months, I hit the darkest depression I'd ever known. People who don't have pets will never understand what it is to lose one, let alone four in such short order. We lost all four in less than six months. If Salvador Dalí had his blue period, this was my black one, made worse by all the problems at school that the administration was so carefully documenting to make its final case to hustle me out of Clemson and into a wretched job market for creative writing Ph.D.s. All that tethered me to anything meaningful during this time was WoW, which I clung to for dear life.

Without warning one Wednesday afternoon, I told an office neighbor that I felt bloodied and defeated from the outrage that had become my existence. I was obsessive, self-centered, and desperate. I seesawed helplessly between anger and profound surrender.

"You're divorced," I said, by way of my unexpected unburdening to him. "You know what it's like to have your world yanked out from under you."

He replied, "I'm the one who dumped her."

❖

In Dean Koontz's wonderful tribute to his golden retriever, Trixie,

The Darkest Evening of the Year, he writes, "Amy believed that dogs had a spiritual purpose. The opportunity to love a dog and to treat it with kindness was an opportunity for a lost and selfish human heart to be redeemed. They [dogs] are powerless and innocent, and it is how we treat the humblest among us that surely determines the fate of our souls."

In this same book, one of Koontz's big bad guys, Vernon Lesley, did some nasty work to fund his alter ego's existence in the game Second Life. "Some people mocked this kind of role-playing, but they were ignorant. Virtual worlds were more *imaginative* than the real world, more exotic, more colorful, yet they were becoming more convincingly detailed by the week. They were the future."

Koontz continues in a way that rings too true to me. "Vern had more fun in his other life than in this one, more and better friends, and more memorable experiences. He was freer as Von Longwood than he could ever be as Vernon Lesley. He had never been creative in his first life, but in his second, he had designed and built a nightclub, and he had even bought an island that he intended to populate with fantastic creatures of his own invention."

Koontz—and Vernon Lesley—might understand me and my relationship to WoW, I realized, a little too well.

❖

In spring 2007, my contract at Clemson wasn't renewed. Just the week before, I'd made an appointment to see one of the many administrators and had gotten a very good report. "You're doing what you need to," she said. Five days later, I was terminated for a laundry list of reasons that seemed to change with each person I spoke to.

Leaving Clemson was like sliding down a ten-foot razorblade barefoot. It didn't have to be that way. The original subtitle of this book was "How a University Professor Lost His Job Due to a Video Game Addiction." In many ways, that was true, although I admit it's a bit misleading. It sounds as if I played WoW so much that I became criminally negligent in my professor duties: stopped showing up for my classes, forgot to grade assignments, skipped department meetings, quit publishing, and generally proved absent in every important way.

None of these things happened. During my four years at Clemson I published eight books and compiled stacks upon stacks of first-rate student evaluations, despite the fact that I was also logging in thirty to forty hours a week of WoW, fully absorbed by the limitless refuge the game offered. What suffered was my personal life, my emotional life, my mental state, my spirit, and my soul. I was running a personal deficit like the U.S. government runs a financial one—take, take, take, even long after the money's all gone. When you hit what you imagine must be the limit, you do what the government recently did with the deficit. You increase the ceiling.

The job never came second, as my wife constantly harped. I love teaching and am a gifted teacher. The universe provided me with this ability, for which I am forever thankful. To inspire another person is to know what it is to matter in this world.

So how, then, can I claim that I lost my job due to WoW? If I hadn't been playing WoW, I might've noticed how much ill will certain administrators and colleagues held in their dark little grinch hearts for me. It might've burst the bubble of higher education delirium I still lived in, where I fancied us all comrades in the shared mission of bettering young people and creating an improved tomorrow. Prior to my time at Clemson, I thought we were all on the same team. I thought all professors taught at universities because they loved teaching and loved students. With competitive class-release time and financial awards, your colleagues often eventually became your enemies.

And I just never got on board with that concept—being a professor just didn't (and still doesn't) feel like a competitive sport to me.

Even good student evaluations and a genuine joy for helping young people won't save you.

So yes, WoW is a major culprit. One of many.

It seems as if I should have more to say about my time at Clemson. I was there for the better part of four years. But I was playing video games. There's not much else to say, since combing through the more than 1,000 days I spent in South Carolina just distills and intensifies something I already know: I am a video game addict.

This is how one accounts for missing time.

This is how one loses a dream job.

Eight

AT WAR WITH MY FAMILY AND MYSELF

> **There is nothing here to suggest that this is a complex physiological disease state akin to alcoholism or other substance abuse disorders, and it doesn't get to have the word addiction attached to it.**
>
> —DR. STUART GITLOW, AMERICAN SOCIETY OF ADDICTION MEDICINE AND MOUNT SINAI SCHOOL OF MEDICINE IN NEW YORK, ON VIDEO GAME ADDICTION

Fifty-eight days, twelve hours, and thirty-four minutes.

That's how much time I devoted to the World of Warcraft. Do the math. That's essentially two entire months of my adult life spent working a deeper ass print into my ergonomic swivel chair while playing a video game in which I accumulated virtual honor, virtual gold, and virtual friends. When you put it out there like that, it sounds kind of stupid.

It's certainly pretty nerdy, but I've always been a bookworm, so that part doesn't shake my core any.

Here's the kicker. Those numbers are from just one calendar year, not the entire two (okay, let's stay honest—nearly three) years I was hooked on WoW.

Here's the other kicker. That was only from *one* of my accounts. I had one for PvP (player versus player, where Horde and Alliance can attack each other on sight at any time), one for PvE (player versus environment, where Horde and Alliance can fight only in battlegrounds), and one for RP (role-playing, in which you always have to be "in character," even when chatting to others). So what was the actual tally from all the accounts? I don't have the guts to find out, but a little quick math puts it close to an entire real-life year.

Here's the final confession. I once spent $224 (real U.S. dollars) buying virtual gold so I could get a big mama-jama epic-level sword and some top-tier armor for Azzkicker, my level-seventy human warrior, so he could beat on other players better.

Okay, here's more. I had seven level-seventy characters (the maximum level after the Burning Crusade expansion, although Wrath of the Lich King allows players to go to level eighty, and the forthcoming Cataclysm will allow level eighty-five) and more than thirty lower-level characters, spread out on various servers so that none of my in-game friends would realize how much I was playing. We razzed the über-dedicated in WoW chat channels for "having no life," although it's more for guffaws than for any serious attempt at WoW playing-time reform, because on some level we all know that if you're actually playing WoW, then you don't have a life, so the levels of irony in these jabs are infinite. It's like alcoholics at AA meetings cracking jokes about pounding vodka.

Here are some sample conversations:

Player 1: Dude, you're *always* on. LOL.

Player 2: Yeah. I think my girlfriend's gonna get WoW for Xmas from me. I'm tired of never seeing her anymore.

Player 1: GFs may come and go, but epics stay with you forever.

Player 2: She's cool. She's a gm [*game master—someone employed to help out characters in-game*] for Everquest.

Player 3: Does she rp in bed, too?

Player 4: Do you shout "for the Alliance!" when you go down on her?

Player 5: W00t! [*geek slang for "hooray!"*]

Me: [*logging on*] Rob, you still on from before?

Rob: Nah. I stopped to mow the lawn. [*lie—he was playing the entire time*]

Me: I just got back on, too. [*lie—I was playing WoW on a different server for the last five hours*]

Player 1: WTB [*want to buy*] a GF.

Player 2: I just had virtual sex with a gnome in IF [*Ironforge, one of the main Alliance cities*]. She was leet [*slang for "cool"*].

Player 1: WTS [*want to sell*] my soul.

Player 3: How much?

Player 4: 2 gold is my final offer.

Player 2: Pfft. 20 copper, tops.

Player 5: I saw that gnome. She had an Adam's apple, man.

Player 2: Ok, ok. 22 copper.

Player 6: OMG. You are all so stoooooopid.

Player 3: [1337] |) | 3 @ |_ |_ | @ || (3 [*translation from leet/geekspeak—Die Alliance!*]

Okay, a bit more. I had a secret Paypal account to cover the fifteen-dollar monthly fees for the two accounts I maintained other than the one my wife knew about.

Forty-five dollars a month. Jeez.

And this. I bought a new computer, a windows XP media center model, despite having a perfectly usable Hewlett-Packard (HP) not two years old. Why? The screen was bigger, it had more RAM, and the graphics card was terrific. In short, it'd play WoW better than my older model, and I was tired of getting killed in battlegrounds because of lag. You'd think milliseconds wouldn't make all that much of a difference, but the way some of those twelve-year-olds play, you'd think they were hardwired into the machine and controlled their characters by thought.

And a final confession. I bought another computer, an HP laptop, explaining to my wife that when I went on all my on-campus interviews for a new university job in 2008, I'd be able to use the built-in camera and Yahoo Messenger to videophone my kids (with our usual bad timing, we had another girl just a few months before losing the Clemson job) and say "Howdy!" from all the hell over. The most compelling reason in my mind to get it, however, was its kick-ass Nvidia graphics card and its wireless Internet capability, which would allow me to play WoW from anywhere, anytime. With a seventeen-inch screen, it'd be sweet to game on.

Dr. Stuart Gitlow of the American Society of Addiction Medicine is wrong. I refuse to let some self-important egghead tell me it's not an addiction when I couldn't stop. I really could not help myself. It sounds like an excuse, but I don't mean it that way. I merely mean it as the most accurate way of describing how it felt, which was that WoW had manifested itself as the most important thing in my life. Body and soul, heart and mind, I was WoW's.

I lied for WoW.

I ignored my wife for WoW.

I ignored my kids for WoW.

I ignored my job search for WoW.

I ignored my writing career for WoW.

I ignored my health for WoW.

I finally nearly killed myself because I couldn't summon the will to quit playing WoW, even when I'd screamed far past the many self-imposed barriers and limits I'd set for myself. Again and again and again.

In the game, certain of the more powerful items are BOP (bind on pickup), which means that they connect with your soul so much that you cannot trade them with another person. You and your Champion's Satin Cowl or Crul'shorukh, Edge of Chaos, are intrinsically linked forever. Sure, you can sell these magical items, but only for a fraction of what they're worth. To get the most of the union, you keep them, use them, or stockpile them for specific key situations or until you grind out some better loot by slaying dozens, hundreds, thousands of mobs (monsters) in the hope of getting that .01 percent drop rate to fall in your favor. BOP items are yours. You are theirs.

I was BOP for WoW.

So I'm just some selfish, stupid asshole with no willpower, you might be thinking. And that's certainly not too far from wrong, but it's not entirely accurate, either. WoW is insidious. It comes at you from all angles at once and hems you in like a rat in a tin can. It gets hold of you and refuses to let you shake free. As of the writing of this chapter, I haven't touched the game in eleven days shy of two years. But I'm tempted every friggin' second to log back on and kick some virtual ass or show off my new epic mount in Shattrath (a major multifactioned city added in the Burning Crusade expansion) or go gank (kill another player, usually stealthily, while he's fighting a monster)

Hordies outside the Undercity (major Horde city) with my Blood-fang-suited Rogue.

I tend not to remember my normal dreams, but I still have the most soul-shakingly vivid ones about playing any of my four dozen WoW characters, and I lurch awake in the dark sweating and thinking I should rush to the computer to check on them, make sure they're still all right, turn on a nightlight, and tuck them into bed.

"You okay?" my wife asks, fearing an asthma attack. Remember—I don't have an inhaler because "it's too costly," but I can manage forty-five dollars a month to maintain three different WoW accounts.

"Just a strange dream," I reply.

"What about?"

I ponder the question and eventually arrive at this: "Nothing. Nothing at all." Not even able to trust my wife with the truth, I settle on silence and the ensuing shame, which sinks deeply into my chest like pneumonia.

If you think I'm full of shit or that I'm alone in this WoW addiction, spend a few minutes scrolling through the tens of thousands of testimonials at www.wowdetox.com, a volunteer-run site "aimed at people with a gaming addiction to World of Warcraft." For those of you who don't have a computer handy, I'll reproduce a few here.

- "I want to stop so badly, but I can't find a way to do it. My life is a mess because I've let everything fall apart while I entirely focus on playing. I play until I'm completely exhausted and then as soon as I stop I am depressed. Sleeping is poor as all I think about is all the things I need to do, quests, honor score, guild issues, etc."
- "I refuse to create yet another WoW widow."
- "i quit wow cuz i came to the realization that 85 days of my life were spent playing a game and investing in gear that becomes obsolete every new expansion."

- "This is my 2nd time quitting WoW. The first time, it really ruined my life. I missed my university application, I failed out most of my school. I lost contact with many friends whom I no longer have any connection with now. My life was getting back on track but I became an alcoholic in college and failed that too. I went back to WoW, I have a dead-end job but there's hope."
- "I was hooked. I had hundreds of days play time, several 70s. I had done old school end game. MC AQ a little Naxx. I lvled again up to 70. Started keying up for the serious raids. WoW was life. I was living with my parents, working a dead-end job, wasting away the hours waiting till the next raid. I regularly ditched social events, friends, girls, everything took a back seat to wow."
- "i will lose my marriage and my job if i dont quit."
- "WoW steals your soul . . ."

Consider that a November 21, 2008, press release from Blizzard Entertainment, the maker of WoW, announced that there are more than 11.5 million monthly subscribers worldwide. Frank Pearce, cofounder of Blizzard, recently admitted that the company is working to develop an application that will allow players to access their WoW accounts from their cell phones.

And then think about how many other MMOGs and the like are working at the minds of people everywhere in vampire fashion: Halo 3. Guild Wars. Doom. Everquest. City of Heroes and City of Villains. Lord of the Rings Online. Warhammer. Dark Age of Camelot. Dungeons & Dragons: Stormreach. EVE Online. Aion. Sims. Second Life. Age of Conan. Perfect World. Even Facebook is doing its best to keep folks like my wife—who says she would gladly shoot the makers of WoW dead if it'd help get rid "of that damn game"—tappity-tap-tapping away for an hour or more a day, thanks to its quizzes and superpokes and the Wall.

WoW never ends.

There's no princess to rescue, which would signify the conclusion of the game.

The princesses in WoW come in infinite variety and supply.

Feeling marooned after school on weekends, I used to waste hours banging away at Super Mario Brothers for the Nintendo 64 or half a dozen Pong variations for the original Atari system. The difference—other than massive graphics enhancements and overall playability—is that most of the old games had a goal, an end point. You slugged away for a few days or a week, and you would save the princess or destroy the head nasty guy or locate the missing magical wand, put the game back on the shelf, and get on with your life (or another game, I admit).

With MMOGs, you can still max out your character levelwise, but there are essentially limitless options, even then. You hit the level cap for a character in WoW, and it opens up a world of high-powered guild and instance raiding, plus the never-ending pissing contest of battlegrounds and arena fighting and grinding for better gear. This is made worse with WoW's new achievement tracker and gear score—another way to whip it out and see whose is bigger. And with expansion modules being made all the time, the phantom "end" is even further from reality. WoW's Burning Crusade expansion sold 2.4 million copies in the first twenty-four hours of its 2007 release; another expansion, Wrath of the Lich King, topped it with 2.8 million units sold in twenty-four hours in its 2008 release; the latest announced expansion, Cataclysm, will probably beat that when it comes out in late 2010.

This cannot be emphasized too much—the game *never ends*. With Zelda or Baldur's Gate or those old Atari games, you sit down to play with the intention of obtaining a goal: win the game. With WoW, there is no winning, only more playing. What the obsession then becomes is not to try to win but to achieve total mastery of the game, a state that exists only in Plato's realm of the forms, not in the real world where people are hooked up to the machines for hours daily, ignoring the real world and everyone in it.

You can never win at WoW.

Of course you can't. Being a writer, I'm no Doogie Howser at math, but even I can figure out this scheme: just 10 million subscribers at $15 per month is *$150 million a month* pouring into Blizzard's bank account. That's not even counting the other "incidental fees" you can incur (twenty-five dollars to move a character from one server to another, ten dollars to change your character's name, twenty-five dollars to change your character's race, and fifteen dollars to change your character's basic appearance).

No wonder that Blizzard does everything it can to keep people cranking along in Azeroth (the name of the virtual world in WoW) through updates, perks, bonuses, expansions, and even holiday content, which currently includes special quests and gear for New Year's Day, Valentine's Day, Easter, Independence Day, Oktoberfest, Halloween, Thanksgiving, and Christmas.

The WoW world feels alive, layered, nuanced, ever changing, and still somehow rooted in the real world you're eschewing to play WoW. And each completed quest gives you the ephemeral euphoria of completion, achievement, and movement toward an end point that other games offer but WoW refuses, the dangling carrot that no cart-pulling donkey ever gets to munch. But the players don't care, because they're part of something bigger than themselves (that type of language sounds dangerously as if I'm describing religion or some noble cause), and they're interacting with other human beings in a whole virtual environment that's staggeringly beautiful to encounter. I used to run some of my Horde toons up to the top of mountain peaks near Windshear Crag and just stand there like Zeus, gazing out upon the scabrous brown landscape that reminded me so much of a long-ago trip to North Dakota.

❖

I can't push WoW out of my mind. I always feel the urge to return to this comic book- and anime-inspired virtual land where the Horde and Alliance factions exist in their uneasy truce while questing, exploring, accumulating great wealth, and fighting one-to-one as well as in large-scale battles. Hell, playing WoW is a good enough pastime for celebrity gamers such as Mila Kunis, R. A. Salvatore, Yao Ming, Jon Stewart, Hulk Hogan, Andrei Kirilenko, Vin Diesel, Ozzy Osbourne, and the lead singer from Korn, among dozens of others.

With many different realms running simultaneous copies of the game that are populated by thousands of players each, there's room for everyone. The game is massive. Blizzard employs 4,600 staff members and uses 20,000 computers systems, 75,000 central processing unit cores, and more than 1.3 petrabytes of storage, according to a September 2009 article on Yahoo!. Rob Pardo, one of the game's lead designers, said that one of the three main goals of the game was to have a "world as toy" effect (quality player versus player combat interaction and a strong adventuring component are the other two). It's supposed to feel new, exciting, captivating, and beautiful, no matter how little or how much you play.

And it is.

Forget the old side-scrolling games in which characters run from the left side of the screen to the right and then have to stop while an hourglass icon appears, the machine whirs, the disc spins (or the cartridge chugs away), and the next screen or area loads. WoW is a seamless 3-D wonder. Rotate the mouse, and you can change the camera view from first person to pulled way back, to down to up or to the side. Aim it any way that you choose, and the landscape appears to go on forever. Use the flying mounts or the transport griffons (or giant bats, if you're aligned with the Horde) and you get a sense of the awesome sprawl of color and shapes that makes up the land of Azeroth.

Yes, it's unrealistic to be playing a bull-headed Tauren or an Undead like the Forsaken, or the Alliance's most monstrous-looking character, the Draenei (blue creatures sporting demon hooves and a long forked tail), but the land is terrifically realistic, as are the characters' movements. And that's not to mention the compelling story line possibilities—witness 6,000 quests to undertake!

The video game industry is a $20-plus billion yearly business ($21 billion in 2008, $18 billion in 2007), and its growth is outpacing that of movies and music. Before long, it's going to be the most powerful and influential sources of popular culture. Already we've got celebrities such as Mr. T, William Shatner, Willy Toledo, Jean-Claude Van Damme, and Verne Troyer endorsing the game in commercials. A $100 million WoW feature film is due out in 2011. Hot Topic has its own World of Warcraft clothing line. Upper Deck has a trading-card game and a miniatures game (the ad for it claims "Magically. Epic. Miniatures.").

There's a series of drinking steins with names like "Tankard O' Terror" and "Blood of the Horde." Fantasy Flight has two board-game versions (eighty dollars and forty dollars), plus two expansions (fifty dollars and twenty-five dollars). DC Comics now has an ongoing WoW series. Blizzard has a WoW credit card whose rewards go directly into maintaining the MMOG account. *South Park* won an Emmy for its "Make Love, Not Warcraft" episode. Twelve-year-old kids wear "Home Is Where the Hearthstone Is" T-shirts because it's cool to be that lame. And the makers of WoW plug back into popular culture with such in-game references as the following:

- Haris Pilton: a socialite in Shattrath who sells Gigantique bags and fancy sapphire pinky rings.
- Ophira Windfury: a woman in a temple northwest of Honor Hold.
- Slim: a merchant who sometimes admits, "I'm neither Slim nor Shady. In fact, I find both references insulting."
- Floyd Pinkus: an innkeeper in Thrallmar.
- Voidwalkers Gone Wild: an Outlands quest.
- Tonight We Dine in Havenshire: a Death Knight quest.
- A Red Rider Air Rifle that occasionally backfires with a "Right in the eye!" debuff. (A *debuff* is the opposite of a buff; it provides a temporary negative consequence for a character, such as decreased strength, DOT [damage inflicted steadily over time], or slower movement speed.)
- Some of the Hungering Dead in Dragonblight yell "Nom! Nom! Nom!" in honor of Cookie Monster as they attack.

I used to think I could get away from WoW by killing my computer: smashing it with a hammer, canceling my subscription to the Internet, throwing the damn PC in the trash. I used to think there'd be a way that I could take the decision out of my own mind and hands. Clearly, though, that's not an option. Our society approves of computers. All my life, people had told me that computers and technology were the future, and the more we utilized and understood them, the better off we'd be.

As Hilarie Cash and Kim McDaniel write in *Video Games and Your Kids*, "We associate them [computers] with intelligence, achievement, convenience, and 'the way of the future.' We want our kids to be computer savvy so they will not be 'left behind.' Thus, many of us feel that whatever our kids are doing on the computer, as long as it is legal, it is acceptable. We assume that if they are gaming, it is fostering, in some vaguely beneficial way, computer literacy."

Yeah, right.

In *Beyond Good and Evil*, Friedrich Nietzsche wrote: "He who does battle with monsters needs to watch out lest he in the process become a monster himself. And if you stare too long into the abyss, the abyss will stare right back at you."

I see the smoky eyes of WoW everywhere.

❖

What sucks so many into it is the social aspect of the game. Even when you're not out questing or grinding mobs, you're chatting with people about equipment, trades, and real-life stuff. Some players just sit in the major cities and talk all night. There's a constant hubbub of activity that is coming from like-minded gamers sitting before their computer screens. It feels active, alive. The game world is dynamic and ongoing.

The real formal structure for grouping is the guilds, a must for any serious WoW player. Joining the right one is the only real way to ensure that you have quality players to do ten-, twenty-five-, and forty-person raids with. There's also a real sense of kinship among guild members: you become an important part of the team, and you're missed when you're not there. There's a penalty for not being a good team player. You miss out on loot drops, you don't gain experience, and you always run the risk of being replaced.

Even if you're like I was and avoid guilds as much as possible, you still have to realize that the only way to really advance well and get the top loot is to group with others. The real prime loot comes from running heroic versions of regular dungeons, where the monsters are supercharged and ready to kick toon ass. The drop rate for heroics is through the roof, compared to the normal rate.

Skip a few days of gaming, and you're left behind. Any status you might've had starts to dwindle as others surpass you—you can almost sense the game passing you behind, leaving you. Take a few weeks off, and poof, you're gone. A lot of the community you loved so much defriends you, drops you from the guild, or finds a replacement in raiding groups. Since all you had by way of connection with this virtual community was the game, if the game isn't constant, the community simply doesn't exist. This is one of the biggest differences between a virtual friend and a real-life one. The majority of virtual relationships aren't as deep, nor are they as lasting or meaningful, even if you open up and share your innermost thoughts.

For most, the social aspect is 80 percent positive and 20 percent negative. For me, it was 50-50. I liked an active server, yet I was equally happy soloing the entire game, grouping only when absolutely necessary. That close-but-distant contradiction to other players suited me well. I wasn't gaming to make friends, I was gaming for the elusive high that most gamers chase.

Even without the huge social aspect of the game, I'd still have played. For me, the magic was the intoxication of the game itself, not the player interaction. I've played on private servers (online versions of WoW not run by Blizzard—many have increased experience and loot-drop rates, sometimes ridiculously so) that were so sparsely populated that the major cities seemed like ghost towns.

And I played on.

❖

"Dinnertime!" my wife's voice rang out through the Bluetooth earpiece of my phone.

My job disaster at Clemson wasn't the complete end of my teaching career—I landed the Jenny McKean Moore Writer-in-Washington position at George Washington University, which allowed us the use of the Lenthall House during my the 2007–2008 school year. This 230-year-old historic four-story townhouse in Foggy Bottom was so spacious that we'd been using the cell phones to talk to each other from different floors. Apparently, houses were much sturdier a few centuries ago, because you couldn't shout from the kitchen on the first floor and be heard from the office area (WoW command central, for me) on the third floor.

A previous resident had left a huge plywood desk big enough to hold all three of my computers. The big desktop PC's function was pure gaming. The second desktop PC kept up www.thottbot.com (a "database for quests, mobs, spells/abilities, maps, and items, updated through players transmitting data from an in-game interface plug-in") so I could readily check game guides or "instance" (identical copies of dungeons in which player groups can explore together and never run into other groups, so each group can kill the same "boss" monsters and complete the same quests independently)information without having to ALT + TAB to switch screens. The third computer, a laptop, was dedicated to www.wowarmory.com (a "vast searchable database of information for World of Warcraft—taken straight from the real servers") and the occasional checking of e-mail.

Students *did* e-mail me from time to time, especially since I hadn't kept consistent office hours in years. I claimed in my syllabi that "office hours by appointment" allowed me the flexibility to meet their schedules, but what it really meant was more time for WoW. If I boomeranged a quick, friendly e-mail within thirty minutes of receiving their notes, most kids didn't feel the need to meet face-to-face, which meant more uninterrupted game time. Considering that most kids just wanted to give me some lip service so they'd get a better participation grade and I didn't really want to see anyone for that type of brownnosing, it was win-win.

"I'll be right there," I told my wife. I was in the middle of a raid with Zip, my new level-seventy Gnome Mage who was running with members of Leper, a raiding guild I was testing out to see if I should accept its invitation to join. I'd been in guilds before, dozens of them, but I'd left just as quickly because of the continual bombardment of lowbies asking my powerhouse toons for runs through Maraudon, Gnomeragon, and Deadmines (popular five-person dungeons), real low-end stuff for a seventy to be doing. You certainly had to help out the lowbies from time to time, but the real reason to be in a guild was for guild instance runs. It's a huge pain in the ass to assemble a halfway decent team to run Black Morass or any of the Outlands dungeons where the best loot was, especially once the Burning Crusade expansion allowed you to crank the dungeon difficulty level up to heroic, which meant the loot was infinitely better, too.

Unless you knew exactly what people you were playing with, like guildmates, you took your chances with a pickup group, or PUG (a group whose members are brought together after they have entered a queue, or a group assembled at random by people who most likely have never played together before).

One PUG member, a Leeroy Jenkins type (a WoW character who became famous after being featured in a viral video in which he charged ahead recklessly and caused a massive party wipe), would usually prove himself wildly incompetent and charge headlong into every situation, which meant a long walk back in corpse-form from a graveyard for everyone.

There'd also usually be some overly cautious idiot worried about getting his precious T2 (high-end) armor scratched, so he'd linger in the back and pretend to help but would mostly just let everyone else do the dirty work so the repair bill for his gear would be low.

Finally, there'd often be a newbie (a beginner player). Oh, he'd be a level seventy, but either he'd be playing on his cousin's account for only the second time or he'd have just bought a toon on eBay for $100 and have no clue how to run his character. Then everyone else would have to do double-duty to cover his less-than-worthless ass. He usually wouldn't last long.

The latest WoW patch updates (fixes applied weekly to correct the many bugs in the game) allow the Kick Player option, in which a group can vote to remove someone who is underperforming or being an ass. Something about the anonymity of the game experience brings out the worst in certain people. Some players go so far as to ninja (steal loot from an enemy corpse) extremely rare loot to which they were not entitled. Ninjaing is a surefire way to get yourself badmouthed regularly in the chat channels and blacklisted among the guilds. Gold farmers, in particular, find it a fair trade to ninja a very expensive item, even if it means some bad in-game PR. If it gets bad enough, they can always do a character name change and/or transfer to another server.

I didn't make it down to dinner that night. Instead I focused on working the immediate-gratification muscle that WoW exercises so well. I took my a new character, Chzball, from five to fifteen as fast as I could, something I'd gotten very good at after reading a few leveling guides that promise you can get to seventy in two days. Maybe it wasn't hard to advance to a new level anymore, but it was like sitting in the main room of a Las Vegas casino—all those bells, all that winning. How do you sit there and *not* drop a quarter into the nearest slot? How do you not say, "I'll just play until I ding twelve"? Then ten minutes later, you decide, "I'm so close to thirteen. I'll just put in a few more minutes and finish off that level." And then the next. And the next.

Eighty minutes later, Victoria banged through the bedroom door and glared. Admittedly, there was no other way to use the doors in this place, since the entire house was moved from 19th and G Streets to 21st and F Streets in 1978, and the house did indeed look as if it had been shoved off the back of a flatbed. Again, this is a testament to the quality of old building practices—if you had dropped the $80,000 one-story I owned in Tallahassee from three feet up, it would have split down the middle and become a pile of cheap rubble in seconds.

If you dropped the Lenthall House, all it would do is develop a little character. The floors mostly sloped at a smooth five degrees, and the door frames were positively M. C. Escher–like. If you opened the hall doors without grabbing the handles quickly, gravity would slam them into the corresponding walls hard enough to rattle your teeth fillings. Considering that the Lenthall House was split into a side-by-side duplex and that this year a stone-jawed law professor from Memphis lived next door with his lawyer wife and amazingly quiet one-year-old, I was worried we'd be sued, since our doors banged maybe fifteen times a day and at all hours, especially with our constant bickering and needling.

"Huh?" I asked as Victoria glared at me. I never yanked my eyes off the screen.

"What's wrong with you?" she asked, but it was a rhetorical question. We'd gone over it 100 times before and were no closer to an answer now.

"I wasn't hungry."

"Why didn't you say that before?"

Valerie, age three, turned on *The Wonderpets* on the twenty-five-inch TV-VCR combo in the bedroom and did her best to ignore us. Our nine-month-old, Veronica, started to sob. You could always tell when we raised our voices too much—the kids let us know.

Feeling the veins in my neck pulse, I said, "Gimme five minutes, then we can talk about it. I'm nearly done here."

"What's the point? Five minutes, five hours. That damn game will still be a problem."

Truer words were never spoken.

❖

Rob and I used to joke about the addictiveness of the game, calling WoW the "World of Warcrack" or "digital heroin" even as we took another hit of it. And it was definitely druglike in our growing dependency on it. Everyone's got an optimal arousal level, and WoW was aimed directly at someone like me with its rapid-fire rewards, its graphical realism, its sense of virtual experience, and the opportunity for regular achievement and advancement. Real life didn't have such power, glory, and freedom, and what little there was got diluted by stress, guilt, shame, and human error. Azeroth, WoW's virtual world, was much more inviting and much more forgiving. If you really screwed up, all you had to do was just roll up another character and try again.

It would be inaccurate to say that WoW had no positive aspects to it. Because we played the game together, Rob and I talked daily, and when we played, we bonded, problem-solving together and learning to depend on each other in what felt like extremely high-stakes situations. We called our ability to know each other's thoughts in a near-psychic connection the "WoW simpatico." It was scary how well we played together with our characters. I flung long-range blasts of ice and snow, and he healed me so I could survive nearly forever, even when I had aggro (the aggressive attention of mobs). Sometimes, to change things up, he went head-to-head with the monsters and absorbed the majority of damage while I sniped away, bouncing and teleporting away from our foes as I froze them solid, then cracked the life out of them blast by blast, the way a malicious cat toys with a mouse. Before long, we could two-man dungeons that would've been trouble for a five-man party.

We also learned about capitalism firsthand through our manipulation of the auction house, the eBay-style system particular to each realm that allows players to buy items and supplies from other players. Some of the best gold-making guides brag about revealing ways to make 200 gold pieces (the virtual currency of WoW, along with silver and copper coins) an hour, which usually involves going to a specific location and killing the same creatures over and over again in the mind-numbing hope of getting the right loot drops to sell on the auction house. Boring! We'd spend less than an hour a day and corner the market on a certain type of item by buying it up and then relisting it at the price we preferred. Five hundred gold in a weekend for very little work was a real possibility.

Maybe it's easier to be weak with someone else, I don't know. But we played a ton—and I mean a *ton*—since both of us remained excited by the idea of characters with extraordinary abilities. If we put in enough time, our characters would level up and develop new skills and thus be better able to mingle with the exotic friends and foes of this fantastic world. *World* doesn't even quite do it justice, because it suggests just a place. Perhaps *spectacle* or *extravaganza* puts the right seductive spin on the word, both being ingredients of good MMOG game play. Putting the best light possible on those months we played together, I'd have to say that we jointly stimulated, challenged, and enriched our imaginations; however, perhaps it wasn't using our imaginations that we were enjoying so much as benefiting from the fruits of someone else's imagination, which is a huge distinction.

All in all, it wasn't enough to justify what came with it, but it was something, I suppose.

People sometimes ask me why I played. It's hard to come up with a satisfying answer. The reasons, though, are legion: My wife is disgusted with me for losing my tenure-track job at Clemson University after four years and seethes with a slow-burning anger that keeps her from talking to me, which is a situation I want to get away from. I've loved fantasy books, games, and stories since I was very young. I like a challenge. I love computers. I don't have a lot of friends, and MMOGs put me in contact with hundreds of people with similar interests (even if it was just a big, often crude-languaged, chat room). I like to feel in control. I like to kill virtual creatures. I like to do things I'm not supposed to do. I like to be rewarded, and WoW is all about quest rewards, talent points gained by leveling, arena rewards, and honor points. I like computers and am mesmerized by technology. I love cartoons and animation. I love to see digital things blow up into a million sparkling pixels. I love the idea of striving to be number one in my guild, in my realm, in all of WoW. I am drawn to its ability to transport me out of this boring, slow-moving, humdrum existence. I am enamored by its beauty.

I also sometimes liked to partner with people other than my main wingman, Rob. So many idiots play WoW that when you keep your mouth shut and just do your damn job in an instance, people not only respect you, they like you. I've done downright heroic things in real life and have been spit on for it, literally. In many ways, WoW is predictable—meaning safe. For someone like me, the concept of a safe zone holds true appeal.

WoW doesn't threaten you with divorce. It's always there, and all it asks is your time and a measly fifteen bucks a month per account. That's roughly the same price as lunch and a so-so tip for your waitress at Applebee's. It's the same price as a pair of Stephen King paperbacks, and less than the cost of a copy of any new hardcover of his. It's the same price as getting a tire fixed when you run over a nail.

WoW is chock full of smart asses talking in the trade channel, and I love smart asses, at least when they're being clever about it.

In addition, WoW lets you have up to fifty different toons per account, so you can have a male Undead Priest, a Female Gnome Warlock, a male Tauren Shaman, and a Night Elf Priest. You start accumulating talent points from level ten on, getting one per level. You dump them into any of the three talent trees that each character class has, and you can specialize further. A warrior can focus on protection, arms, or fury. A Warlock can focus on demonology, destruction, or affliction. And then you gear the toons how you want to, which changes how they look—they can wear a wedding dress or a fancy blue hat with feathers in it—and this modifies even further how well they perform, since after the first few levels, everything you wear will have magic buffs (temporary helpful enhancements) on it that make you stronger, tougher, faster, and harder to kill. The possibilities are endless. You'll never try them all, not in a dozen years.

It's kind of an unmanageable thing to have so many toons—you end up defaulting to one "main" (the primary character you play) and many, many "alts" (the alternate characters that you play simply for fun or when the server your main is on is down). The appeal is that you have a character type that meshes with whatever you're feeling. Angry? Go with Goremax the Deathknight, who does all his speaking with his giant red two-handed mace. Laid-back? Play as Penser the Druid, who can change into cat form and use stealth abilities to hang out and watch battles unfold or even sneak up behind people and rip their heads off before they know what's what. Helpful? Load up Zchick the Priest, who teams up with others and keeps them alive through healing spells and protective buffs. In real life, you're stuck with what you are, how you feel, and who you are.

In real life, I felt plain stuck.

I like WoW because it has an elite level-twenty human boss named Edwin VanCleef who haunts the Deadmines and is the leader of the evil Defias Brotherhood that threatens the human city of Stormwind. Yeah, it's stupid, but I was endlessly tickled to be connected by name to the game I worshipped for so long.

Another way that WoW appeals to me is through the U.S. consumer mentality, which I'm as much a participant in as anybody else. I have a sense of entitlement. When I'm put up in a swanky hotel during my on-campus university job visits, I take the lilac-scented soaps. I swipe the plastic-wrapped plastic cups. I dump the extra roll of toilet paper into my backpack. I take a couple of hand towels to go with the collection of three or four hundred I have in boxes at home. Once I tried to fit a beautiful oil portrait of downtown Pittsburgh into my suitcase. I rationalize that I paid for it by forking out big bucks for one night for the ten-by-fifteen room, so it's mine. If I could've folded up a beautiful bed-and-breakfast room I once had, with its chintz sheets and emerald ocean wallpaper, I'd have slipped it into a zippered pocket and left, whistling, excited that I'd finally have a room that was much nicer than where I lived.

WoW is limitless. And I pay my fifteen dollar a month, so I want it all.

❖

The term *video game addiction* has been devalued by people who use it casually, meaning "I play a lot" or "I overindulge at times" or "I find playing video games to be a very pleasurable experience." But *addiction*, in a scientific sense, means an inability to control one's need for something despite detrimental social, legal, or health consequences. It's a very real thing, and for some (myself included), that word best describes their relationship with video games.

The warning signs of video game addiction include the following:

- Having a strong sense of euphoria while playing
- Feeling empty or irritable when not playing
- Having decreased performance in school or at work
- Becoming uncharacteristically aggressive when unable to play
- Thinking about the game even when not playing
- Craving more game time
- Having an inability to stop playing
- Experiencing headaches, dry eyes, or sore fingers or having pain in the shoulders, neck, or back
- Skipping meals
- Cutting back on personal hygiene
- Sleeping poorly (and dreaming about the game when you do sleep)

I've experienced all of these at one time or another, and I have probably suffered from half of them simultaneously. My wife estimates that I lost five pounds a month when I was really in the throes of WoW. What she doesn't know is that I played so much that the hyperreality of these games transformed how I lived in the real world. I'd be picking up a bag of potatoes and some frozen pizzas at the grocery store, and I'd hear the clatter of a kid knocking over a stack of canned stewed tomatoes. To my ears, it was a Tauren Warrior's war stomp. Worse, I had rehearsed the act of responding to that type of attack so many times that right there—in real life, in that Publix Super Market—I would spin around and ready a blinding powder because I was suddenly my level-seventy Rogue instead of a thirtysomething writer who's never been in a fistfight.

That's the deep connection to a game that its designers are hoping for and that scares the hell out of parents and some experts. "Hit pedestrians, outrun police cars, and get gunned down in a drive-by shooting . . . what LA's really like" invites one video game ad. And there's this one: "The burning sensation you feel is from your broken ribs, not some fireball." The game sometimes becomes your reality even when you're not in it. The games teach you a learned response to stimuli—a pleasurable mix of adrenaline and anxiety. The mind stores away those memories but calls them up again as a response to similar stimuli that don't always happen within the game.

Talk about interactive gaming.

❖

Victoria worked part-time for George Washington University as a university supervisor, which means that she checked up from time to time on student teachers who were fumbling through their craft at area schools in which the students were guinea pigs for the teachers-in-training. It was a horrible job for two reasons: (1) the pay stunk, and (2) she was gone from the house for only a few hours a week, which didn't give me enough unaccounted-for WoW time. She kept track and got really pissed if I played more than two or three hours each day.

I could usually get an hour or three in before she woke up, but I liked a full realm with lots of PvP, lots of auction-house action, and lots of chatter in the chat channels. Daytime is the second-best time for that; 8:00–11:00 PM EST is best, since most of North America is off work and ignoring their families enough to be hammering away at WoW by then, so the servers are almost always bursting at that point—sometimes they're so full that there's a wait time just to enter.

"I'll be back about three," she said, hoisting a near-to-bursting book bag over her shoulder as she ambled toward the front door. "When they get up, don't forget to feed them."

I didn't even consider how insulting it was for my wife to remind me to feed my own children, because I was too worried that Burritothief was going to die. In a sense, it doesn't matter if your toons die, since you're not penalized in any way other than you have to take your newly created ghost from a nearby graveyard and walk him all the way back to where your lifeless body remained, then click YES to the question "Resurrect now?"

Some games do punish you for dying. You lose a level. Or you lose, temporarily or permanently, some of your abilities. In the online phenomenon game of Fate, which my father-in-law logged in seventy-seven hours on in the first two weeks of "casual gaming," one of the death choices was to spend money or lose experience points and fame. Yes, in WoW you do get your gear damaged a bit when you die, but money fixes everything, and after a few hundred hours into WoW, you figure out how to create all the money you need, so even a heavy repair bill isn't much of a disincentive, really.

The joke going through the countless WoW blogs and websites now is that the game should be called the World of Auctioncraft, since higher-level players are making so much money that they max out their virtual money belt—214,748 gold, 36 silver, and 47 copper. At that point, you can't acquire any more money in the game, period. If you pay real-world dollars to one of the better gold-farmer sites to max out your gold capacity, that'd cost you about $1,000.

Still, I felt responsible for and to Burritothief—to all of my toons, in fact. My real life was uninteresting, at best, and stunningly unpleasant and unexciting at worst. The game, in contrast, was a utopia where I could shape and participate in realities that were infinitely more fulfilling than anything I was able to manage in real life. Yes, it was mediated through these toons, but the toons were me, or at least some type of idealized projection of myself. They were truly my avatars. I brought them into WoW. They didn't exist until I came along. In the same way that Valerie sobs when her Digital Doggie Gigapet dies, sprouting wings as it transforms into a beautiful digitized dog angel, I felt stabs of remorse and shame when one of my toons kicked the bucket. I could've prevented it. I could've played him smarter, geared him better, leveled him higher, ran with better wingmen, understood his capabilities more thoroughly. It was my fault.

Guilt was part of the play experience for me.

The last thing I needed in my life was more blame and shame.

Picture this: God at a cluttered desk, head down, phone blaring, self-stick to-do notes everywhere. Some idiot's even banging on the door outside, despite the DO NOT DISTURB sign. God is horrendously overworked. He lifts his head and takes a deep breath, then his eyes fall upon the Bahamas cruise brochure that came to him by mistake, a "sale of a lifetime" advertisement picturing candy-sand beaches and a luscious blue-green stretch of water that's as perfect as monastery window glass. Before he realizes it, he's stuffing underwear and socks into a knapsack and fumbling for his passport, excited for the first time in a long time, but then he wonders: If I'm not running the show, who will? He drops the half-filled bag, settles with a groan back into his chair, his old knees complaining, and he plugs back in, determined to at least do a little better, a little more. He has to. And before long, there is nothing else.

I left Burritothief in the middle of the thickly populated forest outside Shattrath and hit stealth, then clicked the power-off button on the computer monitor because Victoria got up earlier than I had expected and would've seen me playing, and that would've led to the how-long-have-you-been-on interrogation, and I would've lied instead of admitting since 4:00 AM, and she would've known that I was lying because she's an elementary school teacher and has some Spiderwoman sense for lying. I hope she'll leave soon so I can flick back on the power and make sure my guy is okay before some asshole Alliance guy spots him and takes him out without a chance for me to fight back or escape.

A new MMOG, Evony, markets itself to men around the idea of playing without getting caught: it shows a huge-breasted woman coyly looking at you, and the text beneath her says PLAY DISCREETLY AT HOME OR AT WORK. Talk about progress. The only way to top it is with their latest ad, a nearly naked woman leering at you, the words COME PLAY WITH ME, MY LORD, temptingly beside her.

I told my wife to have a terrific day. Victoria turned on the front steps and cut me a look, as though she knew what was roaring through my mind. It's always roaring through my mind. My feet were moving, but I couldn't charge upstairs just yet. She nodded in a way that didn't signify "yes" and headed outside to the car. I waved.

Thank God, I'm upstairs, dashing so fast that my elbow connects with the door frame with a crash loud enough to wake anyone, and I'm praying that the kids keep snoring away because I've got two instances I want to run before they get up, and if the Good Lord remains good to me, I'll have maybe six hours before I have to power down for awhile. Six hours is a nice chunk of time in which to get my daily WoW on. The kids didn't budge, so it was time for some serious WoW.

"WTB mage food. Will pay well," I typed into the trade channel. I'd sent all my food to my fledgling hunter the night before and had forgotten to resupply. For a single gold piece to a bored mage, I'd have enough conjured food to fill a backpack, if I wanted—enough for a whole day of high-powered WoW. You can't send conjured items from one of your toons to others, or I'd have logged onto my own mage and done just that.

"WTB a life!" someone responded.

"ROFL," typed another. Then someone else added, "LMAO."

I laughed, too, thinking that yes, these losers did need to get a life.

Two hours later, in the middle of an increasingly irritating Alterac Valley battle (a battle between Alliance and Horde) in which for some reason the Alliance has its act together and is manhandling the Horde (a rare occurrence), my computer froze. You'd think a university like George Washington, with a billion-dollar endowment, would have kick-ass Internet service, but here at the Lenthall House, it was dicey, as if they might've installed it back in 1794, or whenever the place was built. As often as once an hour it would stop and I would get bumped offline. Sometimes I could go for a few hours with no issues, but then I'd be down for thirty, maybe forty seconds. There's not much you can do about it except log on again as fast as anything, your heart hammering away as you hope that your toon survived the sudden catatonic state you left him in.

Today, though, I was having problems with a few quests, and the stupid gold farmers spamming the trade channels were hounding everyone ("Pleasure to sell WoW gold, best price alive—$9.99 USD guarantee for 1,000 gold. Bonus 10% first-time orders."). This irritated me, because no real gamer needs to buy in-game gold with real-life dollars. That's for lazy people (which I'd been at times, I admit), and it ruins the game's economy. So when I got bumped from a PvP battle that despite losing would still net me some decent honor points, I lost my temper. Yeah, I have an anger issue from time to time—witness the half a dozen broken computer mice in the hallway closet—although usually I keep things well under control. Not this time.

With my anger came a reaction all out of proportion to simply having to reboot the computer: squeezing my fists into my thighs, slapping the desktop, grinding my teeth, storming up and down the room spitting out language that would've made a gangsta rapper cringe. A blinding compulsion to stomp, smack, kick, and destroy bloomed to life.

Why? Because the game was going on without me, and I was certain I was missing out. Also, going a little ballistic provided a noticeable wave of satisfaction that would serve until WoW was back and I was safely plugged into the game again. Being hooked on WoW was like being on fire at the bottom of a dark well and wishing for rain.

Playing WoW makes me feel godlike: I have ultimate control and can do what I choose with few real repercussions. The real world makes me feel impotent and constantly frustrated. A computer malfunction, a sobbing child, a suddenly dead cell phone battery—the littlest hitch in daily living feels profoundly disempowering.

I slammed the mouse down and growled something like "Goddamned, goddamn, goddamned piece of shit motherfucking computer piece of shit-fucker!" while trying to reboot with faster-than-the-speed-of-light results. Valerie was up and whining for a glass of water, and I told her to wait and be quiet or she'd wake her sister, who heard the banging of my fist on the keyboard and woke up from that. Rebooting is a two-minute ordeal, thanks to Microsoft Vista being the worst operating system in the world. Trust me—no one knows about graphics cards, sound cards, RAM, and system stability better than gamers, because we depend on these things. They're the lifeblood of our trade.

"Hold on," I said to Veronica, who was sitting too close to the edge of the bed and looking dazed from sleep. Valerie was singing now, one of her made-to-the-occasion songs: "Water, I need some wah-wah-water. Water, please. Wah-wah-wah-ter. I'd love some water!" And then I smelled that someone's diaper was trashed (if I know my daughters, a number two of epic proportions), and God knows, two kids can't wake up without one of them having pissed, so that would be waiting, too.

I got the computer rolling on the long process of restarting and hurried to Veronica, who was the culprit of the stink. She was crying now, really heavy sobs that suggested she was nearly inconsolable, a state she'd entered more lately than ever before. The only things that helped at that point were 100 percent of Mommy's (not Daddy's) attention, for however long it took, or letting her sob it out by herself. She's a handful.

"Take it easy," I told her, trying to sound calm as I worked the wipies over her bare little behind. Valerie was sobbing now, too thirsty, apparently, to walk the twenty feet to where the glasses and the water were readily available in the bathroom. This set Veronica off again, who was howling now. Then I heard the telltale beep of the computer hitting some type of error in booting up.

"Jesus," I said, finally sticking a semihysterical Veronica into an empty clothes basket while I ran Valerie into the bathroom to change her potty-training pants in Olympic speed fashion. Then she'd gotten some water in a cup but was still crying, complaining that "It's not perfect"—Lord knows what "it" was. Like most little kids, she insists that everything has its place, and if something is broken or—in her mind—wrong or unexpected or less than what she prefers, she freaks. Ignoring her inexplicable complaints, I hurried back to the computer and tried to troubleshoot the startup while bouncing a steadily unhappier Valerie on my knee as Veronica used her weight to knock the basket over. She steadied herself, then walked toward me, smiling, arms out in her pick-me-up gesture. Then she fell face-first over one of Valerie's light-up Elmo shoes that had been left on the floor the night before.

More sobs. Everyone's sobbing. Even I'm sobbing. The insanity of the scene hits me, but I don't know whether my tears are from laughter or from the agony of utter frustration. This day was truly like any other for me in D.C. The sick, unfathomable need to game was upon me like a 1,000-pound weight on my chest, slowly crushing me. It hurt.

"All this for a fucking thousand dollars a semester," I said aloud, weighing the pittance of my wife's salary against the opportunity to play some covert WoW even though it meant having to take some responsibility in the needy-kid realm from time to time. I rubbed at my eyes with a tissue.

"Fucking dollars?" Valerie parroted, and I imagined the horror of my parents, who once instituted the Swear Jar, in which you had to put a nickel every time you used a curse word. As a kid, I once threw in a buck after an errant "Shit!" and didn't bother making change, announcing, "Don't worry. I'll get my damn money's worth."

It took ten minutes to settle everyone down before I returned to my computer. My head was cement-heavy, thanks to a blossoming migraine, and I logged on only to see that I'd been bumped from the battleground, so the whole thirty minutes I had played before that was for nothing, a complete waste. It was crazy to think it, but when I managed an eight-hour WoW day, I still considered even a thirty-minute chunk of time precious. Half an hour ought to be no big deal, but it pissed me off, and I couldn't help cursing again as I got into the ten-minute queue for the next forty-on-forty PvP battleground.

I settled the girls and watched them play in their jammies near the crib; both of them were still snotty from all the crying, but they were content. It wouldn't last. It never did. And I had a mere three hours max before my wife would be back.

Christ.

Behind me, outside my window, was a flicker of leaves as the wind moved the big elm tree. In front of the Phi Sigma Kappa house across the street, two girls were screaming at a kid in dirty khakis who kept shrugging and looking up as if a passerby might help. He really squirmed beneath their barrage. With a frat house and a fire station so close, I rarely registered any noise through the anything-but-soundproof windows. This, though, was new. Maybe those girls would kick the kid and then pummel him senseless there in the street, something I'd normally have paid good money to witness. I did love an opportunity to people-watch, and I found myself doing it from time to time even in WoW: standing around in Shattrath or Orgrimmar, watching the crowds milling about, and listening to what they said.

Now, though, I couldn't care less what was happening forty feet away. The way I was lounging in my swivel chair, I could sort of see it peripherally, but I was focused on the game. The Game. My tunnel vision went back into effect once the operatic theme music cued and the game loaded. A crack in the universe sucking cars off the street in front of my house wouldn't have drawn much notice from me, for once again I was with thirty-nine other Hordies as we decided to right the wrong of the past defeat. Nothing's cooler than the beginning charge of a forty-on-forty battle, all those mounts plunging into a thunderstorm of melee and destruction.

Someone typed: "Let's not !@)$(#*) this up. Stay together."

And we did. We tore through the first group of Allies as if they were blind people playing on some outdated computer from the 1980s. I ambushed, then gouged, then sliced and diced a Draenei Shaman who was trying to run from me, and she was intercepted by a Tauren Warrior who critically struck (a hit that does more than twice the normal damage from a weapon) her with his two-handed flaming axe. She tried to heal herself with Gift of the Naaru (a racial ability for all Draenei), but that Tauren hit her again, so she was down.

I stealthed and threw a garrote over the neck of a Gnome Mage who thought he had a freebie shot on an Undead Priest who was dispelling a curse of agony that some Warlock fired at me. He was toast. Five kills later, I closed in on a Night Elf Warrior who was either AFK (away from his keyboard) or stupid, standing beside a broken-down wagon like that. I feel bad wasting such people, yet not bad enough to not kill them.

Then the girls started screaming over a piece-of-crap two-dollar stuffed animal, a lizard-belly green thing that might've once been a penguin. Valerie was blaming Veronica for trying to swipe it, but Veronica was too strong and wouldn't release her death grip on its flipper. I jockeyed my guy into the closest grove of trees and prayed for some luck as I hurried to the huge stack of kid DVDs I'd gotten for exactly this purpose. I picked *Play Time Maisy*, running time two hours, eighteen minutes.

When I read the June 2005 articles about the South Korean parents from Incheon who had left their four-month-old alone at home for five hours while they played WoW at a PC baang, an Internet café, I was horrified. The story became big news because the kid rolled onto her stomach and suffocated. The real pisser is this: the father's parents lived upstairs. Why the hell didn't one of the parents just go up and ask his parents to watch their kid while they went out? Why the hell couldn't these people prioritize? *Selfish assholes,* I told myself, shaking my head.

I watched my two daughters zombifying in front of the twenty-five-inch screen from the corner of my eye as I knocked out a few hundred more honor points and hoped to reach another 1,000 before my wife got back. I needed another piece of the Gladiator's Vestments set. I had the helm, the tunic, the spaulders, and the gloves, but I really dreamed about the carnage I'd make with the über-powerful leg guards. I was maybe 5,000 honor away from the final piece, which meant I'd also get the full-set bonus, an enhancement that's given when a full set of armor is used on a single character. Major improvement. Way cool.

The connection between my actions and those of the South Koreans (who were charged with criminal neglect of their own child) didn't sink in. It should have, but it didn't. I was in no position to get it, but I still should have. I should've suffered a spasm of self-loathing strong enough to make me quit playing video games forever the moment I read that story on Yahoo!

Instead I had asked Rob, "Which instance are we running tonight? I need to level my Priest so I can get the epic mount. Man, I want that freaking fast horse so bad."

That's the thing about addiction. It makes you a bad husband, a bad parent, a bad friend, and a bad person. It makes you forget to feed your kids sometimes, and when your wife asks you what they ate, you lie, saying not that they were on the second round of *Maisy* on the tube but that they were naughty and refused to eat the corn niblets, crackers, and apple slices you'd so carefully prepared for them and that you'd had your fill of rotten kids and their behavior issues for now, and you just want some quiet time upstairs playing WoW as payback for dealing with so much crap in one day.

Nine

DEPENDENCE

> I don't want the cheese.
> I just want out of the trap.
>
> —SPANISH PROVERB

I hate Tuesdays.

When I was playing WoW, the game was down most Tuesdays for maintenance, patch updates, bug fixes, and so forth. It's hard to think about an entire world being down, as if God himself were taking an extra long snooze and has hit the pause button.

Sometimes WoW would come back up in chunks; only certain realms would be ready to go while the others still sat in limbo. Players will create new toons in the ready-to-go realms and play just to be playing, logging out to check on their home realm every ten minutes or so, just in case. It's for this reason alone that I had characters on nineteen different realms spread over my three accounts.

Eighty percent of the anger I experienced over video games occurred on Tuesdays—not so much because I couldn't play then, but because that was the day I actually did work (reluctantly so, but I did it nonetheless). I wrote a poem stanza or two and then checked to see if WoW was back up. I handled job applications and then checked to see if WoW was back up. I walked the dogs and then checked to see if WoW was back up. I was incredibly productive and useful for a couple of hours every Tuesday morning, which somehow never translated into realizing how much more productive and useful I'd be if I spent Monday through Friday not playing WoW. By 2:00 PM each day, I'd be back on WoW, reimmersed into my home realm, the place I truly belonged.

Tuesday was the proverbial breath of fresh air in a stuffy, closed-in life that was lived entirely at the service of a video game. I felt empty, as if I had a giant hole drilled into the middle of my soul. Wednesday through Monday, the game filled that hole nearly enough for me to forget it was there. On Tuesday, though, it gaped with a fury.

Even though I'm not playing WoW now, I still profoundly hate Tuesdays. I try never to teach on Tuesday. I refuse to drive my kids to school on Tuesday. I tend to just sit around, even today, and mope.

How's that for pathetic?

❖

The psychologist Samuel Gosling says that we can more accurately learn about a person's conscientiousness, emotional stability, and openness to new experiences by having a stranger spend a few minutes rooting through that person's personal space, usually the bedroom, than by asking that person's friends. That's why a quick peek into a medicine cabinet or the basement of a new love interest holds so much appeal. It's not snooping as much as getting a much more immediate look into—behind?—the real person.

Malcolm Gladwell mentions Goslin's study in his book *Blink*: "Just as important, though, is the information you *don't* have when you look through someone's belongings. What you avoid when you don't meet someone face-to-face are all the confusing and complicated and ultimately irrelevant pieces of information that can serve to screw up your judgment. Most of us have difficulty believing that a 275-pound football lineman could have a lively, discerning intellect."

No one knows I'm an addict. My wife sort of understands, but even she doesn't really get it, despite having directly and indirectly experienced it in me for years. She thinks I'm just choosing to be an inconsiderate ass most of the time. She thinks the gaming is a symptom of my asshole-ishness. I couldn't see how much my addiction was hurting her—I only had room to take care of one person at a time, me, and I wasn't doing even that very well. I was ashamed at how weak and disempowered I always felt.

My friends think I've got my shit together. Ironically, more than a few are envious of me for my "stable" life, my "creative" soul, my financial "success," my sixteen published books, my nifty website (www.ryangvancleave.com), my seemingly thriving Amazon business, and my nonprofit poetry press (www.crpress.org).

My parents too think my marriage and my life are great. When I told them I was writing this book, a memoir about my addiction to video games, they changed the subject and never brought it up again, as if I'd lapsed into an uncomfortable moment of word salad like a babbling Alzheimer's patient. I told JT, my old grad school buddy, and he was floored. I told Rob, and even though he was part of the WoW addiction, he was surprised and didn't think I was serious for a few weeks.

Root through my private spaces, though, and it becomes clearer. My office library is full of WoW books, strategy guides, and maps;

rows of WoW figurines line my school office shelves; then there are the printed-out maps, the pages of notes in my writing journal, and the clutter of unused poetry reference books and research materials. I am well-spoken, decently dressed, and terrific in front of a crowd. I'm not Brad Pitt, but I'm a far cry from Quasimodo, too. All in all, people can't get their head around the idea that I'm an addict. I've been an addict for more than twenty years, chasing an elusive high that's harder and harder to find. Whenever I thought of the future, it had WoW in it. Worse, the present was soaked with it, too. I couldn't separate WoW and me any longer. We were one.

Although I've had stretches of lucidity, most of my life has been one of enslavement, complete subservience. That's what addiction is. It's one giant hole that goes right through you.

Addictions don't duck and cover when you scream *air raid*. They might hibernate for the winter or vanish for a long weekend, but give them time—they'll rear their ugly little bastard heads and rejoin you, step by step, throughout your life. Consider Scott Weiland, Britney Spears, Darryl Strawberry, Keith Richards, John Belushi, Kate Moss, Amy Winehouse, or British tennis stud Andy Murray, who got dumped in 2009 by girlfriend Kim Sears because his "seven hours a day" video game habit was too much to bear. This list is a lesson in addiction: these people have advantages the rest of us would kill for, and what runs their life is their addiction. Addiction is insidious that way. Try all the twelve-step programs, group therapy, and drug treatments you want; the best that many can come up with is to vilify the object of their desire, discuss it to no end, and then avoid, avoid, avoid.

It's actually not that hard for me to avoid gambling, drinking, and sex, but WoW meant more to me than everything else combined. I'd have surrendered every drink I'd ever had for a single week of WoW. I'd have turned over every dollar I'd ever won at blackjack for WoW.

I'd have unscrewed every woman I'd ever screwed for more WoW.

This is what real addiction is. It gives you perspective on the other things that you thought were addictions. It beats them up and takes their lunch money. It stands tall and proud and ominous. It declares itself king of its own vast land, and you end up pushing a broom around for whatever wage it pays because you can't say no, you can't say buzz off, and you can't just walk away.

❖

A March 2008 Buzz posting on Yahoo! shows that Dr. Jerald Block of the Oregon Health and Science University gets it. He writes, "Alcohol, drugs, food, sex, and even shopping are all candidates for medical treatment and are recognized as genuine mental disorders, so what about the Internet? Internet addiction—defined as 'excessive gaming, sexual preoccupations, and e-mail/text messaging'—is becoming so common that at least one psychiatrist says it merits inclusion in psychiatry's official handbook of mental illness, the Diagnostic and Statistical Manual of Mental Disorders."

He adds, "Tech junkies display genuinely debilitating behavior, including drug-like cravings, withdrawal, and a constant need for more and better gear—just like a substance addict might exhibit."

Amen, Dr. Block.

Another voice to join the ever growing chorus.

Ten

WHY I COULDN'T STOP

> This is an instruction manual that glamorizes eating disorders and will give your child that extra motivation to become an anorexic or bulimic.
>
> —KATHLEEN ROBINSON, CLINICAL PSYCHOLOGIST, IN A REVIEW OF *WASTED: A MEMOIR OF ANOREXIA AND BULIMIA* BY MARYA HORNBACHER

Let me be straight: this book is not a how-to on being addicted; if anything, it's a how-to on not screwing up your life through addiction (video games, sex, drinking, gambling), or any other type of dysfunctional behavior. It's an account of the slow, spiraling disaster of one man's lifetime addiction to addiction, culminating in a real life-or-death struggle with, of all things, a video game. There is nothing glamorous or outlaw cool or "Professors Gone Wild!" about any of this. If you need help, get help. Too stupid, too ignorant, too proud, and too lost, I didn't get help until I'd sunken so far into a virtual existence that there was damn near nothing left for me to return to in real life, which is why this book begins with me on a bridge at the end of my life.

At the end of my virtual life, not my real one.

Help exists.

If you need help, get help.

If you need help, look at the Recommended Reading and Resource lists at the back of this book.

If you need help, tell everyone—anyone you can.

If you need help, please ask for it.

If you can't find help, tell me. I'm reachable at www.unpluggedthebook.com. Yes, I personally run it, and I read everything that comes in on the contact form.

If it's not you but rather a loved one who needs help, do what you can for him or her. Start by asking, "What can I do to help?"

I wrote this book to help myself. Writing is an act of discovery, I regularly assure my students, and while working on this memoir I uncovered so many things I didn't know I knew about myself and others that it's worth it for that alone. It became, for me, the meaningful therapy that no therapist or well-intentioned friend could provide. There were opportunities for me to get help, yet they never manifested into anything that made a difference for me because too few people really understood what video game addiction was or what it did to you.

Through the writing of this book, I realized that I had forgotten the Mrs. Monroe story for nearly twenty years—an experience most would find forever seared into the forefront of their minds. I had forgotten how much I enjoyed shooting hoops in the front yard of our Palatine, Illinois, house with my father. I had forgotten how the first time I tried to pull a wheelie on my midnight-blue Huffy three-speed bike, I hit an unseen rock and wiped out so badly I had to walk shoeless for a week because my ankle ached so much. I had forgotten the one-eyed chubster claiming to be a private detective and former army medic who liked to visit me at the Amoco station where I worked my senior year of high school, telling me during my 10:00 PM to 6:00 AM shifts about his army days and how he was a world-class tight end at Fremd High School. One day, the last time I ever saw him, he offered me $63,000 to take his one-year-old daughter and leave the state with her, never telling anyone, especially his estranged wife, where I had gone. I had forgotten that for no particular reason one Friday afternoon, I stepped in front of a UPS truck doing thirty-five miles per hour on Rand Road and got flipped twenty feet into some bushes, where I awoke sometime later with a host of bruises, a splitter of a headache, and not one damn broken bone.

For hundreds of reasons, I rewired my brain to work like a computer with a bunch of external hard drives (how ironic—using a computer analogy to talk about my computer gaming addiction). Many of these hard drives have remained unplugged for years, and in some cases, for decades. I'm sure that any psychologist worth his or her salt would recognize that it's a defense mechanism. If things get too scary, just snip the cord to that particular hard drive. Unplug it. Turn off the power. Voilà, you're cured, even if it's still sitting there like a ticking time bomb. I guess I'm just a bit slow at getting on board with the "those who forget the past are doomed to repeat it" theory that everyone else seems to internalize much more easily.

One excuse in my favor, though, is that I've been a creative type all my life. I wrote my first book, *Pigs in Space* (yes, a rip-off of the Muppets skit—if you're going to steal, steal from the best), when I was seven. I've been painting on and off for twenty years. I have three cameras and abuse them regularly through the taking of blurry, poorly framed pictures that would make George Eastman blanch. I sketch second-rate, highly sexualized manga figures in my writing journal alongside the poems. I study tattoo art and have long considered doing my own (six guns and an Old West holster around the waist), although I can't get past the idea that self-tattooing is a bit too much like self-dentistry (another intrinsically bad idea).

Like most creative souls, I am self-critical, perfectionistic, narcissistic, ambitious, and sarcastic, and I tend toward excess. This means that I value the simple act of creation so much that I don't want to waste valuable brain space using my head as a damn filing cabinet. I want a huge megamachine with lots of RAM, not a *Rain Man* model with tons of memory but a Commodore 64 processor.

To continue the computer analogy, this is the reason I never have and never will use drugs. I'm deathly afraid of ruining my internal circuitry—I've seen plenty of otherwise smart kids get permanently spacey after a few bouts of sniffing industrial glue, sucking on crack pipes, or putting down a dozen dime bags of questionable weed over the course of a few weekends. Like the endurance runners who were threatening to boycott the 2008 Olympics because they feared the lasting effects of the air pollution in Beijing that lingered overhead like a thick brown stew, I simply can't risk it. I have too many stories to tell, I'm beginning to realize. I'm sure the drinking never helped, but it never felt as dangerous as drugs seemed, somehow.

Back to my creative-person explanation. Rob, a professional trumpet player in addition to being a very dedicated high school band director, immediately understands what I mean when I explain to him the Filing Cabinet Theory of my mind. He laughed after hearing me spell it out for him. He said, "That's awesome, man."

My wife hates my ability to leave my hard drives detached for great stretches of time; she claims that I'm purposefully withholding information in order to torpedo her in the future with past secrets, shortcomings, and what seem to be "out-and-out-lies." She thinks I manipulate memory. Looking back at what I've written so far in this book, I realize that maybe I do. It's amazing what people can justify doing in order to protect themselves.

"A surprisingly convenient thing," she crabs at me constantly. So it's no shocker that I don't see my ability as "awesome," even though it leaves the majority of my brain free to be creative. Of course, having spent the better part of three years playing WoW and not leaving myself time to actually *be* all that creative sort of puts a thorn in the heel of that idea. Or it simply underscores what a profound waste that time has been.

I said to Rob, "What the heck do you mean? Why 'awesome'?"

Rob explained, "Jazz players throughout history have been trying to empty their minds of the world and let them just create without any interference. That's why so many drank to excess or went wild with drugs. They wanted it all and nothing at the same time. If you can do the same type of thing without downing coke by the bucketful, you're lucky. Most of those cats killed themselves trying to achieve what it sounds like you've taught yourself to do on your own. It's cool. Awesome."

Thinking of how Thelonious Monk's angular twists on melody in "Round Midnight" might have come from LSD or peyote made me wonder. John Coltrane had heroin and booze. Louis Armstrong had marijuana, which he called his "good friend." Billie Holiday too enjoyed a love affair with weed. Charlie Parker was doing Benzedrine (speed) at age thirteen, and he composed "Moose the Mooch" about his heroin pusher.

This jazz analogy, which I wouldn't have thought up on my own in a dozen years, was one I could get behind. One of Rob's great gifts in our friendship is his ability to communicate to me in ways I can relate to, and that doesn't necessarily mean in gaming geek-speak. I have few friends for exactly this reason: we rarely speak the same language (usually the faulty one is me). And the few friends I had, I drifted away from when I became too busy with video gaming to bother keeping up with them. When you're mere hours away from a new all-time best, it's easy to say, "I'll phone you later."

Tomorrow.

Next weekend.

Later.

Never.

❖

Although I have a very strong musical background (I was a professional guitar player for years and played lead trumpet all through college), I don't tend to think in musical metaphors. Speaking with Rob always reminds me that perhaps I should, but it also reinforces the choice I made to move into writing rather than music. It was a decision I made after starting the classical guitar performance program at Northern Illinois University—if you can call flipping a buffalo-head nickel a "decision."

As much as I love—truly enjoy the hell out of—music, my ideas always link up more readily with words, language, books, the text of life. But therein lies the great paradox. *Why can't a person whose life is so enmeshed in language and communication use those skills to help inform and improve his own life?*

I'm blind in every sense of the word when it comes to myself. The connection between my existence and literature is 100 percent absent. The connection between the lives of others and literature is endless and easy to spot. If my life were someone else's, I'd probably say within five seconds of hearing the first chunk of it that it's a lot like James Baldwin's terrific short story "Sonny's Blues," about an unnamed schoolteacher whose younger brother, a jazz pianist named Sonny, is arrested for the possession and sale of heroin. Not wanting to bring pain like his brother's into his own quiet life, the schoolteacher ignores Sonny in prison until he experiences tragedy of a type that only a severely damaged person could appreciate—the narrator's daughter dies of polio. The story weaves the past through the main narrative, telling how the brothers' parents died when Sonny was a teen and how Sonny grew to love the piano, practicing it for hours on his in-laws' piano as if he were "playing for his life."

In a sense, he certainly was.

Baldwin presents Sonny's addiction and drive for creating music as a result of rage, pain, and agony. "It's terrible sometimes, inside . . . that's what's the trouble. You walk these streets, black and funky and cold, and there's really not a living ass to talk to, and there's nothing shaking, and there's no way of getting it out—that storm inside. You can't talk it and you can't make love with it, and when you finally try to get with it and play it, you realize nobody's listening. So you've got to listen. You got to find a way to listen. . . . Sometimes you'll do anything to play, even cut your mother's throat."

If I were someone else, I'd tell myself to read Baldwin's damn story a couple of times and pay a lot of attention to both brothers—in many ways, both seemed to be me. I'd probably then charge myself to read a lot of Edgar Allan Poe, who loves to play with the idea of split personality, two facets of the same soul: the double, the twin, the doppelganger. I'd read "The Fall of the House of Usher," "The Cask of Amontillado," and "William Wilson."

Then I'd further the discussion—sounds like I'm creating a semester-long syllabus here—by asking myself to read Fyodor

Dostoyevsky's *The Double: A Petersburg Poem*, then Guy de Maupassant's "Le Horla," then selections from Franz Werfel's verse trilogy *Der Spiegelmensch*, and finally Oscar Wilde's *The Portrait of Dorian Gray*.

I'd end the semester by watching a few DVDs to close things out with a bit of fun: *The Talented Mr. Ripley*, Vincent Price's *Diary of a Madman*, and a season or two of *Heroes*. Then I'd focus on the ways in which the destruction of the self—literal or figurative—is one way for characters to escape the horror of their second selves.

Throughout the series of texts, my imaginary class would discuss obsession, alienation, the self, human dignity, sin, race, and various issues of ontology and epistemology. We'd talk about how these stories speak to socioeconomic realities, the middle class, and the self-possessed nature of modernity. We'd probably end with an essay complete with a fancy-sounding title, perhaps something such as "Scaring Ourselves: The Doppelganger and Death in Poe's 'The Fall of the House of Usher' and 'William Wilson.'" As a student in that class, I'd probably get an A-.

But I can't get outside myself, not really. And that's a lot of the damn problem, so instead I flounder and grasp futilely at answers I'm unable to supply for myself, even when friends like Rob provide some of the much-needed clues. My life is too much like a partial syllabus in which I'm not even sure what texts I was supposed to read. So with the writing of this book, I'm trying to (re)locate those missing texts, hooking all those dusty, unused hard drives back up so I can finally take a long, deep look at the life I created for myself. In so doing, I might now be able to act from information versus ignorance, which sounds like a much better plan, since the other tactic was a one-way doomed path.

❖

Let me repeat: this is *not* a how-to book.

I don't have a grab bag of tricks and tips on how to finagle more video game time from your already overburdened life. I used one trick, and everyone knows what it is: I chose WoW—again and again and again. Instead of shuttling the kids to Chuck E. Cheese's, I'd play WoW so late the night before that I couldn't wake up the next day. Instead of whisking my wife out on the town for her birthday, I'd get embroiled in a heated PvP match with some idiots from the Gnomercy Warriors guild, and she'd go to bed alone, shaking with anger. Instead of getting ahead by grading student essays on repetition and form in Elizabeth Bishop's poetry, I'd start up a new druid and see how high I could level him in two hours.

It's that simple and that horrific.

If you're going to put self-stick notes anywhere in this book, just do it in the spots where you find yourself shaking your head and saying, "Jesus H. Christ, I'm *never* going to do that!" If that's what this book does—warns those who are teetering on the brink of WoW or MMOG or any type of addiction that scares all hell out of you, great. If it helps others understand how addicts think, act, and live with themselves, and in so doing perhaps shows how others can help the addicts in their own circle take charge of their lives, great. If it simply gets those with a serious addiction to reconsider it—even just a little—great. If it helps one WoW widow get back her (or his—wives, moms, sisters, daughters, aunts, and girlfriends get caught up in video gaming too) life, fantastic. Any of those options pleases me.

This book is *not* a how-to. It's a confession clear and simple. It's a cautionary tale. It's how I am coping. I don't see a therapist these days (I can't afford it, since I don't have health insurance and haven't worked full-time in a couple of years now), and I miss my writing career, which so often took a backseat to WoW because, in the most reductive of explanations, writing is hard work and WoW is fun.

I used to write for two hours every morning, but one day I realized I could knock out half a dozen quests in those same two hours, and that suddenly seemed a better use of my time. I could spend those two-hour blocks writing for a week straight and end up with only two pages of a supernatural thriller, which represented maybe a 0.4 percent move toward completion. In that same time, I might've leveled my new Shaman from five to fifteen—quite a jump! Sure, he's no seventy, but at fifteen there's a range of places he can run around now like an angry Greek god, laying waste to everything he sees, beast or man.

Stack that up against two pages of a first draft of a four-hundred-page novel that probably would be lost for nine months in the slush pile at some $400-million-dollar New York publishing house to one day be glanced at by a nineteen-year-old intern from Vassar who yawns, sips a Red Bull, adjusts her Raspberry Berry lip gloss in a pocket mirror, then boomerangs my book manuscript back at me with a "Dear Writer, Your work was carefully read, but we are sorry to report . . ." letter because she's got an early Starbuck's date she doesn't want to miss.

Yeah, I'm jaded.

Strange how the mind justifies behavior. Having surrendered to antisocial impulses so many times now, I sort of understand the eerily calm man who stands over the body of his wife (or boss or coworkers), the knife in his hand slick with blood, and he tells the cops who approach warily, guns drawn, that "I'm not sure how it happened. I just sort of found myself doing it." Or even "It wasn't me. Really. I swear. I didn't do it."

And he believes himself.

Every second I stay on this non-Internet-connected computer to write this book is one more second I'm not logged on to WoW. I'm the drunk refusing to reenter his old martini bar haunt, the talk-show-caliber obese man refusing the McDonald's drive-through. Maybe that's the secret. Like Penelope staving off her suitors by agreeing to marry one only when she finishes the burial shroud that she secretly unweaves each night, hoping against reason that her love Odysseus would return, I could write and rewrite and tear down and build back up this single book forever, never allowing myself to finish because the actual act of writing it proved to be my salvation. One day, I hope to hop onto a computer at Kinko's or a friend's house or the library and not type "www.thottbot.com" or scan frantically for the Blizzard Game Launcher icon that I used to keep in thc dead-center of my screen, like an unmissable bull's-eye.

That's not today, though.

Soon, I hope.

Soon, my family hopes.

❖

/dance

/drink

/flex

/fart

It's embarrassing, but one of the things I enjoyed most about WoW was the emotes (commands you type in to make your character perform certain actions). If someone typed "/dance," they'd see "You burst into dance" on the screen, then their toon would do a Michael Jackson impersonation or spin like Shakira. Each race and sex has its own special moves based on real-life people and dances. The WoW designers have a sense of humor, creating male Orc boogie moves to mimic M. C. Hammer. Male humans work the pelvis and point in a stylized, sexual imitation of John Travolta in *Saturday Night Fever*.

If you type "Warcraft dance" into the YouTube search engine, you'll see that some people have matched up the toons with their real-life counterparts, and it's hilarious seeing them in action together. I've shown it (there are many different WoW dance videos, but the best is three minutes, twenty-two seconds, added on May 18, 2007) to dozens of nongamer friends, and they all crack up. I can't watch it because anything WoW-related is too much of a hook for me now, but even thinking about that dance video gives me the giggles. With more than 15 million viewings of this particular video as of January 2010, it seems I'm not the only one who reacts this way.

While playing, you can just type "/insult" ("You think everyone around you is a son of a motherless ogre.") or "/fart" ("You fart loudly. Whew . . . what stinks?") or "/moo" ("Mooooooooooo."), and it usually gets a reaction. I can't tell you how many times I tried to flirt or dance or even fart in real life but got no audience response. Zilch. It's almost as if WoW experiences are best-case scenarios the real world doesn't offer. And of course that's what the game designers intend. It has to be easy and attractive, or people won't choose it over real life. It has to be easy and attractive, or people won't pony up those monthly account fees and they'll move on to other games, other distractions. It has to appear to be the other side of the tracks, or you wouldn't yearn for it.

To put on my cultural anthropologist hat for a moment (hey, I can't help it—that Ph.D. made me an academic), I'll say that in many ways the type of interaction between players and MMOGs parallels the way that movies or television became a cultural phenomenon in past decades. By that, I mean it simultaneously informed people's lives, modeled behavior, and entertained them.

But as John Beck and Mitchell Wade note in the preface to *The*

Kids Are Alright: How the Gamer Generation Is Changing the Workplace, "Video games have replaced television as kids' favorite babysitter. But they are much more insidious. They get into our brains. TV is about watching; games are about doing. And doing is where we learn. Even as adults, we learn only about 10 percent of what we watch, but over 70 percent of what we do. And in the formative years, learning from games may be even more powerful."

"Yowzers," I want to say in my best Shaggy voice. (That's Norville "Shaggy" Robert from *Scooby-Doo*, not Shaggy the Jamaican reggae star who in "Angel" announced "Closer than my peeps you are to me, baby.")

A *New York Times* article on June 29, 2003, by Frank Rich has a similarly bleak outlook. "Here's what's wrong with kids in the digital age," he writes. "They live in front of their TV and PC screens. They steal music online. Their attention span is zilch. They multitask on everything and concentrate on nothing except video games. They will buy any trashy product that the media goliaths can sell them, then drop it as soon as the next big hype comes along." The purpose of his article was to discuss the Harry Potter phenomenon and its stunning appeal.

It's all connected, I suppose.

I multitask nonstop (I'm listening to Linkin Park's "In the End" right now, in addition to explaining to Valerie why she shouldn't be eating M&Ms at 9:00 AM, all while trying to write this paragraph and having my cell phone signal an incoming text message). My attention span? Yikes. I buy trashy products all the time. I have a huge collection of Smurf figurines, Beanie Babies (the big ones and the teenies from the McDonald's Happy Meals), and NFL bobble-headed sports dolls. At one time I owned neon red parachute pants and a slick blue Members Only jacket. I've spent piles of cash on teeth-whitening gel, anti–belly fat pills, Baby on Board signs (even prior to having kids), fanny packs in six colors, and three sets of rollerblades.

I am the American über-consumer.

Maybe I have something to blame my video game addiction on other than myself because Blizzard's marketing budget is tremendous—China's big game company, The9, bought the rights to sell WoW in China for more than $60 million, including a guaranteed $13 million in marketing alone. The U.S. marketing numbers dwarf that many times over, although the exact numbers are kept fairly hush-hush. For good reason, I suspect.

So if Frank Rich is correct, then it's not my fault I played too much. It's Madison Avenue's fault.

It's Blizzard Entertainment's fault.

It's God's fault.

But none of these excuses sticks. It's me and always has been me. *Me, me, me.*

❖

I grew up in a generation that was introduced to Pong (my first video game experience), the Atari system, and the Magnavox Odyssey. In terms of computers, I remember the Commodore 64, the Apple IIe, and, my personal favorite, the TRS-80 ("Trash 80"), which featured audiocassette data storage that was so poorly conceived you had to record information on it at least three times to give yourself a decent chance of having saved it. The Trash 80 also had a very expensive expansion interface (which allowed you to bulk up with 48 KB RAM and a real clock) with edge card connectors made of two different metals so you had to regularly clean them with a pencil eraser or they'd oxidize. Good stuff, those Tandy micros.

The students I've had in my classes in the past decade—avid

gamers, many of them—grew up on some serious machines, by comparison. A digital wristwatch has more brainpower than most of those early 1980s computers. Also, these kids simply know how to use computers instinctively, it seems, as though it's ingrained in their genetic makeup. Valerie, who is now five years old, has been playing online Disney games for months and can work a mouse or a touch pad as well as anyone. She's even learned how to open an Internet browser, type in "www.pbskids.org" or "www.noggin.com" and start playing. When she can pound away at a Wubbzy game for an hour straight, I worry. When she begs and pleads to play another round of Smurf Racer on the Wii, I worry. When her Christmas wish list is mostly composed of Barbie video games and Dora the Explorer video games and Disney Princess video games, I worry.

She's not too upset when she gets frilly socks, a scooter, and My Little Pony figurines instead. But someday soon she'll demand an answer to why it was okay for me to game like crazy and not okay for her to do the same. I don't have an answer—and this is her main memory of me from her childhood.

Is addiction learned behavior or something insidious that lies deep in our DNA, like a gene for obesity, flash-fire anger, or middle school myopia?

I worry about this a lot. Especially when Valerie asks me every few weeks why I seem so sad.

"Aren't you going to play your game anymore, Daddy?" she asks, understanding the connection between the two things with the amazing sense of intuitiveness that kids often exhibit. Sometimes she hugs me, saying, "It'll be okay, Daddy."

I hug back, but still I worry.

❖

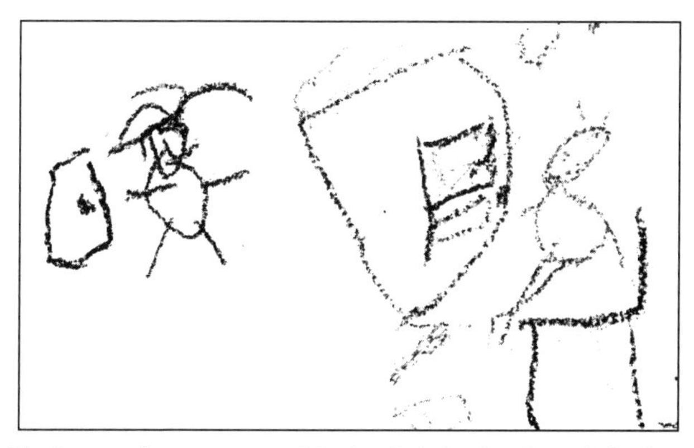

That's me at the computer, and that's Valerie leaving through the door because I was too busy gaming to play. (Valerie drew this at age four.)

❖

Part of being young is wanting to be hip, to be part of something big, the new thing. WoW and MMOGs are hip. If 11.5 million people are playing, why the hell aren't you? Think of it as a gated community, where everything is glitzier, sexier, and more fun on the other side, or at least so it seems when they're paying millions to convince you it's so. Why wouldn't you pay your fifteen bucks a month to bust your way in and see what the fuss is all about? It's like that new downtown club people are talking about (it likely has a funky name like "Medusa" or "Red" or "Element"), only they won't let *you* in. You can stand in line outside, where some 300-pound ex-linebacker with a clipboard and sunglasses says you might have a chance, but it never comes. That only makes you want to get inside the club even more, even if it means jimmying your way through an iron grating over one of the bathroom windows in the rear and falling head-first onto the sticky, tiled floor that reeks of piss and wine and God knows what else.

Even if it doesn't seem glitzier or sexier to be gaming, it's part of the youth culture, and that's a powerful draw to the hip generation. Take

China, for instance. It has 338 million people online, and 280 million of them play online games, according to government surveys. People were hanging out in Internet cafés so often, chain-smoking and downing cough syrup to stay awake longer, that China shut down dozens of online games and got WoW offline for nearly three months in 2009.

The Chinese government believes that online gaming is causing violence and moral depravity (including pornography and drug use): a fourteen-year-old girl learned how to pick up men and have sexual flings from a video game called Audition, and a young man is serving a life sentence for five murders he committed in order to get virtual equipment for online games. To support the claim that video games are the culprit, recent Chinese reports showed that up to 80 percent of the violent criminals in a particular Beijing juvenile prison got into crime because of exposure to it through online games. If that's accurate, that's a shockingly high number.

From the comments on the articles on Yahoo! and other sites about China's crackdown on unwholesome games, it's clear that the United States and the rest of the world is laughing about it. Here are just a few examples of how easily China's attempt to regulate and limit video game usage is dismissed:

- "How absurd. We all know that people who play MMOs in China spend most of their time playing games than actually committing crimes. Consider MMOs a blessing for China to keep most people out of trouble and a way to control the populace."
- "Wow, they're right. I just raced a few mates round the nurburgring and now I have an overwhelming compulsion to kill a child."
- "And China adds another tick to its long, and continuously growing, list of faux pas."
- "I'm pretty sure Genghis Khan used to arrange flowers till he put his hands on a joypad."

Digital media is socializing a new generation with the iPod, MMOGs, and the Blackberry. Digital media connects. It defines. It makes one belong. Want to know about someone? Look at the music on his or her iPod. Check out the faceplate on his or her Blackberry. See which video games he or she prefers. It's all as distinctive and informative as fashion or food choices; moreover, it's far easier now, thanks to social sites like MySpace and Facebook (which, of course, are highly customizable to make it uniquely yours), for people to connect with others who have similar interests.

Back when I was playing Dungeons & Dragons at age eight, we had maybe six similarly aged neighborhood kids to play with. If they hadn't been on board for those old pencil-and-paper role-playing games, I wouldn't have been able to play, because there would've been no other options. It was that simple. Today, you just sign up for a listserv or change your interest section on your personal website(s) or Facebook profile, and wham, you're ready to go with as many new friends (call them *willing participants*, if you want) as you'd ever need. It's like an instant support group for whatever poison you prefer.

And that's how I got my friend Rob into it. I wanted someone in real life to play with rather than the strangers I'd seen from New Zealand, Germany, Canada, and Australia. Don't get me wrong, I enjoyed reading all the chatter (actually, I heard it, once I started using Ventrilo, one of many voice communication programs that MMOGs use) from people who said that the sun was just starting to peek out over the Bombay or Melbourne horizon while I was shirking sleep at 4:00 AM here on the U.S. eastern seaboard. It made me feel very global to know this type of information, to hear them bash George W. Bush and talk about how much they love Kentucky Fried Chicken and how you can buy beer at a McDonald's in Berlin. But it wasn't the same, because I didn't know these people. I mean, it could've been Jeffrey

Dahmer behind one of those toons, or my third-grade teacher, who listened to death metal on headphones during lunch.

Identity is a fishy thing in a digital environment. It's an opportunity for people to remake themselves. It's hard enough in real life trying to read someone, to figure them out. But trying to get a fix on someone who is mediated through a digital avatar that can change with a few clicks of a mouse button? Remember that WoW is happy to change any aspect of your characters if you pay their hefty fees. Identity isn't a constant—it's fluid.

I wanted something I could count on. I wanted a wingman I could put a face to.

Enter Rob.

Like me, Rob throws himself headlong into whatever he's doing, which is terrific if it's a meaningful endeavor but tragic if it's a waste of time, as was much of our undergraduate experience, which included too much partying, too much pigging out at McDonald's (damn those two-for-two-dollars Big Mac deals), too much bad golf at Buena Vista's more-dirt-than-grass nine-hole course, and too little studying. I was leery to show him my new MMOG because I wasn't sure he'd be into it. I feared decloaking and revealing myself for the umpteenth time in my life as a nerd. WoW has elves with pointy ears, and I remember how a five-foot-five Asian kid, Ralph, brought a story into our graduate-level fiction writing class at Florida State, and one of my classmates barked with laughter, saying, "You seriously wrote about elves?"

Ralph sighed, explaining, "Not elves. *Dark* elves."

The room exploded with laughter.

These kind of distinctions mattered to fantasy geeks, a group that seemed infinitely lower on the totem pole of lameness than band geek, science nerd, and chess club guy. Ralph exacerbated this problem later in the semester when he went on a three-minute classroom rant about the nuances of distinction between a werewolf and a were-fox. Oh lord.

I knew the difference between the two, too, from all the fantasy books I'd read. But I knew when to keep my fool mouth shut (at least, sometimes I did).

Rob was a true Halo fiend and had played more than his share of Madden and other highly competitive Xbox games on his own and through Xbox Live, so I suspected that WoW might work for him. Maybe. He was my best friend, too, so perhaps that'd help to sway him, even if it didn't strike his fantasy bone just so, as it did for me.

I'd been playing for a little more than two months before I got him hooked. I might as well have offered him crystal meth as get WoW sparking through his veins through their "Recruit-a-Friend" plan, which gives the recruiter a free month of game time once a friend goes through the ten-day free trial and then purchases a month of game time. I remember thinking that it was a pyramid scheme that I could make work for me. Just get twelve friends hooked, and I'd play free for a year. What a deal!

"How do you aim?" Rob asked over the phone as we played together for the first time, him in Atlanta, me in South Carolina, his Night Elf running circles around a level-one wolf without ever attacking it. The mangy gray animal nipped at his heels, tearing off his pitiful few health points by the second.

"You don't aim, exactly," I said, using my level-ten to one-shot the wolf before it killed my friend's new toon. Dying in your first fight wasn't the way to get excited about a new game. "You target a guy with the tab key or left-click on them, then you choose what type of attacks to use. Use the action bar, numbers one through three."

"So there's no head shots?"

Rob was accustomed to the sniper rifle in Halo, a game in which you could wing someone endlessly and they'd keep on running, but if you popped them in the face or the chest, *boom*, they'd go down. He wanted that type of reward for his accuracy and his skill. Not having kill shots made WoW appear dangerously close to the strategy most diehard gamers disliked: button mashing.

"No," I assured him. "Just choose the right attacks. Set up your hot buttons correctly, and you'll have tons of options."

I thought that WoW had lost him then and there. His wife called to him in the background to get out on the porch and start grilling lunch, so he said he had to go. I told him good-bye and watched his toon disappear from Azeroth. I wondered if he was laughing at me for being so intrigued by this button-mashing, geeky game in which people played as dwarves, elves, gnomes, and trolls. I always wondered if people were laughing at me.

Blasting a dozen more wolves didn't make me feel any better. I hurried to Stormwind, one of the biggest Alliance cities in the game, where hundreds of players' toons streamed around me. Still, I felt overwhelmingly alone. I'd been playing for months and had never once spoken to another player in the game, nor had I ever typed anything into the trade channel, the defense channel, or any channel. Perhaps I was afraid I'd mistype and people would laugh. Plenty of players typed *rouge* for *rogue* and were regularly ridiculed for such sloppiness. Perhaps I simply had nothing to add to the ongoing stream of non sequiturs, which, despite their being often stupid or angry or amazingly WoW-geekish, I still read.

Thinking about it now, I suspect that what kept me from talking was that I preferred silence. If one were silent, one was almost not there. One was ignorable. Think of Buster from *Arrested Development*, the way he'd lurk quietly behind counters, halfway behind a door, bent beneath a chair. For the first three months of WoW, I was worse than Buster, just watching from the periphery of the real action, questing alone, avoiding the battlegrounds, doing my own thing in hush-hush fashion.

It's easy to see now, but I should've just left then, while I still could.

People react to what you say, and as much as you might want to, you can't take back the words. It's not like writing an essay or a poem, which you can revise to make it clearer, better, and more accurate in your intentions. I couldn't risk it. Speaking is high-stakes stuff, especially when thousands could see what you put out there. It's ridiculous, really, when you think about how many people might read this book and forever brand me as a strange, social deviant. I used to worry that one or two people in WoW might razz me because I misspelled a word in the trade channel or didn't know what "OOM" meant ("out of mana")? Talk about needing a little perspective.

It's why I resisted Twitter, MySpace, and Facebook for so long, too, I'm guessing.

When I was sixteen, my mother asked me to be a clown for her preschool class's circus day. I roped Derek, a friend from church, into helping, and we dressed up in baggy outfits with frills, face paint, and big shoes—the whole getup. We arrived that sunny April day at the community building near the family aquatic center on Palatine Road, my makeup smudging along my forehead from the blossoming heat, and I saw those kids (a dozen) and panicked.

"Hey, kids!" Derek yelled, honking on the bicycle horn in his hand.

I said nothing.

Derek danced around and laughed, and the kids responded. I followed him like a shadow. A silent shadow.

"Here's my pal, Ryan the Clown," he said.

I bowed but didn't say a word.

I stayed for the full thirty minutes, and we played with the kids, built a fort with cardboard bricks, blew up balloons, and ate cotton candy. But I never said one word, just as I couldn't find my own voice in WoW. Just as in real life, I was there and not there. I desperately wanted to belong and interact meaningfully, but a sense of impending doom held me in check. I couldn't risk it.

When I logged on the following afternoon, there was Rob's character, a level seven now. WoW had him, too.

"Hey, pal," I typed.

Those were my first words in WoW.

❖

A gaming insider I know—a pal of Ge Jin, the Ph.D. student at the University of California–San Diego who made a widely distributed WoW gold-farming documentary—says that a 2005 *New York Times* article, which estimated that 100,000 Chinese people made their full-time income from MMOGs by selling loot to Western clients, was way off. He says the number is closer to 600,000 now and is growing weekly.

At first, this sounds preposterous. But you can confirm it with Google. Or just type "Wow gold" or "warcraft gold for sale," and you'll get pages upon pages of companies trying to outdo one another with their fast access to ready in-game cash—in some cases, millions, allegedly. It reminds me of the ridiculous days of the pet rock, the idea coined by a marketing guru, Gary Dahl, in the 1970s. For $3.95, you'd get (essentially) nothing. Virtual gold is much more nothing than the pet rock. With the pet rock, at least someone actually sent you a pebble with glued-on googly eyes. You also got a training manual so you could teach it how to do tricks ("Sit" and "Stay" being the easiest). You could pick up the rock. You could smell the rock. You could throw the rock. Try to pick up WoW gold, smell it, or throw it, and you'll see the difference.

Of course, to a WoW gamer like the kind I'd been for years, gold was—well, as valuable as gold. You could never have enough of it to improve your toons. There was always an improvement to make—a new staff, a new trinket, a new piece of chest armor—especially with the overemphasis on gear scores that WoW recently implemented.

It's a genius idea, selling virtual gold for real cash, but it's scary as hell. If you can get people to pay real money for virtual stuff that doesn't and will never exist in real life, what does that say? But hey, you can buy a virtual rose for two bucks on Facebook and give that to a friend to display, and you can purchase all types of virtual birthday cards to e-mail to your pals, too. As each new generation grows up with the electronic world being equivalent to the real world, what will the difference be to them?

It's easy to see why more and more gold farms spring into existence around the world for WoW and most of the other MMOGs, regardless of what the EULA (end user license agreements) warn about trading, selling, and economic abuse. Gamers are into immediate gratification—we want stuff. *Now.* Who wants to run the same three-hour dungeon enough times to kill the final boss to obtain a 15 percent chance of having the sword you want actually drop. And that's not even considering if another party member wants the item, too; then you have to flip a virtual coin to see who actually makes off with it.

Blizzard tries to control the game economy and has banned more than 125,000 accounts for flagrant abuses such as gold farming and running bots (computer-controlled characters) to grind out loot and gold around the clock. But gold farming continues because the rewards are so great for everyone involved.

Making real-world money with virtual goods or services is not unique to WoW. In 2006, Anshe Chung was reported to have become the first real-world millionaire through her land baron efforts in the online game Second Life. And in November 2005, Amazon launched the Amazon Mechanical Turk program, named after the eighteenth-century machine "the Turk," which was basically a wooden Turkish-looking guy who could trounce people at chess. The Turk was later revealed to be a hoax (a chess guru was tucked away and operated the geared arms to make all the right moves), but at the time, people worried that machines might one day replace people. Well, knowing that people are in many ways superior to computers, Amazon pays the subscribers to Amazon Mechanical Turk a pittance to do mind-numbing work that a computer would find problematic.

People from more than 100 countries now subscribe to be part of a large group of consumers, a new global workforce, who are paid to transcribe podcasts, evaluate the visual attractiveness of consumer goods, translate texts, and match colors to a photograph, according to the Amazon Mechanical Turk website. When you consider how little people are being paid—in some cases, one cent per task—it appears that cyberspace has become a vehicle by which to supersede any type of labor laws. All you need is an Internet connection, and you must click on a box to "verify" that you are at least eighteen years old.

Because I do freelance writing through sites like Elance, I find myself competing with companies who outsource assignments to nonnative English-speaking writers at a fraction of what most U.S. professionals would accept. It's becoming a popular tactic to use this type of cheap overseas labor, a practice fundamental to Tim Ferriss's *The 4-Hour Workweek*. Ferriss even explains how to establish your own virtual businesses that make money for you while you sleep, play tennis, and have a wonderful life not working.

My father constantly remarks how impressed he is that I'm able to make money selling stuff online at Amazon.com. He grew up during World War II and fought in the Korean War. Imagine how impossible it is for him to get his head around the idea of virtual economies. If you didn't grow up with computers the way I did and the way my students are doing, it's hard to see the possibilities.

I see them.

Maybe I've read too much Neil Postman, the media theorist and cultural critic who warned in a 1996 interview that the United States in particular needs to educate young people about the social effects, the psychological biases, and the history of technology, so that these young people will become adults who "use technology rather than being used by it." He also famously said, "Children are the living messages we send to a time we will not see."

Call me a Luddite, if you wish.

I too am concerned what those messages will be. I think of Valerie's growing collection of computer games—educational though they may be—and I worry. But to banish them from our home would be to invite that appeal of the taboo. Valerie's kindergarten teacher recommends playing educational video games every week. I know there's value to some games, but she is allowed to play no more than one hour a day. Most days she doesn't even turn a game on.

When will that change? And why?

And what justification will I have to say anything about it?

❖

I started to see that WoW was creating problems in Rob's life long before I saw them in my own. That's the kind of self-deception I was immersed in.

Rob's wife had back problems forever. The shooting tendrils of agony up her back were so bad at times that she couldn't get out of bed for an entire weekend. Surgery was a necessity. Rob said it'd be a serious surgery and even a longer recovery, and he was nothing if not a good husband, so he needed to be by her side, which was his way of warning me that he wouldn't be able to game as much with me as we'd been doing.

"Absolutely, man," I told him through my Bluetooth earpiece. My hands were busy on the keyboard and the mouse playing WoW. I was in the middle of one-manning Maraudon. I drew some type of satisfaction in killing everything in an entire dungeon. Complete monster genocide. After I'd done it a few times, I started timing myself to see how quickly I could bring about a complete dungeon cleansing. I was on a record pace this evening.

Distractedly, I said, "Wish her my best."

"Will do," he said.

Her surgery was scheduled for the following morning. When I logged on at my usual time, 8:00 AM, I found Rob's main toon there, WickedZ. At first I worried that someone had hacked into his account. Plenty of unscrupulous players find ways to insert keylogger programs into the most popular WoW add-on programs in the hope of getting someone's account information. When they do, they play WoW on someone else's dime, and they often sell away all that toon's loot when they're done, then mail the gold in-game to one of their own characters or sell it for real-world cash.

Or they do it just to play for free and screw with others. You hear people bitching about it daily in the chat channels and on WoW blogs and wikis, so it seemed quite prevalent, especially since most players use at least half a dozen add-ons to facilitate better gameplay. I usually had no fewer than fifteen going at once.

"That you?" I typed to him.

"Yeah. Still here in the hospital."

At least it wasn't a hacker. But what did it mean that he was playing WoW rather than being with his wife? I readily imagined that she had chickened out or had had a last-minute surgery scheduling conflict. I tried not to consider medical disasters, but having seen too many episodes of *Grey's Anatomy* and *ER*, I knew words like *aneurysm*, *dural tear*, *deep venous thrombosis*, and *atelectasis*, and they came easily to my mind in a moment like this. I knew his wife from our college days and liked her a good deal. Even if I hadn't known her at all, I'd have cared, because she was married to my best friend and gaming buddy.

"What happened?" I asked.

"With what?"

I hearthed my dwarf back to Ironforge so I could park him safely while I continued to chat with Rob. I hated trying to fight and type at the same time. I usually got my ass kicked while writing something as articulate as "Hye, don't cal me untl myabe 8 tonight. got 2 graed." That would usually be followed by a cry of "carp!" ("Crap!") as I got wasted by a mob or some ganker taking advantage of my semidistracted state.

"The surgery."

"Oh, it's going on now."

"Where the hell are you playing?"

"The waiting room. I found a good signal if I sit by the coffee machine and prop the laptop at an angle. I think it's coming from the Chick-fil-A across the street."

I assumed he was joking, but then thought about it. If my wife were having surgery, what was I supposed to do? Sit around reading outdated issues of *Ladies' Home Journal* and *Fortune*? At the time, killing some anxious hours with WoW made sense to me. Waiting rooms were uneasy, sweaty places. The reason hospitals put magazines on tabletops was to distract people from worrying incessantly about their loved ones' mortality. What better way to escape real-world worries than a little dose of WoW? Hell, escapism is why half of the WoW players probably played. Utterly immersive get-the-hell-outta-this-lousy-earth kind of escapism. A lot of the time, it's why I played.

I asked, "How long do you have?"

"Maybe ninety minutes."

"Let's hit it," I said. And we did.

We ran Deadmines (a low-level Alliance dungeon) for a couple of guildies. Then Rob left. Whether he lost the wireless signal or had to leave for other reasons, I didn't know. Everyone in my house was still asleep, snoring happily away, as they did most days, until noon (my night-owl wife's hours: bed at midnight, sleep until eleven or noon). I headed downstairs to catch Sportscenter and eat some Shrek cereal, which tasted all too much like Lucky Charms but with three times the sugar rush. My daughters craved it, but we let them eat it only occasionally and just as a dessert, three regular pieces for every sugary marshmallow chunk. Breakfast was a rare thing for me, but a couple hours of WoW, especially early-morning WoW, could work up my appetite something fierce. I was not like the fat guy in the Emmy-winning *South Park* "Make Love, Not Warcraft" episode who barely moved as he played. I was the opposite. I jumped, I yelled, I shook my fists, I tensed my neck muscles, I yelled at players the way some people scream at other drivers on the road.

What can I say? Sometimes my fiery disposition really flares up.

After knocking out the entire week's grading and responding to student workshop poems, I logged back on around 11:30 that morning, and there was Rob again. Surprised, I asked, "What now?"

"Surgery's over."

I found myself quickly in a battle as I fought a pair of Bloodscalp Witch Doctors. A Horde Rogue unstealthed and tried to tear my head off with a garrote. I pounded a few keys, froze the jerk, then magicked myself away to safety.

"Stupid Rogues," I said, more to myself than to Rob. Then I added, "Everything go well?"

"We won't know for a few days, maybe weeks."

I sipped at my Hype, a new energy drink I got on sale at Big Lots. Part of my recent growing weight problem was due to all the soda and ginseng and high-octane drinks I downed to stay awake for WoW. I used to skip meals so much that playing made me lose weight. Now it did the opposite. And I slept maybe three hours a night, at most. It was often difficult to function for the other twenty-one, I was so exhausted. Enter the magic boost of energy drinks.

I said, "Where are you now?"

"In Shattrath, trying to find the gem vendor. You know where he is on the scryer side?"

"No, I mean IRL [in real life]."

"Oh, in her room. I found a halfway decent wireless signal here, too. It's not Chick-fil-A's. Maybe someone from the apartments with a booster? I don't know. The lag's awful, but what are you gonna do?"

"I hope it all works out."

"Me too, man. The last thing I want to hear is that we went through all this only to have her still be in pain."

During the next three weeks of her recovery, Rob played more than ever before, logging in four, five, sometimes six hours a day. I know this with certainty because I was online myself to witness it. *What are you doing, Rob?* I asked myself, thinking that he should be available to his wife, especially since he was on winter break and had more time to be home. She could barely sit up, and she needed help getting to the bathroom. But she was probably sleeping fifteen hours a day, so what was he supposed to do? Sit at the foot of the bed, watching her chest rise and fall in the regular pattern of sleep, waiting patiently for her to wake up and need something?

What's interesting is that the preceding anecdote focuses on someone other than me. Sure, Rob had a problem with WoW. He kept playing for months after I'd quit. Sure, he shouldn't have played so much while his wife was going through what had to be one of the scariest moments in her life. Sure, I feel a great amount of guilt over being the one to introduce him to the game. But I'm the one with the real problem. So why do I spend so much time in this chapter not talking about my own addiction?

Denial is a powerful thing. Even here, in a tell-all memoir with the subtitle "My Journey into the Dark World of Video Game Addiction," I'm in denial. I might as well go all out, then.

My name is not Ryan Van Cleave.

I am not thirty-seven years old.

I am not forty pounds overweight.

I do not have a video game problem.

I have never played WoW in my entire life.

It seems that every Hollywood movie about addiction and recovery (*Leaving Las Vegas*, *Permanent Midnight*, *She's So Lovely*, *I'm Dancing as Fast as I Can*, to name just a few) will tell you that the first step in most recovery programs is to admit you have a problem.

I have a problem.

And this is a memoir, purportedly a tell-all, but to recount how many hours I'd committed to leveling up WoW characters and raiding and questing and just screwing around in the trade channel and auction house makes me ill. I mean guilty and empty and nauseous, like an army of frogs stirring angrily inside my belly. If you add up the amount of time lost to WoW (which includes not only the time spent in the game but also the time outside it when I was thinking about it, making plans for it, and talking or blogging about it), it has shaved something like two full years off my life.

And it's not like I chose to smoke Camel Menthols and reduce a hunk of my life on the tail end, when so many people suffer from enough health problems to say, "Who cares if I croak when I'm seventy-six versus seventy-seven or eighty, if I'm downing fifteen horse pills a day and it hurts to pee?" This was my early thirties, my prime time. This was when my daughters were really young. This was when I was starting my first tenure-track job, a career I'd been preparing for after nearly two decades of study, work, planning, and luck.

❖

For the previous section I had wanted to do a change-of-pace humorous thing, something like the Top Ten Ways to Tell You're Addicted to WoW. (Number ten: Your significant other suspects you are having an affair with WoW: even when you're alone with that special person, you find yourself wondering what your toons could be doing right at that moment. Number nine: You play "mental WoW" while driving to work, eating lunch, or even taking a shower.) But I think I'm trying to deflect some of the well-earned shame away from myself here. I'm using Rob as a scapegoat. Yes, he played a lot. Too much. But I played far, far more. I can think of at least ten times I played for twenty-four hours straight. I can think of countless eight- to twelve-hour binges. I don't know when I installed WoW on my office computer at Clemson, but once I did, I kept twenty or more office hours a week because it was far quieter there than to play at home. No other reason.

If WoW were one of those new Japanese life-size animatronic love dolls, I'd have been found dead in my apartment after a few weeks, the smell horrendous as my shriveled form lay atop Betty (yes, I'd have named her), my body so thin from forgoing food that near the end I'd have been able to reach through my stomach and grab hold of my own spine like Buddha during his big fasting.

By comparison, Rob had his shit together.

❖

The other instance in which I saw that WoW could lead to out-of-control behavior was with Rob's oldest son. Maybe it was monkey-see, monkey-do, or maybe it was the boy's love for fantasy books and video games, but he started playing with Rob and me. The three of us quested and adventured together. Even after I quit and was eventually followed by Rob's departure from the game, his son kept playing. He was a preteen who hopped on a few nights a week to game—his life seemed pretty much the same in every other respect. One morning, though, Rob had to run back home an hour after he'd left, and there his son was, playing WoW before he left for school, which was entirely against the agreed-upon rules.

He even tried to lie his way out of it at first.

This was when Rob's eyes opened and he knew that WoW was no longer welcome in his house for anyone. I didn't express an opinion, because it didn't seem relevant, but to see this sensible, smart kid get hooked and change his behavior patterns over a game shocked me. For weeks, I couldn't stop thinking about what the game had slowly done to me and what it clearly had the power to do to others.

In his movie *An Inconvenient Truth,* Al Gore explains how people's view of Earth's growing environmental issues is like a frog that jumps into a pot of boiling water. (He uses a smiling cartoon frog in the IMAX-sized PowerPoint presentation behind him to illustrate the point—very effective). That happy-go-lucky frog immediately realizes something is terribly amiss, so it leaps for safety. But if you place the same frog in a pot of lukewarm water and slowly ratchet the heat higher, a few degrees at a time, then a few more, it'll boil to death unless it's rescued. People recognize radical change. Launch an asteroid at Earth, as in *Armageddon,* and we'll send Bruce Willis up to kick asteroid ass and cheer him on. But subtle change is too easy to ignore, adapt to, rationalize, and explain away.

The water in this frog's pot was 200 degrees and rising before I had the impulse to write this book. Yes, it's late. But as Al Gore says, it's never too late to try, whether you're talking about global warming and carbon emissions or one's personal health and sanity.

Or video game addiction, I hope.

❖

In *Fat Girl,* Judith Moore claims, "Ninety percent of fat people who lose weight regain the lost fat within two years. So many fat people seem helpless against fat." I hope there's no parallel between fatness and playing video games, but I suspect there might be, even though Moore's story is not so much about her own overeating as it is her body's refusal to be thin. The www.wowdetox.com site is full of second-, third-, and fourth-time quitters. Even as I'm writing this book, I've considered slipping back—just for a moment—for "investigative purposes." I don't dare. It's like Moore's final cheeseburger, the one she lovingly describes on the sixth page. She doesn't touch another one for the next fifteen years. She doesn't trust herself.

Would you trust me to go back to WoW for just a taste? Just a single, simple kill-this-particular-boss or retrieve-this-missing-bag quest? Or a PvP duel?

I've touched on this earlier, but it's so unfathomable to me that I have to repeat it to myself to try to get my head around it. Had I read Moore's fine book prior to starting my own, I wouldn't have seen myself in her. I'm a very smart person. I'm well-read, I can muddle through a few different languages, and I am terrifically insightful when it comes to working with young people. I read a book and, by flipping through my mental Rolodex, I see patterns and similarities aplenty. I read Jane Smiley's *A Thousand Acres* and instantly see Shakepeare's *King Lear*. I see a performance of Lorraine Hansberry's *A Raisin in the Sun* and I think of *Damn Yankees*, Stephen Vincent Benet's "The Devil and Daniel Webster," and Christopher Marlowe's *Dr. Faustus*. I read James Joyce's short story "Araby" and I'm all over Adam and Eve, the serpent, and the fruit, as well as the quest for the holy grail. I read Todd James Pierce's *A Woman of Stone* and I see Tim O'Brien's *The Things They Carried*.

I've said it before and I'll say it again: I'm completely blind to myself. I cannot stress this point enough. It's like looking into a mirror and seeing nothing there. I am 100 percent ignorant of the connection between my own life and the texts I surround myself with through teaching and in my own recreational reading. For a gifted educator and a lover of books, this is frustrating—like an opera singer who suffers vocal cord damage and when asked to perform for his parents' fiftieth wedding anniversary, simply cannot perform. When it matters most—nothing.

I could've watched Friedrich Schiler's *Die Räuber* and not seen myself in either brother. Johann von Goethe's *The Sufferings of Young Werther*, Joyce Carol Oates's *What I Live For*, Irvine Welsh's *Trainspotting*, Anne Brontë's *The Tenant of Wildfell Hall*, Philip Roth's *Portnoy's Complaint*—all these would've informed my life in only a passing, casual manner unless some smarter person had come along to point out the obvious relationships to my own life.

Here's how clueless I can be. The first time I watched *American Beauty*, I cried and never wondered why. The first time I read *The Catcher in the Rye*, I thought it was a boring story. The first time I read the poetry of Sharon Olds, I thought she was a world-class whiner. I have the capacity to be debilitatingly introspective about certain aspects of myself, but apparently only the unimportant aspects, such as my sometimes gray, sometimes spinach-green, sometimes ice-blue eye color, or my two-dollar silver pinkie ring that I got from a street vendor in Seattle, or my unusual compulsion for eating warty little pickles and smearing mustard on my French fries. Things like emotional stability, sense of self, self-esteem, anger, and mistrust are unworthy of consideration.

Maybe the British clinical psychologist Tanya Byron is onto something in her March 2008 report, in which she claims that letting children (or idiots like me) surf the Internet is not like letting them watch TV, as most parents believe; rather it's much more akin to opening the front door and letting them run outside unattended. Digital space provides anonymity and ubiquity, which young people in particular are drawn to, making the Internet a terribly tempting place to explore and to test limits. Throw the powerful social networks of MMOGs into the mix, and without some kind of guidance or practice, it's a recipe for disaster. One might easily be overmatched.

Byron offers the example of a real-life benefit-danger arena: a public swimming pool. It's a wonderful place during hot weather, and it's relatively safe, too, but dangers still exist. In her report's press release, she states: "Here there are safety signs and information; shallow as well as deep ends; swimming aids and lifeguards; doors, locks, and alarms. However, children will sometimes take risks and jump into waters too deep for them or want to climb walls and get through locked doors—therefore we also teach them how to swim. We must adopt the same combination of approaches in order to enable our children and young people to navigate these exciting digital waters while supporting and empowering them to do so safely."

Sounds a bit like Neil Postman to me.

Byron's example is an analogy I can appreciate. I nearly drowned in the deepness of WoW. It poured into my mouth, my lungs, my heart. From the moment I plunged headlong through the gateway to WoW's land of Azeroth, every breath I took (apologies to Sting and the Police) was no longer air, it was pure WoW. It's as if I woke up one day with gills instead of lungs. When I was in the real world, I sputtered and choked. When I was in WoW, I breathed freely again, openly, with great relish and delight. When I was in WoW, every moment was life, unlike every moment of my real life, which felt like a tiny death.

And so I played.

Endlessly.

RECOVERY

> Why is it drug addicts and computer aficionados are both called users?
>
> —CLIFFORD STOLL

The day after I was on the bridge, I decided I had to quit. Decided is actually too soft a word. It was a biological imperative that thundered through me. To play again at that point in my life would have been to surrender my marriage, my children, my self-esteem, my health, and quite possibly my sanity. My life would surely follow.

I knew the game was too much for me. I knew I couldn't say no anymore. To play WoW again would be to engage in self-mutilation after years of test cuts and trial nicks on my wrists.

This time, the knife was to my neck. I didn't care that I'd just plugged in the numbers for a new sixty-day time card.

I had to shout, "No!"

I flung myself out of bed and splashed cold water on my face. Shifty-eyed and sleepy from being simultaneously exhausted from restless dozing and jazzed at the idea of going to my computer as I'd done for countless mornings, I moved into the office and shut the door quietly behind me. The ancient floorboards squeaked beneath my bare feet.

"Just another day in paradise," I said aloud as I pulled a "My Monkey Made Me Do It" T-shirt off the rolling clothes rack near the desk and tugged it on. I yawned deeply into the crook of my arm as the computer awoke from sleep mode. With its lousy windows and thin walls, the Lenthall House was amazingly inefficient at heating and cooling. I shuddered at the cold as goose bumps prickled my arms. A second huge T-shirt went over my first, and I turned the heat up from seventy to seventy-five degrees before padding back to my swivel chair.

Irritation at not already playing adhered to me like a burr.

Instead of launching the game, I went into Windows XP's "Add or Remove Programs" feature. I did this regularly to erase unnecessary programs in order to free up space and memory so that WoW would run more smoothly. I wiped out a few dumb programs I never used. I ran an anti-malware program, too, staring at the nail holes in the wall as unwanted cookies and tiny stealth programs were gobbled up and spit into the trash can.

When that was done, I didn't start WoW. I stayed on the "Add or Remove Programs" screen, scrolling down, down, down, trying not to think about what I was thinking about.

There it was. The World of Warcraft.

A gorgeous golden W.

I clicked on "Remove."

The heart-lung machine of my life stopped as the universe paused midbreath.

What would happen next? I wondered.

The second the machine started chewing up pieces of WoW and destroying the world I loved so much, I went crazy. My heart clamored away, and I couldn't breathe. I'd stumbled into making a sudden, unambiguous, irrevocable decision. I had leaped through a curtain of constant pain to try to save myself—I was Princess Peach and WoW was my Bowser, or maybe I was Bowser and it was Peach. The distinction grew fuzzier.

Filled with regret, I didn't care about being rescued. "Take me! Take anything!" I wanted to scream. Let the Taurens and the Dragons and the Forsaken have the girl. Tear her up, rip her to shreds. Anything was fine as long as WoW was there, dependable and constant, as always. "Take me! Please!"

I reached for the computer's power-off button. Too late. The game would be hopelessly corrupted already, even if I yanked the cord from the wall. Stopping it wouldn't make a difference.

Agonizing pain exploded behind my eyes.

Nausea erupted in my stomach.

I couldn't stop shaking, and it had nothing to do with the still-cold air in the house.

The next thirty seconds were grueling. I was Al Gore's frog again, only this time I was sliding down the throat of a big snake.

My kids and my wife were in the next room snoring away. Cars growled past my house on 21st Street as they did every day. The big yellow clock that someone had permanently nailed into the wall kept ticking. I gasped in surprise as I breathed deeply and found the temperature of the air inside my lungs to be shockingly frigid.

I refocused on the computer.

The WoW icon was missing.

WoW was dead.

This wasn't like falling off a cliff. Even when I clicked through the program files and menus and the machine assured me it was over, I didn't hit bottom. I flailed like my old Dungeons & Dragons character, Lucky the Rogue, who'd fallen into a bottomless pit after being cursed by a three-headed demon, his companions looking on with shock as he disappeared into the dark maw of nothingness.

My perspective topsy-turvy, my asthma kicking in, and my mind bewildered at what had just happened, I stared at the computer screen. Absolute betrayal registered.

This wasn't having my affairs tightly in hand. This was a marriage of necessity, me yoking my future to a non-WoW existence that I didn't really want and didn't think would last.

I found myself laughing, a ghastly sound.

❖

My wife had given up on me, so I had no support system in place. Rob was still gaming every day. My guildmates were gaming nearly every afternoon without me. Half of the kids in my poetry workshop played WoW regularly. I kept getting spam e-mails about WoW gold from farmers. Everywhere I looked, there was a WoW advertisement in print, on TV, on websites.

It would've been impossible to feel more completely alone.

From seeing enough TV shows about addiction, I knew I was supposed to get professional help at this critical point, since a relapse was entirely possible in the first twenty-four hours. But therapy wasn't going to work. I'd tried it twice when I was at Clemson, two one-visit attempts with two different shrinks. Both times, the therapist just didn't get it. One didn't know a byte from a Big Mac. The other clearly thought I was making it up. It's not their fault entirely—there hasn't been enough proper research done on video gaming for them to know what's what. Collective ignorance is causing a lot of problems.

I sympathize with them, however. How are they supposed to know anything when the experts contradict each other so readily? Here's a sample:

- "Nearly every study suffers from unclear definitions (of violence or aggression), ambiguous measurements (confusing aggressive play with aggressive behavior, or using questionable measures of aggression, such as blasts of noise or self-reports of prior aggression), and overgeneralizations from the data. Experiments that claim to study the effects of playing electronic games rarely study play at all." —Jeffrey Goldstein, Ph.D., University of the Netherlands
- "Studies generally show that violent video games can have short-term or momentary effects on children, but there is little evidence of long-term changes." —Anahad O'Connor, science editor, *New York Times*
- "Kids learn more positive, useful things for their future from their video games than they learn in school!" —Marc Prensky, *Don't Bother Me Mom—I'm Learning!*
- "Your healthy child can, potentially, become an unhealthy child if he or she is allowed to spend more and more time gaming." —Hilarie Cash, Ph.D., and Kim McDaniel, M.A., *Video Games and Your Kids: How Parents Stay in Control*
- "Our children are being fed a dependable daily dose of violence—and it sells. Now, thirty years of studies have shown that this desensitizes our children to violence, and to its consequences . . . Kids steeped in the culture of violence do become desensitized to it and more capable of committing it themselves." —President Bill Clinton, June 1, 1999
- "When I watch children playing video games at home or in the arcades, I am impressed with the energy and enthusiasm they devote to the task. Why can't we get the same devotion to school lessons as people naturally apply to the things that interest them?" —Donald Norman, author and educator

- "In comparison to other forms of media, video games have a great capacity for interactivity that can make them more personalized and engaging and, by extension, potentially more addictive." —Dr. Jack Kuo, Director of Psychiatric Services at Promises Treatment Centers
- "Although there are some indications of a connection between the content of video games and aggressive and addictive behaviors, more research is needed in this area." —American Medical Association

Common sense would suggest that instead of going cold turkey, I should taper down my playing time: ten hours, eight hours, six hours, and so on. But I knew I'd slip up regularly. There was no nicotine patch to offset the cravings that were sure to come.

With any type of addiction, a qualified medical professional's help is a godsend. I wasn't lucky enough at the time to find one qualified enough to help me. My website now points those who need that information in the right direction. It's easier now because therapists are recognizing that they need more information, more training, and more insight into what some are calling the digital epidemic. Unexpected to me, I'm part of this.

I'm giving at least two ninety-minute lectures at behavioral therapist conferences in 2010 alone. I'd like to think that after my talk, the participants will be less likely to make assumptions, such as that all gaming is escapism, that every excessive video game player is an addict, or worse, that video game addiction does not exist. My experiences as an addict, the writing of this book, and the dozens of interviews I've done to understand how to write about this topic have made me an authority on video gaming. Too few people are being open and honest about what has happened, and those who are may often be ridiculed by gamers and nongamers alike. Too many jeers, not enough cheers. Video game addicts need a spokesperson, and with no one else stepping forward, I guess that leaves it up to me. Shame, guilt, remorse, and blame have quieted too many other candidates.

Let me be clear: I don't want to be laughed at. I can't imagine anyone who does. But no one writes a tell-all memoir without the fear of being ridiculed. It simply doesn't work that way. You bare your soul and try to do so in an interesting, useful way so that others might learn from your experiences. You do it because you have to tell your tale so that *you* might learn from your experiences. You do it to start important healing discussions for yourself and others.

In many ways, writing a memoir (or being grilled by therapists at a conference) is the ultimate act of sacrifice. My parents will never understand this. When my first poetry book came out, they read it—perhaps the first poetry book they've ever read in their lives. My father's response was "Your brother thinks you hate him, your mother is angry because of page twelve, and I'm mad because you used our neighbor's name in a poem." Then, in true Van Cleave fashion, we never spoke about it again, letting the disapproval sink deep into the space between us, softening the bonds, loosening the connections, making everything more tenuous and unsure. I'll wager a dollar to a lug nut they never read a single word from my next dozen books.

Say Hello, my first poetry collection, had one or two nuggets of truth in it. This book is a Mount Everest of truth, crushing me daily beneath its bulk. Some days I feel unable to move.

Let me explain what I'm up to with this book in another way. In *Living to Tell the Tale: A Guide to Writing Memoir*, author Jane Taylor McDonnell claims: "Writing is a second chance at life. Although we can never go back in time to change the past, we can re-experience, interpret, and make peace with our past lives. When we write a personal narrative we find new meanings and, at the same time, we discover connections with our former selves. I think all writing constitutes an effort to establish our own meaningfulness, even in the midst of sadness and disappointment. In fact, writing sometimes seems to me to be the only way to give shape to life, to complete the process which is merely begun by living."

McDonnell gets it. Memoirs are about self-definition, and for me, that's something that's been lacking for too long. Thus this book.

And if you've never heard of McDonnell, here's a writer, thanks to Oprah's March 2008 ten-week Internet event, you probably *have* heard of: Eckhart Tolle, author of the *New York Times* bestsellers *The Power of Now* and *A New Earth: Awakening to Your Life's Purpose.* In *A New Earth*, Oprah's sixty-first pick for her book club, Tolle says that many spiritual teachings encourage people to release feelings of fear, desire, and yearning. That, however, doesn't get to the root of the dysfunction. Tolle goes on to explain: "You do not become good by trying to be good, but by finding the goodness that is already within you, and allowing that goodness to emerge. But it can only emerge if something fundamental changes in your state of consciousness."

That's the point of this book. It signals a change in consciousness for me. It's an attempt to rediscover the good within me that's been tucked away, forgotten, for so long that I'd doubted its existence. I've done a lot of lousy things to myself and others. But I can choose to leave that in the past and make my future rich with possibilities.

Some of you might be thinking, "Your problem isn't video game addiction, but rather a problem with self-control. Self-esteem. Poor attitude. Willpower. All this focus on 'former selves' and 'self-definition' and whatnot is a smokescreen to hide what everyone knows. If you're at all worth a damn, you just man up and do it. In this case, stop playing that stupid game."

That kind of thinking comes from people who don't understand addiction or obsession. We're talking about craving here in a way that shakes me to my very core. When I quit playing WoW, I had withdrawal symptoms: cold chills, 102-degree fever, shaky hands, headaches, heart palpitations. My brain couldn't shut off—I often went three days without sleep before collapsing for eighteen hours. I ached to play even after I had been away from the game for weeks. That's how deep of a hold WoW had on me. I was depersonalized. Without WoW, I felt empty, as though I had nothing. Scary stuff.

Imagine my horror at watching the 2009 NBA Finals and seeing that the sponsor was WoW. The logo was splashed everywhere.

I've read most of the studies on the culture of gaming and video games, and what's interesting is that to speak authoritatively about the games, the researchers immersed themselves in WoW or Everquest or Dark Age of Camelot for months, playing and paying close attention to various facets of the immersive digital experience. Many of them confess to feeling the magnetic pull these new worlds have, and many still play—sometimes beyond what might be considered reasonable as a hobby—long after their case study, article, or book has been written.

We're talking about a subversive pleasure here. In Torill Elvira Mortensen's article "Mutual Fantasy Online: Playing with People," she admits, "[Fun] is a difficult aspect of play to study and so far more researchers of games and game culture have focused on the parts of gaming which can be expressed, described, or observed. The gaming experience itself is elusive, and as the interviews show, almost impossible to express." So to understand, to be in the know, you almost have to play. And once you play, the idea of quitting can easily become the impossible task of trying to put the electronic genie back into the bottle.

Go ahead and say it. "It's a video game. A freaking *game*, for God's sake. Just turn off the computer and move on to something else, like re-reading *The Lord of the Rings* series for the millionth time or [gasp] applying for more jobs. Just turn the game off!"

That's a popular response. I've read it hundreds of times in blogs and online responses to articles about video game addiction. I run my own video game addiction blog, and I get that kind of comment fired at me fairly often through its comments feature or through my e-mail. It's the sort of flippant response a teetotaler gives to a lifelong drunk whose eyes are shot red, whose nose is bulbous and deeply veined, and whose gut is heavy from the constant influx of booze and bar pretzels. It's like telling this person to just stop drinking. No one would imagine that this type of comment could have any effect on this poor fool, would they? It's like the ineffective "Just Say No to Drugs!" campaign. We all know it's not that easy, or the schools that preach abstinence wouldn't also pass out condoms.

The other thing I hear a lot about video game addiction is that it's only the symptom of another problem: usually loneliness, depression, self-loathing, a broken sense of self-esteem, or something along those lines. So the real answer, in this view, is not to deal with the video games but to deal with the root cause.

Fine. But that's the same as a drug addict or an alcoholic, in many cases. The reason they got hooked was that they too had issues of loneliness, depression, self-loathing, a broken sense of self-esteem, or whatever. We acknowledge that there are problems at the root of their alcohol and drug abuse, but we correctly label the drinking or the drug abuse as an addiction and deal with it promptly, because it's downright dangerous.

And for video game addicts, our addiction is dangerous, too. Many have died from it already, and thousands upon thousands more lead lives of quiet desperation. Listen to the pain and torment at www.wowdetox.com and in the interviews in Appendices A and B. For every story I included in this book, I interviewed and heard ten others. The sheer magnitude of human sadness I've witnessed haunts me.

❖

What's it like being addicted to video games?

My mind is dangerous, always ready. If I see Neverwinter Nights on a shelf, I immediately start mentally running dungeons and considering the best race-class combo to roll up. If I see Halo 3 at Wal-Mart, I start mentally reviewing maps and weaponry, replaying past battles, and anticipating future ones. Just mention Castle Wolfenstein, and I'll start to salivate like one of Pavlov's dogs upon hearing a bell ring. Say "All your base are belong to us," the great broken-English subtitle from Zero Wing, and I'm there again, my hands slick on the joystick. Just whisper "pwnage" (gamer-speak for "pure ownage") into my ear, and I'm ready again.

I am forever on the prowl for games to devour or let sit languorously upon my lips, savoring it the way a food addict savors thick applewood-smoked slices of bacon crisscrossed atop a huge stack of buttermilk pancakes doused in butter and thoroughly shellacked in Virginia maple syrup.

MMOGs are the worst because of the constant in-game chatter about the game. The most popular topic of discussion in WoW is WoW. We discuss the best class, the best race, the Alliance versus Horde debate. Which classes are most overpowered? Which patch updates are leet versus suck? Which realm has the best PvP action? Which mods are best? Which professions make the most money? What should be nerfed (made less powerful)? What's the best way to crank out gold?

Think of it this way. Take the food addict I imagined above, put him in a room with 100 or 1,000 other food addicts, and let them prattle on endlessly about strawberry marbled cheesecake, peanut butter cookies sprinkled with confectioner's sugar, chicken tortilla soup, and cilantro cream sauce. They'll never leave. Many of them would stay there forever, if they could, dreaming about food, talking about food, comparing experiences with food, living food with every second of their lives. Now imagine that the world they're in is made entirely of chocolate, pineapple, spicy sausage patties, amaretto apricot soufflés, and frosted cinnamon teacakes.

That's what WoW is. A game addict's pleasure palace.

By writing that, I'm thinking a lot about why I played. The flip answer is something like "escape" or "fun," but that's not it. Not really. I think it's more along the lines of Maslow's hierarchy of needs, the pyramid that illustrates the hierarchical importance of elements and influences in a person's life. Near the middle, right above physiological needs and safety needs, are love, belonging, and esteem. Being adopted and having an assortment of emotional and psychological baggage from that and a few other key life moments, I've probably never progressed farther up the pyramid than these areas. Games give me a place in which I do feel as if I belong, and I'm terrified of giving up that lifeline.

There's also the fact that playing WoW gives me a chance to interact regularly with Rob, someone whose friendship I cherish and whom I have neglected from time to time throughout our lives. Ironically, even though the opportunity to talk about important stuff was always there—Rob and I could just use the chat feature to communicate back and forth through the game while playing—we rarely did. We discussed the game, talked about short- and long-term game goals, and planned dungeon raids. We talked about guilds, spells, and strategies. We talked about quests, talent points, and weapon combinations. We rarely spoke about anything that had to do with the nongame world.

The other thing that comes to mind is that I'm a naturally gifted person. I can pick up a tennis racket and play a solid game without ever taking a lesson. I'm pretty killer at badminton, Ping Pong, and bowling, despite no formal training. The first time I hoisted a golf club, I fired an eighty-four. I hadn't touched my trumpet in ten years, but when Rob invited me to play in the stands with his band during a 2007 October home football game, I cranked out double Fs like no one's business, lasering them through the air with gusto.

The problem is that I never get much better, no matter how much time and effort I put into any of these pursuits. I start disproportionately high on the ability level, but I simply do not improve much thereafter. I suffered through eight years of piano lessons with a lumpy German woman old enough to have shaken hands with Hitler (no joke—she had), but I peaked ability-wise around eighteen months into it. I took guitar lessons for six years, but I was arguably about as good after six months as when I stopped. It's like some unseen ceiling that stops me from climbing higher on the mountain of success.

With WoW, though, I was a monster. No matter what the class, the race, or the gear, I tore that game up. Sure, I had my learning curve, but when I really dedicated myself to the game, I mastered it. The game keeps track of your kills—not how many mobs you've wasted, but how many players. All told, I've taken out more than 75,000 players. In arenas, in battlegrounds, or just out in the realms, I've ganked, blasted apart, burned alive, frozen to death, decapitated, strangled, flattened, smashed, mashed, and shredded so many players that in some realms, my toons had a kill-on-sight edict from the opposing factions.

Being that good at something—it didn't matter what it was—gave me a sense of accomplishment that kept the adrenaline flowing and the dopamine coming. It's the elusive buzz that I first knew thanks to Mrs. Monroe, although if it hadn't been with her, I would've found video games on my own, I'm sure. Considering how many other things I've failed at in life, the chance to be great, truly great, at something, was like an ongoing orgasm. There's no clearer way to explain it.

Some people like to say that video game addiction is just another overblown moral panic, like how reading novels featuring women was a kind of "disease" for young women in the early nineteenth-century, how listening to jazz music in the 1920s led to promiscuity, or how reading comic books in the 1940s led to a life of crime. It should be a moral panic. The numbers suggest an epidemic. But my question is—who's paying attention?

❖

Let's get practical. If video game addiction is such a serious and widespread problem, how does one quit?

The best shot at quitting is if the impulse to quit stems from the gamer. I saw that I'd forever lose my wife and my children as well as any sense of self-respect. It suddenly became quite clear to me as we drove back from Chicago after a Christmas visit to see my parents. I was in crisis mode because all I wanted to do was pull over and find a wireless hotspot to log on to WoW—I was sweaty and irritable because I'd have to be WoW-free for a full day and a half while traveling. Days later, I found myself on a bridge, where I had to make the most important choice in my life. It just took another twelve hours for me to act on it.

Like Doris, the concerned parent in Appendix B, you can force the issue with an intervention. But it's clear from her ongoing worry that sometimes an intervention isn't enough.

So what do you do? There are options, but too many to go into deeply enough here. Visit www.unpluggedthebook.com for resources, treatment centers, and ideas for gamers and their friends, families, and coworkers. I'll do what I can to help. We all have to.

❖

Music used to do what video games did for me. I had long hair and played in a lot of rock bands in high school. At one point, I was certain I'd spend the rest of my life trying to be a rock star. Somewhere along the line—I think it was after my first semester of college—playing music started to feel like work. Whatever joy it once brought me vanished when I was practicing eight hours straight each day. I had tough calluses, but they couldn't hold up to that kind of torture, so my fingers bled all the time. I used to take music breaks to let the skin heal, and that's when I'd play video games. One Friday I put down my guitar for a video game break that lasted for more than a decade.

It's only recently that I've started to play guitar again. It's been, what, nearly twenty years? I have a new appreciation for making music now. Playing guitar helps me through the worst of my video game urges. For others, what helps is lifting weights, dancing, or whatever. For me, playing along to a whole U2 or Metallica album often does the trick. Playing Go Fish with my kids or helping them draw with crayons also makes a difference. I'm also writing again fairly regularly.

Helping a video game addict redirect his or her energies toward a different, more positive activity is one of many ways to help the person get unplugged. Some other options are the following:

- Keep a diary (or write your own memoir).
- Call a long-lost friend and get back in touch.
- Fix a household item that's been broken for a while.
- Rollerblade, bicycle, or hike.
- Organize a block party.
- Take salsa dance lessons.
- Go camping.
- Teach yourself to play a musical instrument.

- Restart an old hobby (coin collecting, painting, fishing).
- Buy a recipe book and try a new recipe every day for a month.
- Reread your favorite books (or read some new ones).
- Make a funny YouTube video.
- Take a class (any class) at a community college.
- Have a movie marathon (I recommend all the Star Wars movies, the Indiana Jones series, or the Godfather trilogy).

The only thing I'd mention here in terms of redirection is to not pick up a new addiction that merely replaces an old one. It's not uncommon for someone trying to quit smoking to pile on thirty pounds from constant snacking. Try to vary your activities—aim for balance in every aspect of your life.

❖

The morning I quit gaming, I wandered through the house like a zombie. Noises from downstairs drew me. My wife had eggs and sausage sizzling in a cast-iron skillet as the kids played with plastic trucks in front of the TV. Resigned to what I'd done, I decided I'd at least get some well-deserved credit for nuking the game. I moved into the kitchen.

"It's done."

"What is?"

"Warcraft. I deleted it."

She poked at the egg yolks with a fork and didn't look up at me. The yellow oozed into the spattering grease. "So what?"

"What do you mean, 'So what?' I deleted it. It's gone."

She let out a long, drawn-out sigh. "I don't believe you."

This got me angry. Injustice didn't sit well with me, and I'd just done the most heroic act in my life here—more heroic than helping the unconscious girl at NIU or bringing some of those sad, sad kids at Clemson to the psychological help they desperately required. Prior to speaking with my wife, I felt like Hercules who had just completed a thirteenth labor: killing the deadly WoW monster.

Part of what drew me to WoW was that I felt underappreciated and undervalued in real life. Here it was again. No credit for a creditworthy act. I wasn't going to ding a level, get experience points, or have a good loot drop.

It took effort not to shriek.

"I deleted it. It's gone," I repeated. "It's not part of my life anymore."

She put down the fork and stared at me. "Isn't it on the Internet versus on your machine? Couldn't you just connect via your laptop or another computer and still get to all your guys and stuff?"

Time zagged sideways. The low-lows I'd thought were gone lovingly purred at my feet like a cat moving stealthily through my legs. Static electricity sent the hairs on my neck straight up.

Of course she's right, I realized. *Of course.*

Twelve

GETTING UNPLUGGED

Just cause you got the monkey off your back
doesn't mean the circus has left town.

—GEORGE CARLIN

January 1, 2008. I called Blizzard Entertainment's billing department and spoke with a very nice-sounding young woman named Sheila. Fortified by my wife's dead-on observation that the game would always be there lurking on the Internet, siren-calling to me, my characters yearning to be dusted off and played with again, I made my request.

Me: I'd like to delete my Warcraft accounts.

Sheila: I can help you cancel a subscription, but I can't do anything about deleting an account.

Me: I need them deleted. I'm talking kill them. I want my

characters completely, a hundred percent gone. I want it all unrecoverable.

Sheila: It's our policy not to delete any accounts. That way, a person can rejoin us at any point down the road. People tell us all the time that they are a hundred percent sure, but then later, they come back. So we don't delete accounts.

Me: I'm certain I won't be playing WoW any longer.

Sheila: It's our policy not to—

Me: I have an addiction and can't stop. If I play anymore, I'm not at all sure I'll ever be able to stop. I have a problem. If you help me now by deleting all my seventies, the epic gear, the gold, all the accounts, everything, I won't start up again because it'd take me forever to get that far in the game again.

Sheila: I can recommend, then, that you consider deleting the game from your machine.

Me: That's not a good plan. I can just buy new discs for twenty bucks or download it again at www.blizzard.com.

Sheila: You're welcome to change the password on the account or assign parental control restrictions—

Me: But if I'm the one changing those features, I can change them back at any time.

Sheila: I'm happy to do what I can to help you with your concerns.

Me: I'm concerned I'll die if I play any more! *That's* what I'm concerned with. I want your damn game out of my life. I want my life back.

Sheila: Sir, it's our policy not to try to police people's playtime or accounts in that way. It's up to the players or their parents.

I slammed the phone down, her words echoing as though they

came from a long, dark hallway. I tried. I really tried to kill the monster that was WoW. I tried to lop off its electronic head once and for all with a phone call I never thought I'd have the strength to make.

Sheila mentioned parental controls. It's an acknowledgment that young people need help, or this game might take over. If there were no danger, you wouldn't need parental controls, right? But the average game player is thirty-five years old and has been playing games for thirteen years. The average age of the most frequent game purchaser is forty. And in 2008, 26 percent of Americans over the age of fifty played video games—an increase from 9 percent in 1999.

Who's policing the parent gamers?

In the introduction to Dave Grossman and Gloria DeGaetano's *Stop Teaching Our Kids to Kill: A Call to Action against TV, Movie, and Video Game Violence*, President Bill Clinton wrote, "I have strongly urged people in the entertainment industry to consider the consequences of what they create and how they advertise it. One can value the First Amendment right to free speech and at the same time care for and act with restraint."

President Barack Obama agrees that video games are a health concern. In a speech to the American Medical Association, he claimed that they are a factor in our current unhealthy lifestyle. But in light of AIDS, the H1N1 flu strain, the nuclear threat in Iran and North Korea, global warming, world hunger, and the sluggish U.S. economy, can you blame people for focusing on other, more immediate dangers than the slow-fuse destruction caused by video games, which are supposed to be fun and provide an escape from our problems?

China and South Korea claim that video game addiction is their most urgent public health problem. What are they privy to that we Americans are not? Is it that so much gaming in Asia takes place in public Internet cafés whereas in the United States we do it privately at home? Is it because we think video games are too cool to be a problem?

One thing is sure, says Eric Gingrich, a Ringling College of Art and Design professor I drank coffee with in Sarasota one breezy October morning. "The industry [people] will never do anything to regulate themselves. The only reason they did anything back when the games were causing seizures was because they got sued. Short of more huge lawsuits against the video game companies, I can't see any change ahead."

This from a man who's been making video games full-time for more than a decade.

❖

I'm not healed.

Every time I pass a World of Warcraft game in a store, I buy a single copy. This used to be because I could resell it overseas to gold farmers for nice pocket money and cover the cost of my own gaming. But then I started keeping a few around, even after that money-making scheme went belly-up and I quit playing WoW. Then it was more, and even more. I've got shipping boxes full of unopened games right now. At $20 a crack, there's probably $1,000 worth just sitting around upstairs—the world's most expensive doorstop. With the U.S. economy in the crapper and my unemployment money long gone, I should be stockpiling cash and cutting back on expenses, but just yesterday I walked through the electronics section of Target and saw the Burning Crusade on the top-seller display rack.

I slapped down my Discover card.

Buying another copy of the game is like a tiny way to hang on to the whirlwind of profound completeness I feel when I immerse myself in WoW. Buying these games is like standing a bit too far on the edge of a cliff just to feel a rush. Buying them is a crutch, I realize, but it's a much more acceptable option than playing again, which I cannot afford on any level.

In many ways, I am still WoW's slave, but at least I no longer log on. And that's saying a lot.

❖

"People assume that, if anything, online activities emanate from offline lives," claims an April 2008 article on Jeremy N. Bailenson, the director of Stanford University's Virtual Human Interaction Lab. "But Mr. Bailenson and his colleagues have shown the reverse. Their experiments demonstrate, for instance, that people who watch their avatars—cartoonlike versions of themselves—gain weight from overeating are more likely to adopt a weight-loss plan in real life."

Perhaps Neil Postman has poisoned me with technophobia, but this strikes me as sinister beyond belief, even without the explanation of how in some MMOGs, players are specifically marketed to after their interactions online are catalogued and recorded. "Our virtual identity is not separate from our physical identity," says Bailenson. This means that if we have our avatar do something, it's likely to be similar to what we'd do in real life. And it suggests that our virtual identity is as much a part of us as our shadow or the little voice in our head. Inseparable.

What does this mean for WoW players, who regularly spit on their foes, scream insults at their teammates, steal from their comrades, and kill lowbies (low-level players) who pose absolutely no threat? What does this mean for me when I've killed more than 75,000 player characters?

Not to get too philosophical, but simply: What does WoW mean? And what does it mean that WoW means anything to me?

In a May 16, 2008 article on www.slate.com entitled "Solitaire-y Confinement: Why We Can't Stop Playing a Computerized Card Game," Josh Levin claims, "We mock solitaire because it is our secret shame." He suggests that despite its simple nature, it's "the cockroach of gaming. You can occupy yourself with an easy variant or one that's almost impossible to win, stare at the screen for five minutes or five hours, and play with an eye toward strategy or with your brain turned off."

He's still talking about solitaire and not WoW, right?

❖

The decision to remain off WoW for good comes down to me alone, which is exactly the worst thing. If I had serious mental fortitude, I'd have axed the addictions on my own in previous decades. I needed help, and it didn't come from compulsively buying up copies of WoW, being screamed at by my wife, speaking with shrinks who still typed patient notes on IBM Selectrics, or playing WoW until I got finally sick of it.

It came thanks to George Lucas, via Yoda's Zen-like wisdom: "Do or do not . . . there is no try." That stupid little green puppet is right. There is no *try*. All that's left is *do*.

Perhaps I should've subtitled this book (with apologies to Robert Fulghum) "All I Really Need to Know I Learned from Star Wars." Big shocker that it was Yoda, too, who wisely intoned, "Named must your fear be before banish it you can."

I am afraid of heights. I am afraid of falling from heights. I am afraid of very large crowds. I am afraid of snakes. I am afraid of the ocean. I am afraid of failing as a teacher, a writer, a husband, a father, a lover. I am afraid of love. I am afraid of being loved. I am afraid of writing this book. I am afraid of not writing this book. I am afraid that this book is about being unloved. I am afraid that my family will never speak to me again after reading this book. I am afraid that Rob will realize what a horrible friend I've been to him. I am afraid of writing a book in which I don't know what the book is really about. I am afraid that I will always be afraid.

But what I am most afraid of is how desperately I still want to play the World of Warcraft. Every day. Even now. And now.

And now.

And even more now.

❖

Eckhart Tolle claims that if we can get past the default dysfunction—the number one big problem—of our lives, we can achieve something great: salvation, enlightenment, the end of suffering, awakening, liberation. Whatever religion you subscribe to has a name for this state of being (Tolle would call it "new consciousness"). We're talking about breaking free here, the act of dropping a lifetime of baggage (physical, spiritual, emotional—all of it) in order to finally move forward.

My default dysfunction is a compulsion to play video games no matter what the cost.

I'm not a rare case. This level of addiction—this type of self-destructive avenue—is available to everyone. We go on living our lives just as we've done before, and the same crappy results we've been getting are usually the same crappy results we'll get tomorrow, and the tomorrow beyond that. And we're almost surprised by it. We howl for change, but we don't know how to go about creating it. So we stay stuck in a rut, disempowered, frustrated, and desperate.

That's why I'm sharing my story. It's part of how I'm shifting from living my present and my future out of the past, and it's part of how I'm recommitting to living an extraordinary life with meaning and purpose. Sounds pretty woo-woo, I realize, but most of the people I've known throughout my life are mired in their own set of dysfunctions. Now that I witness the worst of mine laid out before me like a long row of charred bricks, I can't make the same choices anymore. That way lies hell.

For my wife, my children, my career, and my own sanity, I have to make better choices.

For the first time in my life, I see the paths before me as exactly that: paths. I have choices that I was unable to perceive before—multiple options, choices, opportunities.

I can choose the path I'm going to take. And so with this book I pick a less attractive but better path, as did the speaker in Robert Frost's lovely poem that I've taught for years and only now, today, understand not in an intellectual way but in a purely emotional (Tolle would say "spiritual") one.

> Two roads diverged in a wood, and I—
> I took the one less traveled by,
> And that has made all the difference.

Appendix A

THREE TRUE STORIES

You know what's really exciting about video games is you don't just interact with the game physically—you're not just moving your hand on a joystick, but you're asked to interact with the game psychologically and emotionally as well. You're not just watching the characters on screen; you're becoming those characters.

—NINA HUNTEMANN, SUFFOLK UNIVERSITY

We hear constantly about cyberspace as a place of connections made between all kinds of people who would not have come together before. Perhaps. But every one of them

> has connected by being alone, in front of
> a computer screen, and this is a poor excuse
> for what community has
> meant for most of history.
>
> —PAUL GOLDBERGER, *NEW YORK TIMES*

As I was finishing the first draft of this book, Rob gave me this advice: "You're going to want to have other people's stories in the book, too. This is a big problem. It's not just about one person." And he's right.

My worry was how I'd react to seeing other people living lives of pure delusion and pain the way I once did (and oh so often think nostalgically back to). Part of my addiction to gaming is being too weak to say "No!" to the majestic, beguiling worlds they create. Was including other people's stories in this book a horrible idea? Would it ruin the clean break I'd made from my dependency on the digital world?

I decided that it would serve as a test for me. There's no escaping video games, social networking, text messaging, e-mail, and computers. Until new technologies do away with them, they're here to stay. I had to know if I could resist even when I was staring them down in the worst of conditions, because living in the twenty-first century felt like the worst of conditions.

I had to, once again, peer deeply into the abyss.

I put a call for "The #1 Video Gamer in America" on my blog, my website, and on other message boards. I thought maybe I'd get a few dozen gamers to respond. In three weeks, I had more than 300 candidates who all proudly sent me screen shots, playing logs, high scores, and other evidence of their possible status as the number one video gamer in America. Forget the $100 I'd offered to the top few for using their story in my book—they were out for fame and notoriety along the lines of what "Little Gray," the unofficial world's top World of Warcraft player, got when Yahoo! did a December 2009 feature on him. He'd completed nearly 6,000 game quests and killed 500,000 enemies with his Tauren Druid. Some of the gamers contacting me boasted of two or more years of real-life game time played on the World of Warcraft alone. Others bragged of being an expert in more than 300 different games.

I was stunned by the volume and the sheer enthusiasm of the response. Determined to get a better sense of the range of addiction that exists, I said good-bye to my wife and my kids in October 2009 and headed for north Florida to meet the first significant candidate, whom I'll call Daniel; he originally wanted me to use his full name but then changed his mind once he learned that this book wasn't casting gaming in the most positive light. A few other factors might've played into that decision as well.

❖

The fifty-five-gallon fish tank is empty because the black butterfly koi (Samson, Suzi, and Mathias) got to be too much trouble. Socks litter the floor like two score of crumpled once-white worms. The room—once a guest room of this two-bedroom starter home in north Florida—has the pungent odor of burned toast, coffee, and *eau de locker room*. This is where Daniel spends eight to ten hours a day gaming.

"It's not that much time, really," he quickly adds, pointing out that one of the three laptops on the old closet door laid over cinderblocks behind his big desktop computer is for his e-commerce site for natural hair-care products. "I mean, c'mon, I spend a good hour or two per day handling business."

What he means is that he glances at the more-or-less automated system he's set up, then returns quickly to one of the many screens before him to plunge back into whatever world du jour has captured his attention. For January through May, it was the World of Warcraft. Then he spent three weeks on Sacred II. These days, it's the little game applications on social networking sites like Facebook. He has four or more different ones going at once: Mafia Wars, Organized Crime, the Legend of Spirehold, Sorority Girls, Farmville, and two other kingdom-building simulations—and when he burns through all the energy or stamina on his character in one of the games, he switches to the next. By the time he's done with the last game, the first game's ready to go again, his character recharged and ready for action.

"It's tough to get down the timing," he says, one hand on the mouse, the other cracking open another Diet Mountain Dew.

He has the timing down. Without removing his eyes from the screen or his hand from the keyboard and the mouse, he keeps up a semilively conversation. Daniel is thirtysomething, but his cherubic face suggests he couldn't grow facial hair even if he tried. He looks like a bank teller, or maybe one of those overcologned guys hawking cell phone gadgetry at shopping mall kiosks to hip teenagers.

"Damn it!" he says suddenly, then enlarges one of the games full-screen. A few clicks later, the intruder to his medieval castle is toast—blasted by lightning from a pair of wizards that Daniel commands to attack. He has them rain fire on the corpse of the would-be assassin for good measure, the bright-red pyrotechnics giving his face a ruddy glow.

I repeat a question I had already asked. "What was the first video game you ever played?"

He claims that he doesn't remember. Beyond "I don't know," he doesn't have much to say about high school, his two and a quarter years at the University of Florida, his parents' recent divorce, swine flu, or Barack Obama, either. The more time I spend with Daniel, the less sure I am that he's as high functioning as he repeatedly tells me he is. His e-mail response to my initial call for the number-one video gamer in America and WoW junkies was this:

> Hey, i'm no junky, but i do play Warcraft a good bit. Maybe u could talk to me to show how someone can play games and still kick ass. If you wanna talk to someone all fucked up, I know people like that too.

It takes all afternoon, but I finally get him to crack open the door to his past. He has two older sisters. One got contacts at fifteen, the other at twelve. Daniel got them at age ten. Psychologist Michael Osit calls this phenomenon "modeling down." If you keep giving more and more things to younger and younger kids, where does it go? In his book *Generation Text*, Osit jokes: "I can just imagine toddlers programming their speed-dial numbers into their big, shiny cell phones, calling each other to complain about how their parents don't understand them!"

It didn't stop with contact lenses. Daniel got his own computer at age ten, a Vespa scooter at fifteen, and a "nearly new" Jeep Wrangler at seventeen. Each of his computers has a twenty-four-inch LCD screen attached to it and is juiced with heavy-duty RAM and pro level graphics cards. He's got $10,000 in those computers, and that's not even considering the huge Bose system he's got it all wired into, which (when it isn't blaring the sweeping Wagner-inspired operatic background music of Warcraft or the eerily catchy melodies of Wrath of the Lich King) pumps out old-school Anthrax or Slayer loud enough to rattle the fillings of anyone sitting inside a car out in the street three houses down.

A real problem with modeling is that when these overpriviledged kids grow up, the real world often can't keep pace with delivering what they think they deserve. It leads to anger, frustration, and disappointment.

Worse, so much of the electronic world is predicated on immediate gratification that is furthered by instant messaging, instant texting, and high-speed in-game upgrades "that take fucking forever," bemoans Daniel, while waiting for his Hungry Man meat loaf dinner to finish nuking in the microwave. The expression on his face while he snaps off a text to his sister (who also plays Warcraft, he later admitted, but the middle child in their family does not and "thinks it's lame") reminds me of a hungry Homer Simpson, who, upon hearing that his food would be ready in eight seconds, whined, "Isn't there anything faster than a microwave?"

Daniel's dad became a victim of the recent U.S. economic mayhem, getting laid off from his $120,000-a-year job as a financial consultant. Daniel used to have a Visa card that his dad always paid off, which helped, since Daniel's been underemployed for a decade. He grimaces and reluctantly admits that he hasn't really looked at the bill lately. I do. It's there on floor by the ripped-open box of Wii Sports Resort. It's for $11,000 and change. I'm tempted to ask how well his hair-care business is doing, but I decide not to.

Daniel is answering questions, but he grinds his teeth the entire afternoon in a way that makes me nervous. He looks ready to take a bite out of someone, and I don't want that kind of trouble. For now, his intense attention is focused on an Undead Rogue in Warcraft (Daniel has it running nonstop on one laptop and swivels his chair "to get some WoW on" every twenty minutes or so).

Watching WoW at Daniel's was difficult for me. It was my particular brand of electronic heroin, and I still have vivid WoW dreams, even after not touching it since January 1, 2008—two full years. At one point that day,

I found myself trembling so violently that my teeth chattered. Each exhalation sent me into stutters. That's the type of grip WoW still has on me.

As I watch Daniel expertly maneuver his character and smack the enemy, my heart is booming as if it's ready to burst from my chest. I let out my breath in a rush. I start to reach for the mouse to have the character bow—my own personal victory move. With great effort, I move back from the computer and just let Daniel be Daniel.

Close, I tell myself, still wanting to knock Daniel aside and log on to my own account, which I know is still there, waiting. I've repeatedly heard that the company never deletes an account, even after years of disuse. It seems a waste of hard-drive space somewhere, despite Blizzard's customer service rep, Sheila, assuring me it's not.

Daniel turns to me, scratches at his left ear, then asks, "What were you saying?"

My wife used to tell me that I would growl at her while I was playing if she dared to ask me anything. It's hard not to wonder if this is what she meant. I thought about the months of real-life time that I'd spent on a game at the expense of my friends and my family, and that realization—one I'd had many times before—sat heavy, like a load of cement, in my stomach. *This couldn't have been me*, I told myself, knowing that it was a lie.

The truth bit deep. *I was worse.*

My answer: "Nothing."

During the six hours I spent with Daniel, he had a video game going the entire time. Considering that he had multiple games on at once, I'd guess that he logged close to twenty hours' worth of game play while I watched, my mind struggling to soak it all in. He wasn't some pimply high school kid with anger issues. He had nice clothes (admittedly, crumpled on the floor of his closet). He was relatively handsome—the pictures of his high school prom and some framed snapshots of him at EuroDisney, a ski lodge, and a Key West beach all showed him beaming. He was also articulate (at times) and clearly smarter than many.

But he mumbled his way through every exchange, he didn't seem to notice that I didn't bring lunch (and he didn't offer me any), and he pretty clearly wasn't handling his finances well. Contrary to what he said, I never once saw him actually tap a single key on the laptop he insisted was fully dedicated to handling his online business. I've since Googled the name of the company and can't find anything on it. I'm not sure what that means.

Daniel shook my hand when I announced it was time to leave. The Florida heat was still coming off the blacktop in rubbery waves as we stood on his porch among the stacked-up green resin furniture that had layers of pollen caking it. I wiped at the sweat that suddenly beaded my forehead.

We were nearly the same age, Daniel and I. At one point, I remember thinking I'd love to be living alone again, the way I did as an undergrad and as a grad student, when I could get up at 2:00 AM and game until dawn in the crappy, dark studio apartment my father paid for. That kind of loose sense of responsibility still tempted me, but one look at the dark bags under Daniel's eyes and the nervous tic he had of grimacing assured me that my current trajectory away from video games was for the best. If Daniel were to show up at a face-to-face job interview, I can only imagine the catastrophe that would follow. Whatever social awkwardness he'd surely had as a kid had grown exponentially, to the point that my six hours with him had him on edge enough for the name "Dylan Klebold" to come to my mind.

The journalist in me refused to leave without a final question. I said, "I meant to ask. Do you own this place or rent?"

He grinned, saying, "My grandma used to live here. She died in the porch swing right over there." He pointed to the thick eyehooks in the ceiling from which dangled no chain or porch swing.

A few weeks later, I got this e-mail:

> Hey. book thing gonna happen? or what? My gf moved in and she says u should come back and talk to us both.

I assumed the girlfriend was new, since he hadn't mentioned her during my entire visit. The idea of spending more time at Daniel's place again didn't hold enough appeal to merit the drive, but perhaps he had a point. I'd like to see how a boyfriend-girlfriend combo could lead the gamer lifestyle together. I e-mailed him back, saying, "Sure. I'm happy to come. The book is indeed on and I'm happy to speak with both you and your girlfriend."

No response for two weeks, then this:

> Here but busy. maybe we can talk agin another time. or something.

And then his e-mail account shut down and the cell phone number got disconnected. I kept thinking about that $11,000 credit card bill, which apparently caught up with him. My mind kept saying his father probably bailed him out, but on some level I know that's not likely.

I hope Daniel's okay, regardless. I know his story too well, because I regularly talk to kids in college and twentysomethings who are out of control. For many of them, hitting rock-bottom means financial ruin, unemployment, depression, and sometimes complete alienation from family and friends. I've met two dozen Daniels in 2009 alone.

In the face of such evidence to the contrary, I still desperately hope that all the Daniels get better. I hope their lives leap back on the track and stay there this time.

❖

When I read about Josh Schweitzer's story in the September 9, 2009, issue of the *Los Angeles Times*, I knew I had to speak with him. A twenty-seven-year-old construction manager with a four-year-old son, Josh had recently gotten divorced. What got him through it? According to him, it was the World of Warcraft. "The only people I had to talk to about it [the divorce] were guild people," he told the *Times*. "All of my friends are in Dread Pirates. I don't really have any others."

We spoke on the phone in October 2009 after I tracked him down through Ben Fritz of the *Times*. I decided to include this interview rather than half a dozen others because Josh is the rare person who found balance in his life—of family, friends, work, health, and gaming. For someone like me, who aimed again and again at an elusive bull's-eye but never found the mark, this was a memorable conversation that gave me hope. I needed it, because despite being WoW-free for twenty-four months, I was still struggling without the game in my life.

Q. ***How did the L.A. Times article come about?***

A. This last year, a guild member published something anonymously on the Warcraft forums for our particular server saying, "Hey, if anyone's going to Blizzcon, let's make a list here so we can meet." He put up the list of Dread Pirates—twenty-four people—and Ben Fritz from the *L.A. Times* had planned on going to Blizzcon to write an article about it. Ben came across that post and thought that was a lot of people from one guild, so he got ahold of us to ask if he could shift the whole focus of the article toward us.

We kept it really quiet. We didn't want to let a lot of people on the server know about it, which could create some haters and cause drama. While at the conference, Ben started asking me questions about my life and why I played, and I just opened up. So the article shifted again. I didn't expect to steal the show from the guild, but that's what happened.

Q. *Has anything changed for you since that article came out?*

A. I let everyone know. I put the link to the *L.A. Times* on my MySpace page. I thought it was really cool. I even went on WoW Insider and they had a whole discussion about it, so I got involved in that. Ben also got on that to answer questions.

A lot of gamers were upset about the article. They didn't understand that Ben was writing the piece for people who don't play Warcraft or MMOs. A lot of the snootier game players wanted more facts and real terms put in.

The article happened to have my character's name in it, along with the server I played on, so a lot of people started saying, "Oh, you're the hard-core nerd from the *Times*," and I started getting in-game hate mail. I'm sure that anytime something like that gets posted that people are going to do that, but it got pretty bad. I changed my character name and started playing on a new server.

Q. *So you're not part of the Dread Pirates anymore?*

A. No, I'm not, but it was for a reason. Before the article came out, it was in the works. The article actually mentioned how I asked the leader about raiding at an earlier time with some of my friends, and he shot that down. I had been raiding with them for the last two years, from basically eight until midnight Pacific Time. I'd get up at five-thirty or six every day to work forty hours a weeks. Now my son's five, and I have to take him to school and take care of other responsibilities, and I had to stop raiding after not missing a raid in two years. I had to start taking more care of him because of his age—he just required more time. Plus I wasn't getting enough sleep. I was getting physically sick. Running on five hours a night of sleep is just not healthy.

I got in touch with some old friends of mine who played on a different server in Eastern Time, and now I stop raiding an hour before I used to start raiding with the Dread Pirates. When the article came out and I started getting all that hate and heckling, it was time for me to take my characters and leave. I'm leading things now with a successful guild on another server but at a lot earlier time.

I'm still in contact with the Dread Pirates and everybody there. I join them on Ventrilo every week. I even bought plane tickets two days ago to fly out to Arizona to see a couple of them and go to a Halloween party.

Q. *What about your video game playing in the past? Was Warcraft the first game you ever played?*

A. I've been playing video games in general my whole life—Nintendo, Sega Genesis, whatever. But the first role-playing game I ever played was Final Fantasy VII for PS2. I was so locked in and enthralled with the way the game was. I remember thinking that it'd be so cool if all these people I was playing this game with were actually *real* people. I didn't realize that that was already happening with games like Ultima Online. In talking to my friends about how great this game was, I found out about Everquest. It came out in 1999 and was the first MMOG that really got attention. I played it for a good five years before the World of Warcraft took all the player base and left Everquest in the dust. That's when I transferred to Warcraft.

Q. *It seems like you've managed to negotiate a successful life despite playing video games. You're able to hold down a good job, be a good father, and still find time to enjoy gaming.*

A. I was playing games well before I met my ex-wife. I didn't have a kid back then. When we got married, we both worked, and I knew that gaming could never overtake my family life, and I never let that happen. But things change and people's hearts change. She was younger than me, four and a half years younger. She was eighteen years old and I'd been with her since she was fifteen. She never really did that whole rite of passage dating thing that I did. I'm not making excuses for her, but that's what happened.

At the time I was working for Mercedes-Benz selling new Mercedeses, so we had a sixty-thousand-dollar car, but we didn't have that kind of money. But she wanted to pretend she did, and she thought we were better than what we were, and she went out partying every week, every night, all the time and just didn't want to come home anymore. This went on for about a year, and the only way I could deal with it was through the game because the only friends I had were online. I just started talking to them and telling them that this is what my wife is doing. "I have a one-year-old son and she just leaves us here. Sometimes I don't see her for days." They gave me their advice and their opinions, and they were my only outlet for this really bad thing. They're great friends. If didn't have them, I don't know who I would've talked to or what I would've done.

When things turned the way they did, they were right there for me the whole time. They knew my entire story. I was playing WoW and raiding and talking to them. It was an outlet for me instead of me turning to other things like drinking or drugs or depression. WoW counteracted all that. It was a way for me to get lost in something else besides something negative.

Q. *Do you envision a time down the road when you won't play anymore?*

A. I think about that often. I don't know when that would be. I've met a lot of people who play currently who are there every day—I'm only playing about three days a week. I log on on Tuesdays, Wednesdays, and Thursdays, and sometimes on the weekends. When I don't have my son, I'll play, though a lot of those weekends I'm doing other things, like racing cars.

Q. *How many hours a week are you playing WoW?*

A. About twenty hours a week. I'm playing from three-thirty to eight on those three weekdays, and I do log in on the weekends. I have responsibilities I have to take care of.

Everyone in my guild has my phone number. They call me if there's a problem. This is the second guild I've run, and people look up to me, and we trust each other enough to share phone numbers. I don't have to be online sixty hours a week to be part of things.

Q. *How big is your new guild?*

A. We've probably got sixty-five right now. About twenty-seven are dedicated players who go raiding every Tuesday, Wednesday, and Thursday, and the rest are alts or casual players or are just there for occasional PvP.

Q. *If you were to walk away from WoW today, what's the one thing you'd miss most?*

A. The people, the friends. I think that the single most important thing [is] the relationships that can't be replaced in what you would call the real world. These people know me, they know who I am, they hear my voice every day, and I talk to them, and I'm part of their lives. I've loaned several people money to help pay a bill or cover their rent. Being single now, I've got a little bit of money. I like to help people more than just giving a fistful of gold in the game, especially for those who help me on a daily basis. When I'm at work, there are people who are online doing the things that need to be done to make the guild successful. So if they tell me their heat is going to get shut off, I can give them a credit card number—it's the least I can do.

Q. ***What's your son think about WoW? At five, he's old enough to probably have an opinion of it.***

A. He knows all about it. He used to want to play it really bad, so I would set the controls and let him click the mouse to move the character. I used to let him play Diablo, where all you have to do is click on things and you run up to them and kill them. So I set WoW up for him to play awhile like that, but my conscience got the better of me and I didn't allow him to play it anymore. It was a struggle for maybe a month or two, but he doesn't ask anymore. He plays Xbox now, and he loves that.

A lot of people have negative thoughts about kids and video games, but my son is one of the smartest in his class by far because of them. He has good hand-eye coordination, and his articulation of words is great. It's things like that which kids who don't play video games don't have. It's all within the parents' responsibility to not let it take control.

Q. ***What if it's the parents who have the problem with video games? These things aren't just for kids anymore.***

A. It's getting close to ten years that I've been playing online games, and I've seen some terrible things. I know two people who have committed suicide because of the game. I was there watching TV when a story broke about an online player killing himself—this was about seven years ago—and I knew the guy.

I know some mothers who got their kids playing so they [would have] someone to play with. They don't come out and say it, but I've known people who had kids and then lost custody because of games. On Ventrilo, I've heard kids yelling and screaming in the background, asking for dinner or something, and they're told to wait until the end of an instance or sometimes just to shut up. The gamers don't log off to go help their kids. There's nothing I can really do about that. People would get very defensive about their children if I brought anything up. It would just create conflict and wouldn't help the situation any. And I don't know what their situation is, a lot of times.

A lot of people in my guild—especially all the people from Dread Pirates who I know in real life, and I've met at least twenty-five of them, all of whom I never would have met had I not played the game—are decent, hard-working people.

Q. ***What's your current job?***

A. I'm a foreman for my father's construction company.

Q. ***That's why you have the schedule that allows you to play at three-thirty?***

A. Exactly. I've pretty much always had a similar schedule, except when I was selling cars for a couple of years there when my dad was doing something else and I needed a job. That nine-to-five schedule made it pretty hard to play games.

Q. *What do your parents think about all of this?*

A. My dad? He thinks it's great. I tell him stuff that happened in the game all the time. He doesn't have any desire to play or anything. My mom? She's indifferent. My dad's got no reason to complain because I take care of everything at work for him. He only has to come into work maybe once a week, and that's just to check on things. I've never given him any reason to doubt me. At first he thought it was weird—he didn't understand it. He gets excited for me now and asks, "When's the next Blizzcon?" And [my] making the *L.A. Times*, he was excited about that for me, too.

Q. ***It's clear that you've managed to make gaming an important part of an active, full life. I wish there were a way for others to duplicate what you've done.***

A. Honestly, I know that I'm in the very small minority. It's obvious, especially when you go to the conventions and speak with the people there. Nobody's really talking about this huge, overwhelming purple elephant in the room. Video game addiction isn't just about our nation . . . it concerns the world. More and more people are turning to things like the World of Warcraft or Aion or MySpace or Facebook. Some people say that these things are worse than being addicted to drugs.

Q. *Why is that?*

A. I'm not really certain, because that was my argument when my grandparents and my parents hated it when I was really playing back in the day. I used to get a lot of hate, a lot of flak. "You need to get off that game!" they'd scream.

Why's it so bad? I don't understand it. I stayed home. I didn't

> drink. I wasn't doing drugs. I could be out partying it up like everybody else or I could dump my kid off so my parents could babysit him so I could go out all the time like some other parents. But no, I'm able to take care of my son and do these other things. That's what matters.

❖

A gamer friend who knew us both put me in contact with "Hope." She laughed on the phone when I explained my project. "It's perfect," she said. "I'm a total Facebook freak. Let's get together and geek it up!" But it was that kind of joking, "I have to laugh about it so I don't cry" kind of thing. I knew it well—it's part of the strange equilibrium I maintained with myself for the nearly three years I was playing WoW.

She never ganked anyone. She didn't know the difference between Halo's Gravity Hammer or Mercenaries' Street Sweeper (powerful weapons in these popular shooter games). But I knew my trip to the Buckhead part of Atlanta to see her wouldn't be a waste of time. The NFL fan in me also had been morbidly curious about seeing the Cobalt Lounge, the place where Baltimore Ravens linebacker Ray Lewis got involved with two murders back in 2000.

Hope is Latina, but she didn't offer any type of specific background information, so I didn't ask. I watched her at work—it was her suggestion to meet at the restaurant that employed her, one of those ten-dollar hamburger joints with beer-battered onion rings, eight-dollar margaritas, and waitresses who congregate to clap and sing a smart-ass rendition of "Happy Birthday" on cue as a molten chocolate cake arrives. She's fluid as she moves from table to table, keeping up at least five stop-and-start conversations without a hitch.

It's no wonder she can multitask like that—she follows 2,145 people on Twitter and boasts nearly 4,000 friends on Facebook. I nodded when she told me this, unable to fathom the true network of connections that this number represented. I saw her in the middle of a room with thousands of silver filaments stretching off in every direction like a giant spiderweb.

"It's exhausting," she confessed, wiping her forehead with the back of her hand when she took a moment to chat during her ten-minute break. I offered her some of my onion rings. She made a face as though she had just eaten bad French cheese.

"God, no," she said. "I don't *eat* here."

But she did whip out her iPhone and log into her e-mail while we were speaking. In my opinion, the intrusion of the electronic world in a real-world situation is rude. For someone her age (maybe twenty-two?), it's completely normal. The electronic world is just another normal way of communicating, and for someone who e-mails, listens to music, watches TV, and IMs somebody all at once, simultaneously talking to me and texting someone is not using that many neurons, I suppose.

"Justin's an a-hole," she muttered, then tapped onto her iPhone some more. Before I could ask her who Justin was, she announced, "Three thousand nine hundred fifty-nine." It took me a moment to realize which earlier conversation this related to: the exact number of friends on Facebook—she checked. She thinks she can hit 4,500 by Christmas, 6,000 by the end of next year. Last time I checked, which was weeks ago, I had 300, which made me feel pretty hip, although I confess I don't know about 40 percent of them, who seem to be friends of actual friends that I have. Most simply spam me with requests to help them with Mafia Wars, save the rain forest by keeping up a virtual fish pond, or planting pretend flowers in a pretend garden.

My mind reeling, I finally asked Hope, "What do you want that many Facebook friends for?"

She glanced at her watch, snapped her gum, and said, "Back to the salt mine." But she did answer my question—sort of. She cocked her head and gave me a look. "What's wrong with having friends?" Then she became the brown-and-green whirlwind, easily moving food and handling chitchat with customers at every table. I nibbled at my cold onion rings and thought about my reluctance to get a pager years ago. Few of my high school friends seemed to have one, except for the two juniors who drove pizzas for Domino's and were sometimes "on call" (for what, I don't know). They were very cool and always had cash for soda, movies, whatever.

Having a pager made them seem important. I considered getting one for a while so I could impress girls with how damn important I was, but I eventually decided not to, because I simply didn't want to have an electronic leash. Sometimes I didn't want to be found. This same thinking kept me from Facebook even while my wife was racking up friends by the dozens, delving all the way back to elementary school to reignite relationships.

Is there such a thing as 3,959 friends? I don't think I've even met that many people in my entire life, and that counts sixty or so new students each semester for more than ten years as a teacher. My skin prickled at the idea of the near-lethal level of guilt and shame I'd feel over not wishing the right people "Happy B-day," commenting on their newest posted pictures, or telling them "Feel better soon!" with some kind of frowny, sick, sad emoticon that always made me think about the WoW emotes I used to love.

Two hours later, Hope emerged from the kitchen in a shiny blue dress with spaghetti straps that my wife would not approve of, but I was here for an interview, I told myself, as we got into my Grand Caravan and worked through the Buckhead tourist traffic. Girls that pretty didn't have to own a car—someone always volunteered to give them a ride. It was part of our arrangement, anyway: I would drive her home, and we could chat the whole way for my book.

"Where to?" I asked her as I realized we were passing the Cobalt Lounge. It looked like every other upscale drinking joint in the area. It was incredibly anticlimactic. But what was I expecting—police tape from the nine-year-old crime? Oh well. The real world was often painfully anticlimactic to me. WoW always delivered. It was a fleeting, ghostly satisfaction and pleasure, but with the constant updates and expansions, and the ability to play new characters on a whim, it at least felt fresh and exciting. It was almost tailor-made to my desires.

"Up ahead, then left," she said, not looking up from her phone. While we drove the forty minutes to the apartment she shared with a graduate student from Georgia State ("Bailey," she said, making a yuck face), she told me about the two semesters she spent at Kennesaw State College as a communications major. "I wanted to be a news anchor," she said.

It didn't take much prompting to find out what had happened. She had started up her own Facebook page when her pal Jennifer, a saxophone player in Kennesaw's jazz band, got one, too. They raced to see who would get to 100 friends first. Jennifer won, which burned Hope to no end. Soon they both got iPhones. They both set up Twitter accounts. They jointly created a blog called "Dr. K Sux" to bash a wildly unpopular history teacher who gave them both Ds.

Halfway through the first semester of her sophomore year, Hope flunked out. She'd been slowly skipping more and more classes—to work on her MySpace page and create music mash-ups, combining bits of her favorite songs and synching them with clips of her favorite shows (*South Park*, *The Daily Show*, and *Dexter*). When midterms whooshed past without her, that was the last straw, academically speaking (although I wonder if that antiprofessor blog would have gotten her nailed eventually, anyway). Honestly, she didn't strike me as all that interested in academics, unless Socializing 101 was on the course list.

dog walker for a while, then a Facebook friend
e restaurant. Better tips," she explained.
into her parking lot beside some shirtless yahoo drinking beer in a speedboat up on a trailer. He nodded at me, then saw her and gave us both a conspiratorial wink. Hope made the yuck face again. I tried not to take it personally, although the undergrad in me felt profoundly belittled—and old as all hell.

"Four hours a day," was her answer to how much time all that tweeting and Facebooking took up. The way she constantly fiddled with her iPhone, I suspected she was skewing the real number down. Or maybe that's all she thought it was. I remember thinking that I didn't have a Warcraft problem—I was playing maybe five hours a day. Then my wife kept track for a week, making little marks on a sheet for every fifteen-minute increment that I loafed at the computer. That week I was on for sixty-two hours. I would've gone before Congress and sworn it was thirty hours, max.

"You probably think I'm some kind of retard," she said.

I shook my head no. "You seem rather smart, in fact. I should know. I used to be a professor."

Again, no response. My wife regularly assures me that I am not funny. It's times like this that I wonder if she's right. As I said, old as hell and feeling older by the moment.

I said, "Have you ever thought about just, I don't know, cutting the cord? Deleting your accounts and going back to school? Or getting a full-time job?"

"I make more than my dad does."

She does. He makes $25,500 as a janitor in a nearby warehouse district. She cleared more than $30,000 last year as a waitress and an occasional sleepwear model. Hope's got a point. Throw in all the free rides, free drinks, and God knows what else, and she had it fairly good, by most standards.

"Why did you agree to meet me?" I asked, since she didn't seem as that interested in anything I had to say.

"To see an addict up close, I guess."

That was the same thing I thought about coming to see her—like going to the zoo to see if the lions were going to kill each other. A bloodbath. A freak show.

We sat there, the two of us: Me, forty pounds overweight with glasses and a little chin acne. Her, five feet ten with legs to die for and a breathy laugh that made me think of wind. Addicts do come in all sizes and types, I decided, as she thanked me for the ride and slid out of the car. Guiltily, I watched her disappear into her apartment building, convinced that I could charm that dress off her in five minutes flat if I were a few pounds lighter, a few years younger, and single again. Without WoW to make me feel powerful, I needed every little boost to my confidence I could muster.

The idiot in the boat laid on the air horn, startling me out of my little mental fantasy. He couldn't stop laughing as I sped away fast enough to squeal tires.

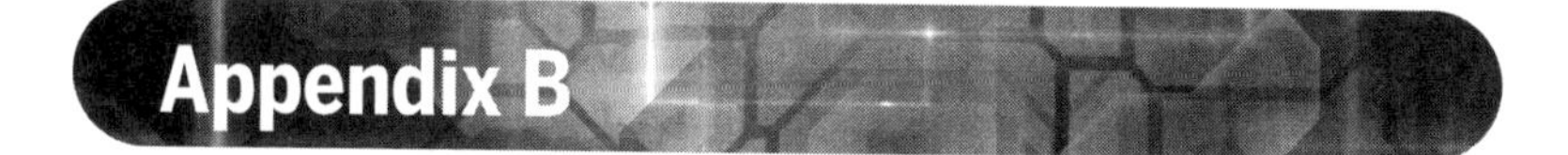

Appendix B

WHAT THE EXPERTS SAY

Advice is what we ask for when we already know the answer but wish we didn't.

—ERICA JONG

When we ask advice we are usually looking for an accomplice.

—CHARLES VARLET DE LA GRANGE

***Expert:* (n) a person who has special skill or knowledge in a particular field;** a specialist; an authority; (adj) demonstrating or involving great skill, dexterity, or knowledge of a subject, often as the result of experience or training.

In most books, an expert is someone with a Ph.D. who teaches a bunch of eighteen- to twenty-two-year-olds from fall through spring and who writes thick tomes that consist of case studies and footnotes and that bear subtitles such as "The New Legitimation of Consumption Practices through Cultural, Normative, and Regulative Influence." When it comes to video games, the Internet, and social networking—all those things that make up digital culture—I was a little surprised to find experts in a variety of fields and with a shocking range of backgrounds: a graphic designer, a high school band director, a syndicated cartoonist, a homemaker and part-time commercial real estate agent, and a college professor. Others I spoke to who could echo these stories include a police officer, an elementary school janitor, a philanthropist heiress, a bestselling crime novelist, a professional oboe player, a Wendy's assistant manager, a recreational-vehicle mechanic, and an unemployed interior decorator. The faces change, but the stories remain the same.

Each of them comes at video game addiction and the digital world from a different angle. Some of what they offer is abstract, and some is quite practical. Some is from personal experience, and some stems from hundreds of hours of working directly or indirectly with others. Some is anecdotal, and some is scientific. Some is amusing, and some is anything but.

The following offers a great deal of insight into the new and growing phenomenon of digital addiction, as well as its sources and some possible cures. If nothing more, it at least offers a better sense of the size and the scope of this mounting issue in the United States and around the world. It's a larger issue than most think, and its effect is like the Six Degrees of Kevin Bacon game—most of us don't have to search for more than one or two people in our network of friends and family to uncover someone who has a less than healthy relationship with the digital realm. This is for you and them both.

Here's a chance to carefully and critically peer behind the veil at that captivating, immersive, pixellated world.

My Own Cross to Bear

Rob is the director of bands at Creekview High School outside Atlanta. He also plays trumpet professionally. And he's my best friend—the same Rob who is woven throughout this book. He has gamed nearly as much as I have, so it's no surprise that I talked on the phone with him a lot for this book to discuss what we did together and to hear his thoughts on video game addiction. He told me, "Other than being a video game aficionado myself, I see a number of kids every day who play video games nonstop. I see students who spend every spare moment with their noses in video games (PSP, Nintendo DS, and cell phone applications). They take every moment to escape into another world. When I try to have a conversation with them as they're playing their games, I get a lot of 'Uh-huh' and 'Sure' responses. When I say something that they don't understand or that requires a bit more thought, I get 'Wait—what?' It's crazy to think about how fully a person is able to be sucked into another world without any regard for the one you're standing in."

We should know—we gamed away months of our lives together. We've turned that into a strength by being able to talk the other one out of a relapse, which the writing of this book nearly precipitated half a dozen times. "For research reasons" was nearly our excuse.

"One of the biggest misconceptions people seem to have," Rob told me just a week ago, "is that video games conform to a particular personality. I would suspect that the general 'video game junkie' would be a seventeen-year-old boy with glasses, zero social life, and acne. The reality is that video gamers conform to no stereotype. Gamers are made of all types: people who are successful in their careers, people who are in need of personal help; rich, poor, analytical, creative, and tons of others from all walks of life.

"The idea that all gamers are of one mold is preposterous. I think that the best video games—the ones that have millions of buyers and players—have the ability to serve those who fit several molds. For example, some games allow those who are analytical to advance quickly, while creative spirits and souls are able to advance just as quickly, but through using different means. I think that's the genius of a well-made video game. Advancement is something that is bred in us very early and often in life. The allure of guaranteed advancement, regardless of our strengths, is very difficult to resist."

"Tell me the story of how you quit, Rob," I said. I knew the story well. It happened in March 2008—two and a half months after my own exit from the game. My quitting really put a crimp in our relationship, becoming the massive elephant in the room that no one wanted to mention, although we spoke at least three times a week about whatever else was safe to talk about. I wanted to join him in WoW so desperately, but somehow I was able to resist. I'm thankful that he never asked me to play, because I bet I would've.

"I was in a hotel in Savannah, Georgia," Rob said, taking a deep breath as if preparing himself. "I'd been playing the game for hours. The weather was beautiful, and the city of Savannah has much to offer. I was in a hotel room, and all I did was sit there and stare at a computer screen. I can't remember who pointed me to the site www.wowdetox.com, but I went there that day. The stories on that site were *my* stories. They weren't just similar to my own story—they had it completely pegged.

"I couldn't stop playing Warcraft. When I wasn't playing the game, I was thinking about it. Before that, it was Halo. I made so many bad decisions surrounding those games that I'm really embarrassed about who I was back then. I would stay up *way* late and sacrifice the quality of my performance at work because I was playing. I wasn't a good father, good husband, good teacher, or good man. When I discovered this, the pattern of my addiction became very obvious. Since then, I've realized that my pattern isn't only about video games—but also about electronics in general as well. I seem to have a problem being 'disconnected.'"

Rob worries that he's failing at remaining disconnected, or unplugged. He laments, "It's Facebook these days. I keep replacing one addiction with another. I'm hoping for the next addiction to be lifting weights or practicing my trumpet. I'm trying to battle it, and I'm certainly aware of it, but the future seems completely out of my hands. I really hate that I will probably be dealing with this for the rest of my life. I guess we all have our crosses to bear."

He's wrong, though. He's not failing at anything. Rob's very involved in his kids' lives, and he tries to be a good husband, teacher, father, and friend. He is the director of a church band, and he loves it. He's got a strength of character that I can only aspire to. He suffers from temptation—at least twice this past month, he's admitted the "WoW jonesing [craving]"—but he handles it well. When he spent too much time on Facebook, he simply deleted his account and that was that.

He's got a terrific life and too much to lose. It didn't take perching atop a bridge and contemplating self-destruction for him to figure it all out. The cumulative weight finally got him: me quitting; his wife's ongoing anger; his kids' shame and disappointment over the loss of their time together; the tiredness he felt getting up at 6:00 AM for school after being up until midnight gaming. Given all that evidence, WoW had to be gone. I have faith that any other addiction that flares to life for him will be similarly squashed.

He doesn't believe it, but he's an inspiration to me, and I hope that he can be one to others, too. We have to make better choices, just like Rob does every day.

The Power of Pop Culture

I knew of Shaun Boland though his syndicated cartoon, *Bol's Eye*. He's written about video games often enough in his comics that I suspected he'd have a lot to add to the subject. I e-mailed him, and soon enough we were on the phone chatting about it like old friends.

He said, "I think that people have a tendency to make the assumption that if something gives them pleasure, that more and more of it will make them happier. And this simply isn't the case. Everything in life has to be balanced, or other aspects of life will become unbalanced. Even healthy activities, such as eating and exercising, can be damaging when done in excess. Therefore, it's no shock for me to hear how dangerous gaming addiction can be."

He's exactly right. I kept thinking that by playing more WoW, I'd get more and more of that little burst of joy I felt upon first playing the game. The reward grew less accessible, however, despite my increased gaining, and this made me incredibly frustrated and dissatisfied. You'd think those feelings would've caused me to leave the game, but the opposite happened. I gamed more. It's along the lines of the gambler's "logic": I've lost six times in a row, so I'm due for a win.

No one wins with WoW.

It's a lot more like a life sentence in hell than anything else.

Shaun continued, "To me, the allure of video games to children, and even adults, lies in the ability of people to enter a virtual existence with no real risk or danger. It's much easier to play a video game than to set goals in life, take chances to reach them, and to face the possibility of failure. Although I do enjoy video games, for me there's nothing more exciting than the game of life."

Although we spoke much longer, his comics supply enough commentary to stand alone. What they suggest is disconcerting and socially relevant. For continuing the conversation in such a public way (these were all published and reached a wide audience), I thank Shaun. Any voice of sanity and common sense on this tumultuous topic is much appreciated.

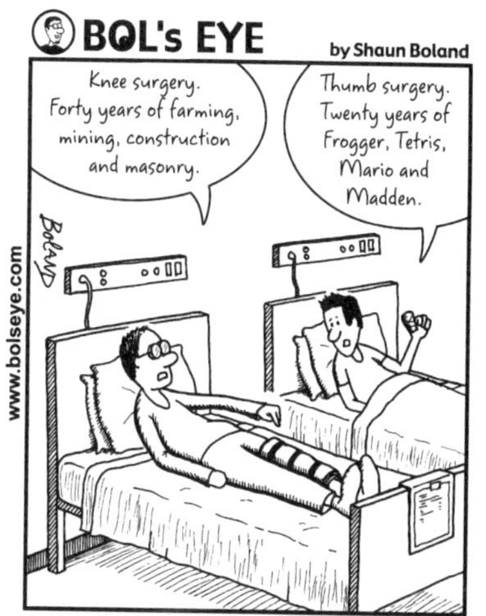

A Conscious Approach

I met Steven when I moved from Washington, D.C., to Sarasota, Florida, in 2008, right after my one-year position at George Washington University ended. I went there to be the creative director of a film company that intended to make a movie along the lines of *The Secret*. Although the company disbanded without managing to do much beyond spend a lot of initial capital, Steven proved to be an invaluable source of information on many subjects. He's been involved in TV, film, and graphics production since the mid-1980s, working for such companies as Blockbuster, IBM, McDonald's, and Universal Studios. In an effort to improve his own life, he's amassed more than two decades of training in spirituality, alternative health, consciousness, and personal transformation. The latter expertise seemed particularly useful to my understanding of video game addiction.

What follows is a fast-paced Q & A that happened in Long Boat Key, Florida, one afternoon in August 2009 while we sat on his porch and watched the sun pink the horizon and finally disappear, leaving us there with heavy thoughts and a blanket of stars overhead that stretched beyond comprehension.

Q. ***How have you encountered video game addiction in your own life?***

A. I've been involved in computer graphics and animation since the beginning, back in 1987. I was one of the first three students at our art school who worked with computers, and we were ridiculed for it. It was considered a false art at the time. Nobody could foresee how computers were going to play out. I never got really all that involved in video games. Still, somewhere along the line the game Oddworld caught my eye—it looked visually like a movie. It looked fun. It wasn't about going out and killing people. You basically caught bad guys and turned them in.

I bought an Xbox just for this game. I went out on a Friday night to Best Buy and picked up a unit and this one game, then I came back and set it up and started playing it. Monday morning, I realized that for two and a half days I had been sitting in my room playing nonstop except to use the bathroom and eat. I had lost complete sense of time and space. That was really shocking.

Q. ***And the experience of your marathon gaming session was like—***

A. While playing, I got nearly to the end of a hard level, then lost and had to start that level over. It was very challenging, and I didn't like that. I remember feeling like I should've been able to do better at the game. If I just played a little differently, shot the webs from a different angle, I'd be able to capture him and move forward. The game itself was fun to look at and it was cool, but I was addicted to my inner feeling of frustration. It wasn't healthy for me. I didn't feel good after those three days, despite winning the game. I walked away feeling lousy, like I'd gone through hell. I'd simply lost two and a half days of my life. I'm a single guy, so it was pretty easy for me to do this—I didn't have a lot of external things in the world pulling me away. Yet it was pretty dramatic, since I had things to do that weekend and I didn't get them done.

Q. ***What type of insight do you now have on what happened back then?***

A. When I took the time to really reflect on what happened, what I got was that on one level, I was really just competing with myself. It was just me overcoming my skills. The only thing you really "win" is an emotional response. It's not as if winning the game has the Xbox spill coins or hand out a "You're great!" banner. My own emotional reward wasn't satisfaction, in this case. It was me versus me, and I was so frustrated. I threw the game controller and screamed at the TV. I hated it. My guy kept dying, and I was going crazy trying to overcome the feeling of hating the feeling I was going through. I was trying to fix it—something in me—that seemed not good enough, not capable enough.

Something I've also come to realize is that anytime people or events in life push my buttons and get me to react, causing me stress, I realize it has nothing to do with them. It has everything to do with my own inner conflict that I'm trying to resolve that they're simply reflecting. With video games, it's the same thing, when it's just you versus the Xbox, though I still feel the same emotion I feel by being stressed by others.

With these massive online games, it's all amplified. I'm dealing with people I might actually know, so there's more at stake to "lose" if I don't look good or perform well. How are they going to look at me? People addicted to the global gaming systems have a heavier amount of internal strife. In general, people are either trying to look good or avoid looking bad, and I think that's what's playing out, too, in video games. These games are just an extension of our consciousness. It might seem like an escape, but it's not.

If the video game affects my real life in any form—[if] my emotions are tied to it, my thoughts are tied to it, or my interactions with my family or friends are in any way affected by it and the frustration over winning or not winning, looking good or not looking good, or conquering or not conquering—then the addiction is pretty obvious. Players aren't addicted to the video game as much as they are to the emotion of passivity that the video game [gives] them. Oddworld had complete control over me for three days. I was angry that my body needed food and that I had to stop playing to eat or use the bathroom. That's real evidence of a problem.

Q. ***Let's talk about the addiction side of it some more. How do you understand addiction?***

A. People do a thing in order to get something out of it. We go after a certain job or approach a new relationship because we feel, on some level, that with it we're really going to get something that makes us happy, that we're going to like. Games—especially fighting, battling, and creating strategies to kill other things or beings, which is really what a lot of these games are about—are great for people who don't have the ability in their social structure to actually go out and exhibit anger, hate, domination, brutality. It's just not socially acceptable. So a lot of people have suppressed their anger and their fear and their pain because the world basically says, "Don't show us those things, because they make us uncomfortable."

And so video games have been birthed out of our unconscious to help us exert or exhibit or dive into some of these realms to help us through them. They [the games] are fascinating—the artistry, the worlds they create, are captivating, and now games are being created with karmic choices. What's interesting is that on the surface it may appear that what they [the players] are getting is a release, but what's hidden underneath it, part of the addiction, is very much in the spirit of Buddhism, which says, "Life is suffering." It sounds counterintuitive at first, but what we develop an underlying addiction to is the pain and the suffering, not the expected catharsis.

Let me put it another way. The pain of losing is really what the gambler is going for. Playing video games is, in a sense, like gambling. You're basically cheating the dice to see if you're going to win something: better armor; a kill. This oversimplifies it, but I think it's useful to see it this way. The whole deal with a gambling addiction is that the gambler is there to lose—all of his conscious effort is toward winning, yes, but unconsciously there's a self-sabotage mechanism that's addicted to the process of losing.

Q. *Some of the people I run across who hear about my own problems with video games think it's a joke. They write it off not as some tricky self-sabotage or spiritual yearning, but rather just a double helping of geekiness or laziness or something like that. It's something better laughed off than taken seriously.*

A. People who say there's no such thing as video game addiction are wrong. It's hugely widespread. Someone who plays video games and isn't addicted to them on some level is a rarity, simply because what's going on in human consciousness on a deeper level that's so pervasive throughout all of life is being mirrored in video games. I'm talking about that inner passivity of things having power over us or us being powerless.

Q. *Is it fair to expand that idea into the whole digital world? Do the Internet and all these new communication technologies also provide outlets and reflections of ourselves and the way our world is?*

A. What I see is that they're a filter that keeps us one step away from being able to deal with and handle these things in real life. It's another veil to suppress us and keep us further away from the truth of our being and being able to interact in real relationship with real people.

In some way, shape, or form, every human being has been

separated from [his or her] true spirit. My whole journey in consciousness has been to come back to find my own spirit. Ultimately, for every technique and tool I've learned, the goal of it all has been to get me back to me, to reconnect to my true inner spirit, my power, to my direct source. We all have a heart and the capacity for genius. We all have our own intuition, creativity, brilliance, and power—the only reason that we play out these dysfunctional things is that something has pulled us away from seeing, believing, and really understanding who we truly are. All these veils that we go through—gambling, alcohol, drugs, sex addiction, video game addiction—they're all basically there to cover up, hide, or filter these issues and make them a little easier for us to handle so that we can feel powerful through the video game, the cigarette, the alcohol. It's because we've lost our sense of personal power.

Q. ***The way you talk about veils and self-deception, it's a surprise that more of us don't suffer from one type of addiction or another.***

A. That's exactly right. Even though I'm not addicted to video games, I knew addiction—I was addicted to my work. I was addicted to looking good professionally, achieving something, being somebody—not to myself, but to my family and to the world and to my peers and to other businesses that were like mine. I wanted to be seen as an achiever and somebody who was great. I had this dream that if I were the best animator at the best visual effects house, the best computer graphics guru in South Florida, it'd all mean something. But I lost all my relationships as a result of striving for those goals. I was married to my work, not to the people in my life. I had to fly to Miami from Sarasota for Christmas Eve—a three-hour drive away—because

I was working up to an hour before my flight. I was trying to look good and not look bad to others. My profession was my codependent way to feel good about myself.

It's just like what we're doing in the world with real wars. It's a never-ending thing. You can go and kill and battle and destroy continents and civilizations and peoples and religions all you want, but you don't really win. Nobody wins.

Connected to all of this is the idea that the more people show how strong and powerful they are, the more it's all an admission of how weak they actually feel. When you see a limitation in someone else that's a problem, it's because on some level, that's your limitation, too.

Q. *Describe what a good relationship with video games would be.*

A. The first thing is to move it out of the consciousness of what would be "good." The whole idea of good-bad consciousness is the root of where a lot of these addictions come from in the first place.

Q. *Okay, try this: What would be an effective relationship with video games?*

A. That's a useful question. First, it's important to understand that people are still going to play the games that their consciousness is most aligned with. If people are feeling the consciousness of war, or they're feeling personally beat up in the world, then they're going to be attracted to games in which they can overcome that, or be strong in that world. So there's an essential part of those games playing a role. As I've evolved in my consciousness, the video games that attract me are ones where I'm being creative and have the opportunity to create healthy relationships, or where I am evolving, like Spore, which is a game I have some interest in. I have yet to play it, but there's something in my spirit that attracts me to it mainly because I think there's a direct relationship to the reality we live in.

You know, it's a whole aspect of evolution, growth, development, tribal states, civilization states. Just look at our planet—we're all a species going through this. Spore condenses all of that into a forum where you can go out and create civilizations, you can build buildings, you can create creatures, and that's fun. Some of the other games are probably quite fun, too, like Warhammer and Warcraft. There's some fundamental aspect of fun involved.

If I were in charge of all this—playing God, or a benevolent being looking out for our most powerful state of being and choosing to help us be productive, happy, nourished, loved, supported, and fulfilled—I'd ask, "Does this game and its content and format support you in all of those ways?" If the answer is no, then I'd seriously question the ultimate outcome of that game.

Don't get me wrong—I love seeing things explode. I'm in the visual effects industry. I got into it because I liked watching how things blew up and particles flew around. I love animation. I'm aware that there's an attraction there. My new state of being, though, asks me what I'm getting out of it to see things blown to a million pieces and blood everywhere.

Q. ***So asking that question of the games you encounter is a step toward a healthier relationship with video games?***

A. Yes. My little nephew, he's nine years old, has never had a conversation with me except in the context of video games. He doesn't call or talk to me unless it's to tell me what he achieved in a video game, or [to ask] if I would support him in getting a video game that he really wants. He relates everything he sees in the world to video games, like when we go to the beach and he says, "Oh, that's like in the Star Wars game, when . . ." I don't know if he has any basis for reality that satisfies him outside the gaming world. He doesn't know how to relate to people. He's had a tough time, and he's resorted to video games to survive. As we've been having this conversation, I've been thinking about him more and more, and I'm now really questioning what his life is going to be like.

He doesn't hide his connection to video games, though. Once someone gets to the point where they hide, lie, or disassociate themselves from the very thing they're doing, that's when it's a huge, deeply unconscious problem. It's going to take a lot to deal with it. Anything that we lie about or hide is less than healthy.

Q. ***One of the main ideas you've come up with over the years is codependency. How might that play into video game addiction?***

A. Codepency is what we're taught. It's in our news. It's in our knowledge base. Everything is based in external sources. It's always outside us, and we have to go to it to get what we want. We have to give up certain rights to have the government protect us. There are so many codependent relationships going on in our lives that I don't think any of us really fully remembers what it means to be coempowered, to be able to have fun and be powerful without having to play a video game.

Q. ***"Coempowered" would be a state in which multiple people are self-reliant versus depending on one another for everything they need?***

A. Yes. Though there's an element of giving to one another that's essential, it's part of our nature, but to *need* it is when it gets problematic. I'm talking about: "I cannot survive and be happy and be who I need to be in my world without X." X could be a girl, a mentor, a behavior, a thing.

Q. *So what do you do if you or someone you care about has this unhealthy relationship with video games? If the X is a video game?*

A. Overcoming addiction is a difficult thing—it requires confrontation, and it requires someone being fully present with absolute consciousness and love. The addicts can't do it themselves. [They] need help from others to get it started.

For me to change myself, I needed to be shown what I was doing. Even then, my first reaction was to deny it. My second reaction was to dismiss it. My next step was to walk away and go do it again. Another further step is often to blame the people who are trying to help you—attacking them, saying they don't know what they're talking about.

You end up returning to the addiction, the game, trying to reclaim the payoff you always thought it would deliver. But ninety-nine percent of the time, what you really get is frustration. I'm not good enough. Why didn't I score higher? Why didn't I play better? Why didn't I feel the same high I did before? It's frustration, that feeling of inner passivity. It's the sense of I can't get what I want, it won't let me, something's in my way. That frustration is the key to knowing it's an addiction—the person gets frustrated easily, by anything.

Q. *That frustration sounds like a powerful weakness.*

A. From your weakness is your greatest strength returning. That's from the Bible, by the way. If you come to understand why the weakness is there, it becomes your area of strength. The most powerful question I've ever used to stop people in their tracks when they're derailed—when they're reacting, pushing buttons, frustrated, or emotional—is simply, "What are you doing right now?"

Only good things can come from asking that of people and receiving honest answers. It keeps going deeper as long as it's asked until light shines on something they've never seen before. They're so caught up in the drama that when you show them to go deeper to see what it really is, it's a "Eureka!" or an "Aha!" moment.

Q. ***It took me a lot of years before I got to my own "Aha!" moment with video games. Any other insight into these elusive "Aha!" moments?***

A. Here's one last thing, another potential "Aha!" moment that might offer some useful perspective. I'm paraphrasing from P. D. Ouspensky's book *The Fourth Way* here, which is based on the teachings of G. I. Gurdjieff: "Every single external technology that man has ever created, no matter what it is—to print, to fly, to transport himself, to see better, to hear better—every single one is simply a compensation for an inner technology that we already have but have lost connection to."

Steven has decided to put aside his career in animation and instead focus on teaching these days. It's clear to me that his future is bright and that he has a lot to offer. Many problems in the world demand his attention and passion. I wish him luck.

Parenting a Video Game Addict

"Doris" is a divorced Chicago homemaker with two kids and an occasional commercial real estate agent who sought me out after finding my website accidentally while she was scrambling for help with her children. She knows the cost of video game addiction as well as anyone. What she wanted more than anything was answers on how to cope with the addiction and how to better parent her kids.

"There are no easy answers," I assured her, "and a lot of the information out there isn't helpful."

"Tell me about it," cracked her voice over the phone.

When I asked her about WoW, she said, "Just hearing that name gives me the shivers. My oldest, Ronnie, got into all that while he was at college. He played video games on and off throughout high school. We paid attention and made sure he kept up with sports, girls, and school. He's a good kid. But the moment that game entered our lives, he changed."

It took zero prompting for her to explain. This story was bursting inside her, desperate to get out. I opened a Diet Coke and turned on my digital audio recorder as she explained.

"He started lying, for one. He ignored his friends and stopped dating. But the thing is, he did this at college, so we didn't know about it until he came home for the summer. Every other summer, from the time he was sixteen on, Ronnie had a job. One time he worked for the local park district. Another time he painted houses. This past summer he lied about looking for work and stayed in the basement office playing that game. He'd be there from the time he got up until lunchtime, then again until dinner. Sometimes he'd stay playing until midnight or so. The only times we saw him were [when he wanted] food or when he needed a shower, which was less often than we'd prefer.

One night I had a stomachache and couldn't sleep. I heard a noise downstairs at three in the morning, and I thought, 'God, we've got a burglar in the house!' Turned out it was Ronnie playing on the computer again. At three A.M.!"

Doris is a good parent. She pays attention to what her kids watch on TV and what they're learning in school. She keeps them in clean clothes and feeds them well. But as she points out, a parent can't police everything 100 percent of the time. And worse, she doesn't really understand computers, let alone video games, so trying to help Ronnie seems like an insurmountable task.

"I feel like a complete failure," she said, emotion making her voice thick. "What the heck did we do wrong for him to think this was right? Throughout high school, he had a solid three-point-five GPA. He's a bright kid. It's so upsetting."

As sometimes happens with kids, the problem seemed to resolve itself. Maybe he's not an addict but just someone who overindulged more than he should've, I thought. But then Doris said, "He started up again a month or two later, and it's worse than before. Around July we'd had enough. We got the whole family together—even his uncles came down from Oshkosh. We had an intervention. I'd been watching that A&E TV show *Intervention* and got the idea from it. I asked Ronnie to head out to Schlotzsky's to pick up some smoked turkey sandwiches for lunch. When he came back, we were all there, and we wouldn't let him back down.

"It was the most awful thing. Things got hot, and a lot of things were said that no one should've said. But Ronnie finally said he wished he could quit. So we went right downstairs and watched him delete it—What do you call them? Characters? Players?—off the computer and his laptop, too. The last six weeks of summer were pretty quiet. He never did find a job, but he did start playing basketball with some old friends. He also dug out his old skateboard. We had our old Ronnie back for awhile."

I knew this story well. My wife had threatened me with violence, told me the kids would need years of therapy down the road, and said half a dozen other things to make me "see sense." I nodded, swore to do better, then got up after they went to bed and started massacring murlocs in WoW as if doing so wasn't going back on my word. Real-life promises simply didn't apply to the virtual world. They were two completely different things.

For Ronnie, too, it didn't work. Doris admitted, "His father visited him at college when he had a business trip downstate, and the report wasn't good. Ronnie's roommate went to Applebee's with them, and all he talked about was that game. We think they're in it together. We called the school to see if the Internet could be shut off in their dorm or if the two of them could be split up.

"We just don't know what to do. Maybe Ronnie's making good choices and going to class, but we don't think so. He doesn't return our calls for days. If this were my husband instead of my son, the ink on the divorce papers would've dried long ago. But he's our son. So what the heck are we supposed to do? Especially with Jim, my ex, living ninety minutes away?"

"A lot of parents and spouses have the same questions," I replied. "What are you going to do?"

The pause that followed told me more than anything. She was frustrated, angry, hurt, and confused. *This* was the reason I was writing my book, I realized: for Doris and people like her who were forced to witness spouses, parents, and children destroying themselves and everything they cared about. I couldn't swallow the shame I felt even though I'd never met Ronnie and most likely never would. I'd brought that level of discomfort and anger on my own family and loved ones. Every time I witness the carnage of someone else's gaming, it's like being slugged in the gut for me.

Finally, Doris said, "Jim thinks we should hire a professional intervention specialist and try again. Maybe we didn't do it right the first time. I'm thinking that we might stop paying for school so that he has to come home, where we can watch him. But Ronnie's threatened to move in with friends before, and we don't want to push him over that edge.

"Greg—Ronnie's favorite uncle—had a similar thing with his stepson. That kid was into cocaine. Greg says the only thing to do is wait until they hit rock bottom and just be there when that happens. But the thing is, we're talking about video games, not drugs. And no matter what, this is our son we're talking about! How can we sit back and watch him throw his life into the garbage like this? Where did he get the idea that this was okay?

"We don't know what to do, but I swear to you, we'll keep doing something. Ronnie needs our help. My son needs my help, even if he doesn't know how to ask for it. I'd cut my left arm off if I thought that'd do any good."

I gave Doris information on how to get a medical professional to evaluate Ronnie. I also passed on the titles of useful books and websites. That was six weeks ago. I'm still hoping for a good report, but with addiction, you never know. You hope for the best and prepare yourself for more disappointment and sorrow.

But if anyone's going to make it, I reasoned, it'd be someone with a parent who loves him or her as much as Doris loves Ronnie. That was going to be the difference, I decided. Self-sacrificing love like Doris's, like the kind my wife had for me, can save someone when things are at their worst.

The Insider

I wanted a good sampling of diverse voices and opinions in this book, and the one I knew I was missing was a video game industry insider. I started teaching writing at the Ringling College of Art and Design in Sarasota, Florida, in the fall of 2009, and this was a school that had degrees in computer animation, motion design, game art and design, and graphic and interactive communication. One of the newest Computer Animation Department faculty members, Eric Gingrich, had spent thirteen years in the video game industry and has been credited with fifteen titles on eleven platforms and in nine genres. The only thing it took to get his insight was to buy him a cup of Starbuck's coffee. The following is our conversation, which took place outside Ringling's Idelson Studio in October 2009.

Q. ***How did you get into teaching?***

A. Mostly it's because of the economic downturn. The studio I was working for went under. I'd never considered being a teacher, but once I found out about this place and came here and saw what they were doing, I was pretty impressed.

Q. ***The classes you teach in Ringling's Computer Animation Department have a lot of future video game makers in them. What are they like?***

A. Hardcore. They work hard, and most are really strong artists. They're excited and intense.

Q. ***What's your own history with video games?***

A. I've been playing video games since Space Invaders in 1979. It was unbelievably cool that you could actually interact with something like that and actually blow the things up yourself versus watch them being blown up. I used to ride my ten-speed to the arcade after school every day throughout middle school. Arcades finally went away, which I was surprised and saddened by.

I eventually got an Atari 400 computer. I didn't actually program any games on it, but I learned BASIC and played games off the tape drive. I kind of missed out on the whole Nintendo thing somehow. At college, we had Amigas for creative arts—this was before there was a computer arts program. Those Amigas were advanced computers, so I started playing games on them. I got a degree in video and ended up working in the broadcasting industry. I taught myself 3D, and I taught myself computer graphics. Through doing that I met a game programmer in Alaska who was making games on his own. I made some graphics for him, and he got a job in the industry, so that's how I got my own start.

Q. ***In the biography on your website (www.ericgingrich.com), you refer to yourself as being a video game addict. Let me ask it flat out: Is video game addiction real?***

A. I think I used the term loosely in my biography, but yes, it does exist, though I've tried to avoid it myself. Going down to the video arcade as a kid was my life. I was getting out in the sun and riding my bike on the way there and back, which is far different from staring at a screen alone in a room today.

The World of Warcraft came out in 2004. Obviously the people I work with are into video games, and one by one, they all started playing it a lot. I checked Warcraft out and played enough to get a feel for it, then put it away and never touched it again. I decided I didn't have enough time for it and didn't want to get sucked into it.

As far as addiction of that kind goes, I'd say television is an addiction. When you come home after a hard day of work, you're tired and want to zone out. You just want a beer and some passive entertainment. It's basically a waste of time. Take your memoir, for instance. Watching TV is going to suck up that time that you could've used to write your book. Millions and millions just passively sit in front of TV screens.

I have a four-year-old daughter, and it's really hard to limit her TV time because you have to get stuff done, and sometimes you just want to sit the kid in front of the TV for a couple of hours. She loves TV. It's totally an addiction for her. If you let her, she'd watch TV all day long. She'd never go outside or do anything else.

Facebook is another addiction, right? I use Facebook a ton. And right now Facebook is more important to me, since I'm away from all the people I've ever known in my life. It's the only way I keep up with them. Once again, Facebook is something that you have to manage. What I've found is the more I interact, the more it draws you in. It's kind of a genius thing they have going. If you comment on a photo, post something about yourself, or even identify an interest of yours, then you get an e-mail about it. I mean, how many distractions can you handle per minute? You get an e-mail saying, "Joe Bob has commented on your status." You haven't heard from Joe Bob in six months—what's he up to? So you stop working and go find out.

You have more friends than you've ever had. Usually you lose touch with people. There are three or four people from high school or college that you keep up with—but now you can keep track of them all. I have two hundred friends now, going back to high school. And if I were a bit younger, I'd probably have them all the way back to middle and elementary school.

Q. ***Is the idea of addiction ever talked about in your classes?***

A. We just talk about the structure of games and how to create all the stuff that goes into a good game. We don't say, "Oh, and be sure not to addict anyone!" You'd be lucky to addict someone. It'd be an achievement. As a designer, you'd be successful if that happened. I assure you, it's not easy to do that.

Q. *How long does it take to develop a single console-system game?*

A. Years. The ones I've worked on are mostly low-budget titles, so maybe thirty people working for a year and a half [can get one done].

Q. *Versus a big-budget title?*

A. For something like Assassin's Creed or Halo, you'd have a hundred or more people working for maybe three years. Look at the credits for Gears of War, though, and you'll see it's hundreds and hundreds of people.

Q. *What's the future of video games look like?*

A. In a couple of years, there'll be another generation of console games that comes out to replace the old ones. The graphics will get better—hopefully they'll do something more with the AI [artificial intelligence]. Something I'd like to see be improved is how they handle physics. Like being able to have a character walk across the room without having to animate it. In Grand Theft Auto, if a car bumps into you, your character will push off the car realistically. That's great stuff.

Other than that, it'll be more of the same. Better graphics and bigger teams. Basically, it's all going to get bigger and bigger and bigger, because the expectation will get so much higher. The difference between a Playstation 3 and a Playstation 2 is huge.

It's getting to the point for me that a big-budget game is more enjoyable than a blockbuster movie. If you play Assassin's Creed, Gears of War, or Halo, you're going to get an interactive experience that is beyond what a blockbuster movie now delivers, in my opinion.

Q. ***How has our relationship with video games changed, due to their accessibility? We have them on our cell phones, our home computers, our DVD players, our console units, in social networking forums, even in our cars.***

A. We were talking earlier—the average gamer is what, thirty-five? And has been playing for thirteen years? My generation is now old enough to produce a president. Obama probably has played a video game or two, which I personally think is kind of nice. Most people my age or a little older than me don't understand what the deal is with video games. They don't get it. It's a foreign thing to them.

But there are people like my uncle—he's eighty and plays solitaire on the computer. Video games are becoming less of a weird thing that only kids are doing. It's going to become such an everyday part of life that no one's going to worry about it. No one's going to say, "Oh this is a video game, or this is a movie." It's going to be an interactive experience that can be used for all kinds of things. You can use it to teach your kid stuff—my kid goes on www.sesamestreet.com all the time and plays games there. Just the fact that she is able to use technology to interact is a big thing. Technology is already such a part of our lives. An integral part.

I think it all comes down to the person. Parents will eventually understand what the World of Warcraft is, because everyone uses a computer now. When I was a kid, I was a computer geek by the very fact that I used a computer. Nowadays they're ubiquitous. The same thing's happening with video games. Everyone knows what a game is. It's not some crazy black hole you can blame all the ills of society on.

I'm going to know anything that my kid does on the computer—I'm at least going to have a clue about it. That's the good thing. But my cynical side says that's going to happen with anything. It comes down to the person. It comes down to the parent. It doesn't matter what you're addicted to—it's ultimately about the person being able to look at it and deal with it, or not, because of whatever issues [he or she] may have. It's not the medium, but rather the psyche of the people and what they do with their lives.

Q. ***On the most basic level, what's good about video games?***

A. They can provide a release, an escape from day-to-day life. They can be an educational experience, just like *Sesame Street* is for TV. Similar to going to see a movie, a video game can make you feel good and deliver a message, even if it's just a horror game that can give you a rush and take you away from your life for a little while. If it's a violent game where you're shooting stuff and blowing people's heads off, then maybe it can release some of that tension—take out your aggression in the video game versus doing it in real life.

I've mostly worked on kids' games, but I've also worked on Wolverine and Call of Duty. Now, Call of Duty is an exception to your typical game in that it's a World War II shooter—you can get away with a lot more in that because you have your basic good and evil, pure good and pure evil, which we really don't ever encounter in real war. That's a good thing for some people to experience.

With video games, you have much less anxiety. And if there is anxiety in the interaction, you can instantly and easily get away from it.

When you get down to it, we're driven by two things. We avoid pain and we seek pleasure. That's our entire existence. We're preprogrammed in a lot of the ways to go after those two things. So when people go to make a movie or a game, they're trying to tap into those things. It's surprisingly easy to do, though it's hard to do well.

It's a lot like when you go see a magician. You know what he's doing is a trick, but the way he presents it to you completely blows you away. You're completely enthralled.

They say that one of the reasons people enjoy movies is that we can learn from watching others avoid pain and seek pleasure. This is a kind of scientific way to understand why we enjoy it. Maybe the same thing goes for these games that are so complex now. Maybe people are learning things. If you're a healthy person with a healthy psyche and you're playing Warcraft, maybe you're learning how to interact with people better. Perhaps you're learning how to be a bit freer so in the real world you can feel less constrained around others, if that's an issue for you. The closer these games come to real life, the more likely it is that they might be able to teach you something about the real world.

Q. ***What about the flip side? What are some of the negatives about video games?***

A. I don't look at it from that standpoint. I do look at derivative games that don't do anything new or interesting or are poorly made or don't tell a story the way they ought to, and I see all that as a negative thing. As far as society goes? Just like any other medium, some things aren't suitable for children. I definitely don't want my kids playing a mature-rated game. That's not very well enforced, especially on the Internet, where all you have to do is type in your birth date and you can just put in anything you want. Again, this requires parents taking an active role in what their kids are doing.

As far as a negative impact on society and me having a negative impact as a designer? I really don't see that. I'm doing a job. The content I create is meant to be inspiring and have a positive message, but at the same time, it's just a job. I don't view this job as having a built-in social responsibility. I try to do the best job I can—I try to produce something good that people are going to enjoy.

Q. ***Do you ever envision a time when the video game industry will be regulated beyond the current rating system?***

A. Saying that the rating system isn't enough is like people blaming McDonald's for making them fat. It's their choice. Eat there or not. Play the games or not. People want to blame someone else—and maybe it's the parents' fault to a degree—but ultimately, it comes down to the gamers themselves. Trying to blame video games for anything that comes out of the individual person is a mistake.

Q. ***What is it about video games that make them so addictive?***

A. I think a lot of the addiction comes from the social aspect of video games. I don't see people getting hooked on any game that doesn't have a clear social aspect. Most games have a beginning, a middle, and an end, and then you're done. Maybe you'll play it again a few times. Maybe not. The single-player experience is going to end, at some point. You might move on to another game, and then another, however, but each of those is a different experience. That's a lot more like watching a movie and then moving on to another movie. But you add in multiplayer games, and you suddenly have a dynamic, ever-changing social component—especially with an MMOG like the World of Warcraft.

I remember when I first started using the Internet back in 1993 or so, and they had IRC [Internet Relay Chat, or real-time messaging]. That was all there was—IRC. Just like sitting in the World of Warcraft or Second Life and chatting, I got addicted to that. I was in an OS/2 Warp chatroom and I realized I could talk to people throughout the world. This was mind-blowing. I was like: "Oh my God! I'm chatting with people in New York." I found myself sitting there just being mesmerized by their conversations. And night after night, I started to become involved in their lives—that was a bit of an addiction for me. After a few months, I finally cut it off, saying, "What the hell am I doing chatting with people in New York City?" That's kind of what I see as one of the main addictions to the World of Warcraft or Second Life. I mean, what do you do in Second Life? You do all the things you do in real life.

What that comes down to is not even the game—that's today's world that we live in. That's the Internet. That's the connectedness that we have. We're connected here in this moment because you and I are having a conversation, but you're connected to the world through your cell phone, the GPS in your car, and other ways, too. So yes, connectedness happens in games, but it also happens outside games.

But all of that has a positive side, too, because you can meet and find anybody you want. If you need a certain type of social interaction, you can probably find it on the Internet and through video games.

Recommended Reading

In order to better understand all that I suspected wasn't working in my life, I read the books listed below between 2007 and 2009—not because they were the best books or bestsellers, but because most of them were easily accessible. That's all. Other fine books on these subjects exist. For me, this collection provided enough insight and introspection for me to write this book and gain some much-needed perspective and insight. For that, I sincerely thank the authors, editors, and publishing houses associated with these titles.

Addiction

Capuzzi, David, and Mark D. Stauffer. *Foundations of Addictions Counseling*. Boston: Allyn & Bacon, 2008.

Peele, Stanton. *Addiction-Proof Your Child: A Realistic Approach to Preventing Drug, Alcohol, and Other Dependencies*. New York: Three Rivers Press, 2007.

Ruden, Ronald, with Marcia Byalick. *The Craving Brain: The Biobalance Approach to Controlling Addictions*. New York: HarperCollins, 1997.

Anger

Birnbaum, Jack. *Cry Anger: A Cure for Depression*. Don Mills, Ontario, Canada: General Publishing, 1973.

David, Daniel. *Your Angry Child: A Guide for Parents*. Binghamton, NY: Haworth Press, 2004.

Diamond, Stephen A. *Anger, Madness, and the Daimonic: The Psycho-*

logical Genesis of Violence, Evil, and Creativity. Albany, NY: State University of New York Press, 1996.

DiGiuseppe, Raymond, and Raymond Chip Tafrate. *Understanding Anger Disorders.* Oxford, England: Oxford University Press, 2007.

Feindler, Eva, ed. *Anger-Related Disorders: A Practitioner's Guide to Comparative Treatments.* New York: Springer Publishing, 2006.

Gaylin, Willard. *The Rage Within: Anger in Modern Life.* New York: Simon and Schuster, 1984.

Kassinove, Howard, ed. *Anger Disorders: Definition, Diagnosis, and Treatment.* Washington, DC: Taylor & Francis, 1995.

Marcus, David. *What It Takes to Pull Me Through.* Boston: Houghton Mifflin, 2005.

Moeller, Thomas G. *Youth Aggression and Violence: A Psychological Approach.* Mahwah, NJ: Lawrence Erlbaum Associates, 2001.

Digital Culture

Guernsey, Lisa. *Into the Minds of Babes: How Screen Time Affects Children from Birth to Age Five.* New York: Perseus Books, 2007.

Steyer, James P. *The Other Parent: The Inside Story of the Media's Effect on Our Children.* New York: Atria Books, 2002.

Zengotita, Thomas de. *Mediated: How the Media Shapes Your World and the Way You Live in It.* New York: Bloomsbury Publishing, 2005.

Sexual Abuse

Carnes, Patrick, and Kenneth M. Adams, eds. *Clinical Management of Sex Addiction.* New York: Brunner-Routledge, 2002.

Davies, Michele. *Childhood Sexual Abuse and the Construction of Identity: Healing Sylvia.* London: Taylor & Francis, 1995.

Mudaly, Neerosh, and Chris Goddard. *The Truth Is Longer Than a Lie: Children's Experiences of Abuse and Professional Interventions.* Philadelphia, PA: Jessica Kingsley Publishers, 2006.

Oz, Sheri, and Sarah-Jane Ogiers. *Overcoming Childhood Sexual*

Trauma: A Guide to Breaking Through the Wall of Fear for Practictioners and Survivors. New York: Hayworth Press, 2006.

Suicide

Blauner, Susan Rose. *How I Stayed Alive When My Brain Was Trying to Kill Me: One Person's Guide to Suicide Prevention*. New York: Harper-Collins, 2002.

Cutter, Fred. *Art and the Wish to Die*. Chicago: Nelson Hall, 1983.

Paris, Joel. *Half in Love with Death: Managing the Chronically Suicidal Patient*. Mahwah, NJ: Lawrence Erlbaum Associates, 2007.

Video Game Addiction

Beck, John C., and Mitchell Wade. *The Kids Are Alright: How the Gamer Generation Is Changing the Workplace*. Boston: Harvard Business School Press, 2006.

Bennet, Steve. *The Plugged-In Parent: What You Should Know About Kids and Computing*. New York: Times Books, 1998.

Bruner, Olivia, and Kurt. *Playstation Nation: Protect Your Child from Video Game Addiction*. New York: Center Street, 2006.

DeMaria, Rusel. *Reset*. San Francisco: Berrett-Koehler Publishers, 2007.

Dovey, Jon, and Helen W. Kennedy. *Game Cultures: Computer Games as New Media*. Berkshire, England: Open University Press, 2006.

Gee, James Paul. *What Video Games Have to Teach Us About Learning and Literacy*. New York: Palgrave Macmillan, 2003.

Grossman, Dave, and Gloria DeGaetano. *Stop Teaching Our Kids to Kill: A Call to Action against TV, Movie, and Video Game Violence*. New York: Crown Publishers, 1999.

Gunter, Barrie. *The Effects of Video Games on Children: The Myth Unmasked*. Sheffield, England: Sheffield Academic Press, 1998.

McAllister, Ken. *Game Work: Language, Power, and Computer Game Culture*. Tuscaloosa, AL: University of Alabama Press, 2004.

Osit, Michael. *Generation Text: Raising Well-Adjusted Kids in an Age of Instant Everything*. New York: Amacom, 2008.

Selfe, Cynthia, and Gail E. Hawisher. *Gaming Lives in the Twenty-First Century: Literate Connections*. New York: Palgrave Macmillan, 2007.

Williams, J. Patrick, Sean Q. Hendricks, and W. Keith Winkler. *Gaming as Culture: Essays on Reality, Identity and Experience in Fantasy Games*. Jefferson, NC: McFarland, 2006.

Williams, J. Patrick, and Jonas Heide Smith. *The Player's Realm: Studies on the Culture of Video Games and Gaming*. Jefferson, NC: McFarland, 2007.

Resources

The following organizations are concerned with issues related to video games and video game addiction, and many offer useful resources, information, and advice. During the production stage of this memoir, one of the biggest organizations that deals with video game addiction, Dr. David Walsh's National Institute on Media and the Family (www.mediawise.org), fell victim to economic troubles. Other organizations might meet a similar fate, but others are likely to take their place in time. In order to find the most current information on new and existing organizations, feel free to visit my own website (www.unpluggedthebook.com) and check out its links, or use your favorite search engine. The information below is a fine place to begin.

American Psychological Association
750 First Street NE
Washington, DC 20002
phone: (800) 374-2721
public.affairs@apa.org
www.apa.org

The American Psychological Association is a scientific and professional organization that represents psychology in the United States. With 150,000 members, it is the largest association of psychologists worldwide. Its website contains an extensive database of books, journals, videos, software, and reports.

Canadians Concerned About Violence in Entertainment
167 Glen Road
Toronto, ON M4W 2W8
Canada
info@c-cave.com
www.c-cave.com

C-CAVE, as the group is generally known, is an independent national nonprofit public interest organization. It is committed to increasing public awareness about the effects of cultural violence on society. It maintains an article archive, audio and video clips, a list of relevant books, and an extensive links page.

Center for Media Literacy
23852 Pacific Coast Highway, Suite 472
Malibu, CA 90265
phone: (310) 456-1225
fax: (310) 456-0020
cml@medialit.org
www.medialit.org

The center's website provides the following features:

- A downloadable MediaLit Kit, which provides a vision and directions for successfully introducing media literacy in classrooms and community groups from pre-K to college
- A consulting and speaking bureau
- Links to media literacy education organizations
- A reading room, which is an online reference center for background articles, core research studies, and timely reports. It also serves as a historical archive that documents the development of media literacy in the United States.
- Best-practices information
- FAQs

Center for Successful Parenting
P.O. Box 3794
Carmel, IN 46082
csp@onrampamerica.net
www.sosparents.org

The center's website states, "Our culture used to protect the innocence of our children. Today our children are constantly exposed to sex and violence. Our vision is to move parents, leaders in health, government, business, education, public safety, and other vocations to action by changing our culture to protect children from unhealthy media in all formats." The website provides news updates, a brain-scan research video, parenting tips, culture-changing tips, and a list of resources.

Center on Media and Child Health
300 Longwood Avenue
Boston, MA 02115
phone: (617) 355-2000
cmch@childrens.harvard.edu
www.cmch.tv

The center's website states, "The Center on Media and Child Health at Children's Hospital Boston, Harvard Medical School, and Harvard School of Public Health is dedicated to understanding and responding to the effects of media on the physical, mental, and social health of children through research, production, and education." The website provides information for researchers, parents, and teachers as well as clips of press coverage.

Common Sense Media
650 Townsend Street, Suite 375
San Francisco, CA 94103
phone: (415) 863-0600
fax: (415) 863-0601
www.commonsensemedia.org

Common Sense Media is dedicated to improving the media and entertainment lives of children and their families. The website states, "We exist because media and entertainment profoundly impact the social, emotional, and physical development of our nation's children. As a nonpartisan, not-for-profit organization, we provide trustworthy information and tools, as well as an independent forum, so that families can have a choice and a voice about the media they consume." The website contains reviews of media products, educator and parenting resources, a press room, and age-specific content for children.

Entertainment Consumers Association
64 Danbury Road, Suite 700
Wilton, CT 06897-4406
phone: (203) 761-6180
fax: (203) 761-6184
feedback@theeca.com
www.theeca.com

The Entertainment Consumers Association (ECA) is a nonprofit organization established in 2006 to serve the needs of those who play computer and video games. It is an advocacy organization for consumers of interactive entertainment. The website states, "Today, more than ever before, gamers need to stand together to defend against political activity that is threatening the creation and publishing of video games. On behalf of the gaming community, the ECA lobbies legislators directly as well as launching grassroots digital initiatives to preserve our rights as gamers." The website contains the following features:

- Links to other gamer advocacy groups
- Forums and message boards
- Publications: *GamePolitics* (a "game news site focused on anti-game/gamer legislation and political issues that affect gamers"), *GameJobs* ("the industry's leading career portal and job board"), *GameCulture* (a "mass market publication which publicizes the

positive impact games and gamers have had on society"), and *ECA Today,* a nightly newsletter.

Entertainment Merchants Association
16530 Ventura Boulevard, Suite 400
Encino, CA 91436
phone: (818) 385-1500
fax: (818) 385-0567
emaoffice@enmerch.org
www.entmerch.org

The Entertainment Merchants Association is a nonprofit international trade association dedicated to advancing the interests of the $33 billion home entertainment industry. Its mission, according to its website, is to "promote, protect, and provide a forum for the common business interests of those engaged in the sale, rental, and licensed reproduction of entertainment software such as DVDs and video games." The group holds an annual convention and sponsors a scholarship foundation. Its website contains a job board, a press room, a technology glossary, industry resources, and information on ratings enforcement and government relations.

Entertainment Software Association
575 Seventh Street NW, Suite 300
Washington, DC 20004
esa@theesau.com
www.theesa.com

The Entertainment Software Association is "exclusively dedicated to serving the business and public affairs needs of companies that publish computer and video games for video game consoles, personal computers, and the Internet." It offers a range of services to interactive entertainment software publishers, including a global antipiracy program, business and consumer research, information on government relations, and intellectual property protection efforts. The website contains industry facts, public policy information, news releases, and an article series called "Games in Daily Life." The association also sponsors a foundation with grant and scholarship opportunities.

Entertainment Software Rating Board
317 Madison Avenue, 22nd floor
New York, NY 10017
www.esrb.org

The Entertainment Software Rating Board is a nonprofit, self-regulatory body established in 1994 by the Entertainment Software Association. The board assigns computer and video game content ratings, enforces industry-adopted advertising guidelines, and helps to ensure responsible online privacy practices for the interactive entertainment software industry. Its website contains education and outreach information, parents resources, rating categories, consumer research findings, and FAQs.

International Game Developers Association
19 Mantua Road
Mt. Royal, NJ 08061
phone: (856) 423-2990
fax: (856) 423-3420
contact@igda.org
www.igda.org

The International Game Developers Association is the largest nonprofit membership organization that serves individuals who create video games. It has chapters that sponsor events and parties, engages in anticensorship advocacy, and maintains a speakers bureau. Its website contains a LinkedIn private group, special interest groups, forums, white papers, a wiki knowledge base, columns and articles, and casual games reporting standards.

Mothers Against Videogame Addiction and Violence

www.mavav.org

This is a parody website that is "dedicated to educating parents of the world's fastest growing addiction and the most reckless endangerment of children today." Although it is meant to be satire, the site is commonly mistaken and cited as a straightforward video game addiction website. Many of the comments on its blogs and message boards speak to key issues in video game addiction.

Media Awareness Network

1500 Merivale Road, 3rd floor
Ottawa, ON K2E 6Z5
Canada
phone: (613) 224-7721
fax: (613) 224-1958
info@media-awareness.ca
www.media-awareness.ca

The Media Awareness Network is a nonprofit organization founded in 1996 to pioneer the development of media and digital literacy programs. According to its website, it promotes "media and digital literacy by producing education and awareness programs and resources, working in partnership with Canadian and international organizations, and speaking to audiences across Canada and around the world. MNet focuses its efforts on equipping adults with information and tools to help young people understand how the media work, how the media may affect their lifestyle choices, and the extent to which they, as consumers and citizens, are being well informed." The website is multilingual (English and French) and contains a resources catalog, media issues articles, free educational games, a blog, and information for parents and teachers.

My Addiction
phone: (800) 401-3218 (24-hour treatment line)
info@myaddiction.com
www.myaddiction.com

This online recovery resource website is a good source of treatment information. It contains information on support groups, a list of treatment centers, a blog, addiction videos, articles, and a glossary of addiction terms.

National Parent Teacher Association
541 N. Fairbanks Court, Suite 1300
Chicago, IL 60611
phone: (312) 670-6782
fax: (312) 670-6783
info@pta.org
www.pta.org

The PTA remains the largest volunteer child advocacy association in the nation. It provides families with a powerful voice with which to speak on behalf of every child and with the best tools to help children be safe, healthy, and successful. The PTA holds numerous conferences and conventions and publishes *Our Children* magazine, which is available both in print and online. The website contains tip sheets and articles on student-related issues; photos, videos, and podcasts; and networking opportunities through a bulletin board and a great idea bank.

On-Line Gamers Anonymous
104 Miller Lane
Harrisburg, PA 17110
hotline: (612) 245-1115
www.olganon.org

On-Line Gamers Anonymous (OLGA) is a self-help fellowship along the lines of the other twelve-step programs (Alcoholics Anonymous, Gamblers Anonymous, Narcotics Anonymous, etc.). Its website states, "We share our experiences, strengths, and hope to assist [one another] in recovery from the problems caused by excessive game playing, whether it be computer, video, console, or on-line. Our community includes recovering gamers, family members, loved ones, friends, and concerned others." OLGA, and its companion group for an addict's family members, OLG-Anon (like Al-Anon) was founded in 2002 by Elizabeth Woolley, whose son committed suicide after becoming addicted to online video games. The OLGA website contains an anonymous chat room, an active message board, and a list of professionals and groups that specialize in video game addiction.

Serious Games Initiative
1300 Pennsylvania Avenue NW
Washington, DC 20004
phone: (207) 773-3700
bsawyer@seriousgames.org
www.seriousgames.org

The goal of Serious Games Initiative, according to its website, "is to help usher in a new series of policy education, exploration, and management tools utilizing state-of-the-art computer game designs, technologies, and development skills." The initiative holds yearly conferences, and its website contains discussion lists, a YouTube channel, a Flickr stream, and slideshare features.

Video Game Addiction
phone: (866) 869-4530 (for treatment program information)
www.videogameaddiction.org

"When video games become more than just games," this website warns, you might need to check out its comprehensive articles, parenting tips, list of symptoms and treatments, wilderness program information, and links to similar sites.

Youth Free Expression Network
275 Seventh Avenue, 15th floor
New York, NY 10001
phone: (212) 807-6222 ext. 22
fax: (212) 807-6245
ncac@ncac.org
www.ncac.org/YFEN

This network, according to its website, provides "in-class workshops that address student rights, while fostering creative ways to combat censorship in schools and on college campuses." It seeks to "fill an enormous void as the first coalition of youth and adults committed to shifting debate beyond overly reductive sound-bites and toward policies that enhance young people's access to information, and ability to express their views, as well as increased participation in the political process." The Young Activist Speaker's Bureau presents panels on a variety of issues at conferences throughout the United States. The website contains interactive workshops for high school and college students and faculty, as well as articles on issues faced by American youth.

About the Author

Ryan G. Van Cleave was born in Neenah, Wisconsin, and raised in the Chicago suburbs. He has taught writing at Clemson University, Eckerd College, Florida State University, George Washington University, Ringling College of Art and Design, University of Wisconsin–Green Bay, and University of Wisconsin–Madison, as well as at prisons, community centers, and urban at-risk youth facilities.

The author (or coauthor) of sixteen books, Dr. Van Cleave's writing has appeared in *The Christian Science Monitor*, *Clean Eating*, *Harvard Review*, *National Geographic Adventures*, *The New York Times Book Review*, *People*, *Psychology Today*, and *Writer's Digest*.

His work has been featured in such books as *Mooring Against the Tide: Writing Fiction and Poetry*, *The 15th Annual Year's Best Fantasy & Horror*, *Never Before: Poems About First Experiences*, and *In a Fine Frenzy: Poetry Inspired by Shakespeare*.

Dr. Van Cleave lives in Sarasota, Florida, with his wife and two children, where he works as a freelance writer, a writing coach, and an addiction and recovery consultant. He also serves as director of C&R Press, a nonprofit literary organization based in Chattanooga, Tennessee.

Dr. Van Cleave welcomes comments, questions, and feedback through his website for this book, www.unpluggedthebook.com, and through the book's blog,unplugged.hcibooks.com. He is also available for speaking engagements, workshops, and class visits, as well as one-to-one or group consultations.